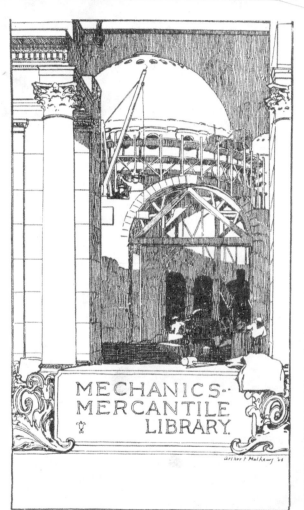

THE TURBULENT WORLD OF FRANZ GÖLL

THE TURBULENT WORLD

of

FRANZ GÖLL

An Ordinary Berliner
Writes the Twentieth Century

———

Peter Fritzsche

HARVARD UNIVERSITY PRESS
Cambridge, Massachusetts
London, England
2011

Library of Congress Cataloging-in-Publication Data

Fritzsche, Peter, 1959–
The turbulent world of Franz Göll : an ordinary Berliner writes the
twentieth century / Peter Fritzsche.
p. cm.
Includes bibliographical references and index.
ISBN 978-0-674-05531-5
1. Göll, Franz, 1899–1984.   2. Göll, Franz, 1899–1984—Diaries.
3. Berlin (Germany)—Biography.   4. Men—Germany—Berlin—
Biography.   5. German diaries—Germany—Berlin—History and criticism.
6. Germany—History—20th century—Biography.   7. Germany—Social
conditions—20th century.   8. Germany—Politics and government—
20th century.   9. Germany—Intellectual life—20th century.
10. Berlin (Germany)—History—20th century.   I. Title.
DD857.G6F7 2011
943'.155087092—dc22
[B]
2010039754

To Lauren

Contents

Preface   *ix*

1   The Case of Franz Göll, Graphomaniac   *1*

2   Franz Göll's Multiple Selves   *32*

3   Physical Intimacies   *78*

4   The Amateur Scientist   *108*

5   Franz Göll Writes German History   *132*

6   Resolution without Redemption   *187*

Notes   *229*

Index   *256*

Preface

I discovered the remarkably rich diary of an obscure man in the state archives of Berlin in the spring of 2003 while I was working on another book. I quickly realized how extraordinary the Franz Göll diaries were. Born in 1899 and writing the diary from 1916 to his death in 1984, Göll commented on the state of the world across almost seventy years: from Kaiser Wilhelm II to Ronald Reagan, from World War I to the Cold War, from the age of Darwin to the age of Aquarius. I was immediately struck by Göll's evocative portraits of Germany's political and economic calamity: we see the hungry winters of World War I, the unemployment lines, and the rise of the Nazis; Göll walks through that showpiece of the Third Reich, the 1938 exhibition "Degenerate Art," which he finds provocative rather than repulsive; and he describes the brutality of World War II, which crashes into the basement of his tenement building in April 1945 when he witnesses Russian soldiers raping his neighbors. Göll composes poems about bombs falling on his city at Christmas, he nurses his mother after her toes are amputated in the bitter winter that followed the war, and he questions the nuclear policy of the new superpower, the United States, all the way into the 1980s. Göll was a poignant witness to the violence that saturated the twentieth century.

As I continued reading Göll's plain handwritten notebooks, I was astonished by how these observations served as springboards for Göll's effort to explore the very structure of modern life. Göll tries to figure out what the keys to self-fulfillment might be as he negotiates what he realizes is the modern imperative to make his own way, to compete in an unyielding work world, to fashion a consumer "lifestyle," to define his sex life in an ever more promiscuous age, and to adapt to a city torn by war and revolution. The diary reflects on everything from the nature of Göll's self, his sexuality, and his phobias and desires to the evolution of the universe and the nature of God. What Göll does is to investigate himself as a social, biological, and psychological subject, and he goes on to analyze the world with the aid of a lengthy syllabus of self-assigned readings, his hand-built aquarium, and the lens of his camera.

IN WRITING THE BOOK, I profited immensely from my discussions with Thilo Schimmel, my former student and research assistant who transcribed the diaries in exemplary fashion. Thilo took a harder line on Göll than I did, but he remained fascinated by the diarist and the diaries and offered helpful insights and bracing questions. I would like to thank the "German Colloquium" at the University of Illinois and especially Harry Liebersohn and Matti Bunzl for a critical reading of the manuscript in fall 2008. As the book neared completion, my colleagues Mark Micale and Mark Steinberg spent a wonderful evening discussing with me the text and the issues it raised. My parents, Sybille and Hellmut Fritzsche, both of whom were born in Berlin, also read and commented helpfully on the book. Special thanks to Dorothee Brantz, Kathleen Canning, Kristen Ehrenberger, Geoff Eley, Moritz Föllmer, Michael Geyer, Jochen Hellbeck, Karen Hewitt, Jonathan Huener, Susanne Kothe, Alf Lüdtke, and Franziska Schubart for their help and encouragement. The Research Board of the University of Illinois generously supported the research and writing of this book. I am grateful to the Landesarchiv in Berlin for making it possible to reproduce photographs from Franz Göll's albums. Many thanks also to my agent, Chris Calhoun, and to my editor, Kathleen McDermott. I dedicate this book with all my love to my daughter, Lauren.

I

—

The Case of Franz Göll, Graphomaniac

From Aachen in the west to Königsberg in the east, Reichsstrasse 1 in Germany follows an ancient trading route stretching from the north Atlantic ports to the "Great New City" of Novgorod in Russia. For centuries merchants, pilgrims, and knights traveled along this principal highway. It provided the geographic axis of the growing might of Prussia in the early modern period and a thoroughfare for immigrants and ideas about everything from Marxism to pan-Germanism in the nineteenth century. Later it traversed the "bleeding" borders along the Polish Corridor that divided Germany after its defeat in World War I. It accommodated the soldiers of the Third Reich who invaded Poland and then the Soviet Union in World War II, and it filled up with German refugees fleeing westward, in the opposite direction, at the end of the war. Reichsstrasse 1 is a Route 66 through the windings of German and European history.

In Berlin, Reichsstrasse 1 enters the city at the famous Glienecke Bridge near Potsdam, the site of spy exchanges during the Cold War. It travels through Zehlendorf, Steglitz, and Schöneberg, the old incorporated townships that pulled Berlin west and south to make it the fourth-largest city in the world at the turn of the twentieth century, crosses the dense traffic of Potsdamer Platz at the former site of the Berlin Wall, and exits the capital via the long, straight-ruled Frankfurter Allee to the east.

It was along Hauptstrasse, as the highway is designated in Schöneberg, that Franz Göll, born at the cusp of the new century on 16 February 1899, apprenticed himself to the big city and prowled its neighborhoods, where he shopped and looked for work, where he scouted his first love, Klara Wasko, who lived at Hauptstrasse 152 ("rear courtyard, first side wing, 1. staircase to the left"), and where, farther up the street, on Potsdamer Strasse (116), he might have bumped into the young Marlene Dietrich, an almost exact contemporary (1901–1992). Reichsstrasse 1 skirts the Rote Insel (Red Island), a narrow triangle of a working-class neighborhood formed along two sides by the railroads converging on the center of the city and known for the left-wing politics of its inhabitants, including the socialist Julius Leber, who paid with his life for resisting the Nazis and was a legal client of my grandfather, Herbert Lauffer, who lived in nearby Steglitz. Inhabiting a small apartment on Rossbachstrasse, Franz Göll lived all his life on the "island." But although Franz never moved, world history moved through him, and it was from this perch that he reported on what he saw in the voluminous diaries and notebooks he kept for nearly seventy years, from 1916 until his death in 1984.

What makes Franz Göll's diary unusual is not simply the extremely long time frame—from Kaiser Wilhelm II to Ronald Reagan—but the author's deliberate task to examine modern life amid bewildering political, economic, and intellectual upheavals. Uneducated but highly intelligent, the son of a luckless typesetter and a barely literate mother, Franz authorized himself to compose a "symphony" out of the "everyday music" he heard around him.[1] His diary entries, which were usually composed about once a week in a series of twenty-three notebooks and are astonishingly eloquent in antique German, offered far-reaching commentaries on the world that took shape in the twentieth century. Göll detailed the history that thundered along Reichsstrasse 1, from World War I, the rise of the Nazis, and the onset of Hitler's wars to the Cold War and the jeopardy of nuclear war. He described the densities and confusions of city life, the dissolution of social milieus, and thus both the imperative of individuals to find their own way and the possibility to make their own way. He also commented continuously on the scientific breakthroughs of Darwin, Freud, and Einstein and on the competing ideas of capitalism, Nazism, and Communism. All this was part of twentieth-century life. But so was Franz's desire and ability to see for himself, to make examinations and accounts, which he did through the syllabus of readings he prepared, the aquarium he built, the camera hobby he cultivated, and the master vocabularies he assembled from the natural sciences, especially biology and psychology. The diary entries registered the turbulence of the century; they also revealed the work of a mapmaker and place finder who produced his own intimate version of modern German history.

In many ways Franz Göll was an ordinary man. The routine of work dominated his life, whereas most famous diarists were much more indolent. It is fitting that Franz bears the name Alfred Döblin gave to his most famous character, Franz Biberkopf, in the quintessential big-city novel, *Berlin Alexanderplatz* (1929), to denote someone near the bottom of the social heap. Franz Göll worked as a clerk, postal employee, night watchman, and publisher's assistant, sometimes earning promotions, other times losing his job in hard times. Like many twentieth-century Berliners, he enjoyed steamboat excursions on Sunday afternoons and countryside holidays in the summers. Franz went to the movies, often more than once a week, and he wore fedora hats, ate spice cake, and drank beer and schnapps. Like many low-level white-collar workers, he displayed a penchant for order, sought the embrace of a structured community, and was both suspicious of and attracted to the century's new freedoms. Thus many of his judgments about the Weimar Republic, the Third Reich, and Germany's defeat in World War II express the responses of ordinary Germans.

But, as is often the case, when you scratch ordinary lives, you glimpse the marvelous possessions they contain. Franz Göll's diary provides this scratch and reveals many strange things that come tumbling out. Franz had a knack for taming birds, indulged in a mania for collecting postcards, and sustained a lifelong passion for reading, mostly fiction, biography, and natural history, which he annotated in scientific notebooks that were the foundation of the work of genius he believed he had been called on to produce. In his self-appointed role as a scrupulous, even obsessive, observer, he proved to be an independent, insightful commentator on world history. A loner, he was prickly with friends and family, and as someone who considered himself middle class, he insisted on a measure of deference (and the formal "Sie") to distinguish himself from the blue-collar workers who made up Berlin's majority. This was a man who shoveled war rubble wearing a tie.

Franz Göll was officially Franz von Göll; his father, also Franz von Göll (1864–1915), was born the illegitimate son of Gertrude von Göll (1840–1915), a minor noblewoman who abandoned the baby boy to her sister in 1864 but left him her name. The patronymic vexed the son; although it gave him a bit of social capital, it also served as an unmistakable reminder of his family's dwindling fortunes. His father had dropped the "von" altogether. Still, Franz always referred to himself as "Franz von Göll." It seemed to affirm his sense of mistaken identity and unrecognized genius—he even wondered whether he was related to Charles de Gaulle.[2] In fact, von Göll is a very uncommon name, although Thomas Pynchon introduces us to Gerhardt von Göll (an imaginary German filmmaker) in his novel *Gravity's Rainbow* (1973). I have decided to drop the "von" entirely because it invites misunderstanding about the nature of the diary project, the value of which derives from the fact that it was undertaken not by a proper nobleman in a castle but by a *kleiner Mann,* a modest, uneducated, impoverished Berlin shop-man living in a crummy two-room apartment. The perspective of the diarist is of a person who felt beleaguered and perplexed rather than entitled.

What the diary reports on first of all is the extraordinary violence of the twentieth century. The "struggle for existence" *(Kampf ums Dasein),* the catchword of popular Darwinism at the end of the nineteenth century, dominated the way Franz saw the world. The ideas of competition for food and space and of adaptation and development to changing environments provided the interpretive keynote of his philosophical readings and natural history studies and the foundation of his observations of aquarium and terrarium life. Also following Darwin, Franz conceived of struggle in zero-sum terms, so that "improvement" here entailed "extermination" there.[3] Franz saw this struggle for existence confirmed in his autobiography: he embarked on the diary just after his father died in December 1915, an event that impoverished the family. In the middle of World War I, his mother was forced to take in work sewing sandbags for the German army but could not pay off the sewing machine. The world of work that Franz himself entered in 1916 was one he found corrupted by competition, suspicion, and self-promotion. What Franz regarded as unfettered capitalism had destroyed the security of social hierarchies he imagined had once been in place. Especially in the Great Depression, in the early 1930s, millions of twentieth-century contemporaries felt the same anxiety about having been somehow abandoned to their own meager devices. But Franz also displayed a characteristically twentieth-century German mistrust of political and social conflict and desire for the stability of community even when he prospered personally.[4] Franz took the world wars to be an extension of the predatory patterns he observed at work and in nature, although he always thought of himself as prey, intimidated as he was by the aggression and racism of Nazi predators, only to find himself bombed and his neighbors raped by the victorious Allies. Moreover, in his view, the post-1945 settlement rested on the expropriation of Germany by the United States and the

Soviet Union and remained tense into the 1980s as a result of the United States' nuclear brinkmanship. Not only was violence in life the norm, but also the very effort to create some sort of normal life—to save money, to redo the apartment, to go on vacation—had to be accomplished in the emergency conditions of the Third Reich and the Cold War. The diary offers genuine insights into the social psychology of Germany's extraordinarily violent twentieth-century history.

For Franz, the struggle for existence was compounded by his evaluation, which he shared with many modern artists and intellectuals, that modern life left the individual increasingly alone and insecure in conditions of moral and political insecurity that extended even to the foundations of knowledge itself. Although this abandonment could be considered the basis of the autonomous personality, and in many ways Franz took advantage of the new opportunities of an increasingly free society, Franz tended to take into account the collateral damage of the risks to which the individual was exposed and the self-reliance he was forced to cultivate. Although the diary is an example of the self-authorization he in fact achieved, Franz felt a profound sense of alienation and even humiliation and shame in his relations with society. He was a physically small man, uneasy around people, unsure of how to approach women and manage his sexuality, and frightened of the brutality of collective life. His report on the modern nature of twentieth-century life underscored the persistence of struggle, and his response to this uneasy state was to develop an ultrasensitive register of melancholy emotions in which he dramatized everyday challenges, endeavored to order his universe, and honed his alertness to social pressures and individual inadequacies. Franz Göll depicts himself as an injured individual as he reinterpreted the world; he was not the cool, flexible man of disguise celebrated by modern realists, but the melancholic accountant of loss, worthlessness, and incapacity as he wrote down the entries of his diary.[5] Franz's melancholy gave him something to say about the world. It enabled his self-reflexivity, his energetic curiosity, and his literary industry.

Although Franz's testimony about social decomposition and loneliness is telling, it is not entirely representative. The 1920s and 1930s, the years of Franz's young adulthood, gathered Berliners into an astonishing variety of interest groups, political parties, and leisure organizations. Nazis, Communists, and Social Democrats all raised large political armies, and workers, employees, and other middle-class constituencies energetically organized to protect their economic interests, a dramatic contrast to Franz's sense of isolation. Franz also did not take an interest in competitive sports, the games of winning and losing that preoccupied millions of soccer enthusiasts, boxing junkies, and bicycle-racing fans. What he did share with his fellow metropolitans, however, was movie mania, what Germans call *Kinosucht*. These escapades into twentieth-century mass culture contradicted his sense of social distinction.

At the same time, Göll did not adopt the widely held view after World War I that divided the world into Germany's friends and foes; his failure to develop strong ties of association and loyalty left him disinclined to identify with the German nation, to bewail its postwar travails, or to excoriate its enemies. He made a poor nationalist, and he had little to say about the Treaty of Versailles or Germany's thunderous rearmament under Hitler, topics that impassioned millions of Germans between the two world wars. One reason for Göll's reserve was that he never served in the army, which was highly unusual for German men of his generation (he was called up in June 1917 but was deemed medically unfit, and his employers kept him at home in January 1940, when he might have been conscripted as a reserve policeman in Poland). As a boy, he preferred to play with dolls rather than soldiers, and during World War I he identified with housewives in food queues rather than with infantrymen on the front lines. His opposition to the Nazis, after initial enthusiasm in 1933, also put him in the minority. It is rare to find an ordinary diary that attacked the Nazis as relentlessly as Franz Göll's did. Even so, Franz demonized the "Asiatic" Russians who occupied Germany after its defeat in 1945, a clue that his non-Nazi sensibilities went only so far. Nonetheless, he was well ahead of German public opinion in his support of détente and Ostpolitik and in his criticism of American nuclear policy in the 1950s. At the end of his life, he disparaged Ronald Reagan. For Franz, the struggle for existence was a fact of life that his observations confirmed again and again, but it was not a premise for nationalist mobilization. In this regard, Franz Göll was not a typical German of the twentieth century. He thought in the global categories of natural history, which made more sense to someone who worked on his aquarium, gazed at the night sky, and developed ideas about evolution and God.

That Franz deployed the term "struggle for existence" from Darwin and his popularizers in order to make sense of the new social and political world around him indicates how scientific interpretations of the natural world worked themselves into twentieth-century life. The diary takes up all sorts of biological and psychological vocabularies. Physiognomic categories, usually in pairs founded on the strong and the weak, but also in the threes and fours of more elaborate typologies, were both passed on and reworked, so it is possible to see how twentieth-century scientific language inhabited contemporaries and how contemporaries personalized the expert concepts they borrowed. Twentieth-century life also consisted of observing trends, making comparisons, and constructing a case for oneself based on evidence. Franz Göll the diarist, the reader, and the amateur scientist actively participated in the process of apprehending the world and constructing descriptions of its meaning, case studying and picture making that the philosopher Martin Heidegger regarded as the characteristic attribute of the modern age. Insofar as the modern "subject" knowingly possesses a view of the world, "each subject is, to that extent, an artist." Understood this way, Göll's diary is a work of twentieth-century art to which history, science, and medicine contributed methods as well as themes.[6]

World wars, economic calamities, and scientific discoveries further stimulated the general urge "to 'get the hang' of world affairs as a whole."[7] Indeed, the very activity of applying science to life was typical of the twentieth century. This was a period when more and more people felt the need to figure things out because custom no longer seemed a reliable guide to understand scientific and technological transformations, to achieve professional self-advancement in a more socially mobile society, to find the right marriage partner, or to acquire new hobbies and explore new interests. The travel guide Franz bought before he went on holiday in Mecklenburg in 1921 was illustrative of a whole new approach to daily life; Franz and his contemporaries actively engaged in fashioning lifestyles for themselves. Franz attended lectures on sexuality, bought self-help books, and devoured books by great popularizers such as the naturalist Wilhelm Bölsche, a best-selling counterpart in Germany to H. G. Wells in Great Britain or Will Durant in the United States. Lifestyles may have been more or less conventional, but the deliberate task of construction they presupposed was new.

Göll's act of writing a diary is not idiosyncratic. The interrogative nature of keeping a diary collaborated closely with twentieth-century history. Of course, neither the diary nor biographical reflection was a uniquely twentieth-century literary form; the genres had flourished for at least two hundred years before Göll began writing his life. In our own times, as Jeremy Popkin has noted, "far more people keep diaries than engage in any other form of regular writing."[8] Indeed, the twentieth-century context of war and social mobility and new ideas about the independence of the self fostered self-examination. In turn, the unprecedented stress that war, mobility, and self-reflection laid on individuals to act for and think about themselves as individuals makes autobiographical texts extremely useful for understanding the psychology of twentieth-century developments. Without ever moving from Rossbachstrasse on the Rote Insel, Göll experienced four political regimes: the Wilhelmine monarchy up to its demise in 1918, the Weimar Republic, the twelve years of the Third Reich from 1933 to 1945, and, finally, the Federal Republic; he lived through two world wars, saw many of his contemporaries killed—so many, in fact, that a photograph of the fiftieth-anniversary reunion of his confirmation class in 1963 shows sixteen women but only five men—and contemplated nuclear annihilation;

he faced financial ruin after the great inflation in 1923 and again after World War II; and he witnessed the expansion and fall of European imperialism on a global scale.[9] The consciousness of vast historical change propelled the diarist to write in an exercise of self-location as his private rooms on Rossbachstrasse collided again and again with world history. Moreover, as the great scholar of the diary form, Gustave Hocke, notes, the sheer power of twentieth-century political forms made the soul feel "lonesome." Beleaguered and tyrannized, it coaxed the "internal monologue" of the diary to speak up.[10] This was especially the case for Jewish diaries during World War II. The commitment to "bear witness" certainly fortified Victor Klemperer's (1881–1960) will to continue writing a diary, even when it became dangerous for a Jew to do so. In many ways the testimony of the diary is a kind of conceit in which the diarist persistently dramatizes the impact of social, economic, and political change on the individual self. Giving voice to the individual, diaries such as Klemperer's could also reconcile. Klemperer the diarist regarded the troubled present in such a way that Klemperer could continue to live among Germans in a post-Nazi future; his Germans were poisoned, but not generally poisonous.[11]

Even more fundamental to the advancement of the diary was the perception that the individual was no longer embedded in traditional social milieus or traditional institutions such as family, craft, or religion. What followed was the recognition that individuals had to take their own lives in hand, which alternatively produced disturbing feelings of homelessness and a liberating sense of spiritual discovery, but in any case strengthened notions of individual autonomy. Even though many theorists distrust the idea of the unified self, belief in it was, according to Paul John Eakin, "a fact of contemporary cultural experience," especially in times of stress when the self appeared to be vulnerable.[12] Franz was extremely alert to this condition of displacement, which he interpreted in psychological as well as social terms. The requirement to construct autonomy, to be oneself by producing oneself, made the self more strategic in its dealings with others, more self-reflective in the contemplation of its own subjectivity, and more apt to take up the role of diarist to advance and chronicle the struggle of selfhood. Indeed, the diary can be imagined as a sustained protocol recording the effort to develop a program for life. Twentieth-century diaries such as Göll's flourished because they monitored the complicated relations between the newly propelled self and society, the demands and loneliness of self-reliance, the anguish and disappointment of self-promotion, and alienation from the mass of outsiders. In this regard, the diary should not be seen as the newly discovered authentic voice of the self but as a tool used to construct the self in the arduous modern conditions of social fluctuation. In Mark McGurl's terms, "personal experience" became the grounds for the work of "reflexive modernity."[13]

"Autonomy can only be preserved by virtue of a constant reflection on the self by the self," explained the nineteenth-century novelist Gottfried Keller, and "the journal is the best way to achieve it."[14] But the autonomy Keller prized was hard won because, in the words of Jerrold Seigel, self-reflection often created "a split, sometimes perplexing and painful, between our actual being, with its persisting limitations, and our expanded consciousness." As the psychologist Lewis Sass concludes, "Each new perspective on oneself brings, along with the legitimate insights it may offer, new and perhaps even more tortuous possibilities of ignorance, self-alienation and self-deception."[15] The burden of observation was not simply the pain of close examination but also the acknowledgment of the incompleteness of the self and even the ungovernable "proliferation of ourselves" that the Portuguese poet and diarist Fernando Pessoa (1888–1935), identified; Pessoa felt that he was constituted by "beings of many sorts in the vast colony of one being, who think and feel differently."[16] Thus diaries often produced their own copy as diarists returned again and again to observe the constructed self, the incomplete self, or split, multiple selves. Given the demand to build the autonomous self and the likelihood of finding it insufficient or flawed, diaries, even in the hands of the most alert social observers, tended to move from the sociological to the psychological and even the biological level and to focus on individual failure rather than general approval, giving the texts a melancholy and narcissistic cast. "I am a character in a novel that remains to be written," wrote Pessoa.[17] The subject was available, but the role to be played was uncertain, so that subjectivity often became burdensome and the conditions of its unfulfillment, whether they were seen to derive from society or the self, loathsome. Other autobiographical genres such as the memoir, which Göll experimented with as well, are more sociological and less self-absorbed, but also less painfully direct.

In sum, autobiography in the twentieth century should be taken as a literary response to the violence of war and revolution, to the requirement to build an increasingly autonomous self, and to the proliferation of technologies of self-observation. It was also a privileged means to understand those same developments. The form of the diary gave personal voice and individual shape to the collective calamities of the twentieth century and added poignancy through illustration. Autobiographical texts allowed writers and then readers to situate themselves in history. The diary indicates as well how social processes such as more scientific lifestyles or more self-reliant life programs or more open sexual practices worked themselves out through individual choices. Finally, the diary reveals one of the main stories of the twentieth century: the flamboyant self-consciousness about making choices and acknowledging perspectives. What is remarkable about Franz Göll's diary in particular is that it combines extraordinary commentary on world history with an alertness to the various optical instruments the modern observer used and refined. The diary thus contemplates the nature of seeing and reporting. This too was part of twentieth-century life.

Göll's diary developed out of broad trends in twentieth-century history, but it remains an unusual text. Not only is the diary nearly as extensive as the century, but Franz's seventy years of commentary cover an extraordinary range of themes: his battered self, the history and politics he experienced as a German and a European, natural history, sexuality, the origins of religion, and finally, theories of knowledge that double back on the nature of his writing and reporting. Moreover, the diary is composed of different genres that choreograph different versions of the self. What Pessoa regarded as the "proliferation of ourselves" in the process of observation emerged quite openly in the juxtaposition of Göll's diary, his memoirs, which he wrote in the 1940s, and his detailed household account books from the 1920s. To imagine multiple selves or to introduce the decentered subject at the level of metaphor is thought-provoking, but to uncover them substantially via different autobiographical genres is quite remarkable. Göll's autobiographical texts also included poems, a reading diary, scientific notebooks filled with excerpts from the hundreds of books he read, and a single political manifesto from the year 1921. Reading and writing constituted the "principal task" of his life; "everything else was of secondary importance."[18]

To open the first volume of the diary and to read the introspective entries is to become aware of how the diary took note of the particular conditions of its own production. The diary continuously struggles to account for Franz's efforts to realize his literary and scientific ambitions, which were reflected in the vast ground of inquiry opened up by the popularization of science at the beginning of the twentieth century but were also instigated by personal crises. The entries quarrel with Franz's passivity but are also the product of his inactivity and maladroitness. The self of the diarist emerges in his disassociation from society, and both become the objects of Göll's lifelong scrutiny.

In 1916, seventeen-year-old Franz Göll believed that he was at a crossroads. Since 1914 the terrific war in Europe had demanded months and then years of daily dying. He found his course of study at a *Präparande*, a grim evangelical academy for prospective primary-school teachers set up in three primitive rooms off a back courtyard on Kronprinzenstrasse in Berlin-Lichtenberg, "schematic" and "intellectually deadly." Without "the ability to freely develop the mind" or any other goal, Franz saw in front of him an "unbearable present-day situation." Then in December 1915 his father died suddenly at the age of fifty-one after complaining of shortness of breath and developing ulcers and swellings on his arms and legs. Because she had misplaced insurance receipts, Franz's mother received a reduced pension, far less than his father's income as a type-setter. "The way it was with us," Franz noted, "was the custom in the village whereby important papers were hidden amid the washing in the laundry hamper. But because our hamper contained less washing than all sorts of junk such as carpet remnants, used corsets, broken umbrel-las, and other utensils carefully stored away, the documents easily went lost in the clutter."[19] Later in life Franz, an obsessive collector, would never tolerate such "clutter." In the meantime, however, there was not enough money, even after trips to the pawnshop and handouts from his moth-er's relations in Kladow. "Moving in with us is the misery," Franz real-ized at the beginning of the new year 1916.[20]

One of Franz's poems from this period, "Premonition and Present," the title of Joseph von Eichendorff's long romantic novel about decline, described his feeling of abandonment, the "foulness" of friendships, and the "passing away" of home. But his mood was more defiant than mel-ancholy. Franz considered his future brightly, just "not here at home any more." What is more, he hoped to make his future far away "in the dis-tance" with his "happiness," the girl with the "brown braids," the "small red jacket," and "a little black cap," Klara Wasko, who lived around the corner on Hauptstrasse.[21] At the same time, to force his luck, Franz vis-ited a fortune-teller who foresaw a "second career," not the stultifying *Präparande,* but something else. It was at this point, on the first day of 1916, that Franz Göll began to write the diary. The idea had "preoccupied me already for some time"; "so today the idea has been put into action." The tension between idea and deed troubled Franz for the rest of his life, a life he always felt was incomplete and unfulfilled, but in the case of the diary he resolved to undertake the task, and he wrote and wrote for the next seventy years. Begun after the "breakdown" of his father's death, the diary was to have accompanied Franz's "breakout," the new start for himself and Klara in the future. The feeling that his "spiritual journey" no longer corresponded with the ideas of his mother but aimed at its own purposes inspired him to set down his reflections on paper.[22]

Franz's newly won sense of himself as a genius reinforced the desire to record and monitor and thus reaffirm the new directions of his life. His ability to write poems to Klara, to undertake the effort to keep the diary, and to note down other scientific observations awed him. "The poet came to life in me," an eye-opening revelation that fortified the writing process because truth telling was, as he saw it, the special responsibility of genius.[23]

Klara was a name, wrote the novelist Joseph Roth, that "was so simple, so healthy, so trustworthy, so dependable, so honest."[24] But disappointments quickly accumulated. In spite of the makeover the fortune-teller had predicted, Franz failed to find a job at his father's old print shop. For a while he stayed on at the teachers' academy, until money worries forced both him and his mother to work as low-paid clerks for the German Women's Fund for Children of War (Kriegskinderspende deutscher Frauen). Over the course of 1916 and 1917 the diary came to serve Franz as a place to register the discrepancies between his expectations and the deeds he in fact carried out, between "the wide vistas" that the fortune-teller had predicted for his life and the fear that laboring as a clerk would transform him into "a machine," between the call to genius he felt and the absence of any outward confirmation of such a calling.[25] His poems about Klara began to express growing doubt and anguish. Later verses no longer announced his animated love but suspected its forsaken nature. For months Franz carried the poem "Riddle" around with him, but he never found the opportunity to give it to Klara. He followed her along Hauptstrasse but never talked to her.[26] The sheaf of poems he sent out in the fall of 1916 was rejected by one publisher after another—Velhagen und Klasing, Reclam, Westermann.[27] His last attempt to address the outside world, a 1921 manifesto, "A Path of Salvation," a call to rehabilitate postrevolutionary Germany, was also returned by all the (left-wing) newspapers to which he offered it: *Welt am Montag,* the *Berliner Morgenpost,* the socialist daily *Vorwärts,* and finally the *Berliner Volkszeitung.* He kept on writing, but nothing happened. In his rooms on Schöneberg's Rossbachstrasse, Franz added continuously to the archive in which he reported on his passivity. He wrote as someone who had arrived "too late," as the critic Theodor Adorno once remarked about the romantic poet Eichendorff.[28] But with his writing, Franz created for himself a "room for growth" from which "ignorance had otherwise locked him out."[29] Franz himself connected the diary's "sentimental portraits" to "the passive role that stamps itself on my life." "I am and will remain simply an extra, a bystander, at most an observer," he noted.[30] The sidelines were his preferred vantage point, and they licensed his graphomania as he wrote continuously about himself, the nature of the universe, and world politics.

When Franz matriculated at the teachers' academy in October 1913, he also discovered the local library. Thirty years later he tried to describe how the library opened up the world to an otherwise unremarkable boy: "I registered with the municipal public library and could finally read books. Not 'moldy' schoolbooks" such as those assigned in the *Präparande* "but those of my own choice with life-giving contents. A whole new world of unimagined greatness and richness opened itself up to me, and I made the happy, uplifting discovery that in this new world I was not alone or a stranger." Although he had never seen his mother hold a book, "here on the threshold to the world of creative endeavor, I could see a path illuminated for me, and I gingerly entered this place of magic and wonder."[31] Libraries facilitated what literacy had made possible: the reading boom that began in the late nineteenth century as more and more people educated themselves by their own efforts. Public reading rooms were established in Berlin only at the turn of the twentieth century—Schöneberg's dates from 1901—but by 1920 there were over eighty libraries in the city. And although most Berliners did not read regularly—less than 2 percent of the city's inhabitants owned a library card—those who did, including Franz and Klara, whom he glimpsed in the library almost every evening in October 1916, read avidly, checking out an average of about twenty-five books a year.[32] Observers were never quite sure what to make of these industrious readers. On the one hand, there were patrons who read nothing but "kitsch literature," which was "almost more dangerous to good taste than trashy pulp fiction." On the other hand, there were plenty of readers who sought out books on philosophy, natural history, and technology, participating in the great popularization of scientific knowledge.[33]

For Göll, as for many other readers, "the craving for books" was linked to "new light," illuminated by Darwinism and its insights into the development of the natural world and its suggestions about the improvement of political and social conditions.[34] At the end of the nineteenth century, natural history reopened human history. Ordinary working people grabbed the volumes of Darwin's popularizers, Ernst Haeckel and Wilhelm Bölsche, because they held out the promise "to crush superstition, to inform, to liberate, and, indirectly, to democratize." Bölsche's works alone sold over 1 million copies in Germany by 1914;[35] among male workers surveyed in Leipzig in 1924, Bölsche was the fourth most popular writer, after Goethe, Schiller, and Tolstoy.[36] If Nietzsche scorned contemporaries for seeing no further than the horizons of their fathers and grandfathers and for drowning all that was possible in the self-satisfied "shallow waters" of nineteenth-century culture, Göll felt differently, pulled as he was into an unfamiliar but enticing "place of magic and wonder."[37] Night after night he sat in the library until it closed at eight, and once he understood that science was "no closed book," Göll thought of himself as a "young bird" flying over a "free, wide sea" toward "new shores."[38]

A "craving for books" well describes Franz's astonishing reading program as a young man. Between 1913 and 1916 he read nearly 250 books in the Schöneberg library, ranging from literature, in which classics mixed with popular romances (Edward Bulwer-Lytton, Eichendorff, Theodor Fontane, Maksim Gorky, Bernhard Kellermann, Heinrich von Kleist, Jules Verne), to geography (On The Rio Negro or The Sahara), philosophy (Haeckel and Otto Weininger, for example), and natural history (everything from Darwin and Bölsche to Snapshots from Berlin's Zoological Garden). Indeed, in the reading diaries he maintained until 1980, Göll carefully categorized and tabulated his reading choices.

He showed a clear preference for literature and natural history.[39] He also laboriously took "scientific" notes, filling volumes in chronological order, to create a hand-crafted encyclopedia for personal reference. "Even then my efforts," Franz admitted in 1943, "were directed toward an overall view, a survey; I searched for overarching connections and associations."[40]

With classificatory zeal he worked mightily to hold on to this fabulous new world lest it disappear like some schoolboy's fantasy. Franz remembered that when he was a small child, his grandfather entertained him by cutting out pictures of animals and mounting them on cardboard. This was the foundation of Franz's vast picture collection: "I carefully saved these animal cutouts, bought new ones, and collected them in a shoe box, and one box was quickly followed by a second one. My eagerness to collect was stimulated and developed already back then. I became expert at cutting figures out and even pared away the blank parts between the legs and around the neck, head, and breast in order to get an image of reality as true to life as possible."[41] Ambitious plans in 1916 revolved around sorting all his animal pictures according to the classification scheme employed in Alfred Brehm's *Animal Life*.[42] At the same time, the chocolate bars that kids purchased at newly installed vending machines around the city included pictures from an interesting series: "Landscapes from exotic places, customs and traditions of strange cultures, animal pictures, agriculture, colors of the sky, types of sailing vessels, etc." Among Schöneberg's boys "the passion for collecting was in full bloom."[43] But Göll did not want to trade pictures; he wanted to assemble them, all of them. His purpose was "to fix and fold fast the present and its inventories, and to give it a commemorative or souvenir form in order to keep it from completely sinking into oblivion." Hence his collecting mania: an inventory on 20 February 1916 yielded 2,000 pictures; by October the collection had grown to 5,730, all systematically cut out of magazines from the years, as he faithfully reported, "1896, 1897, 1899, 1900–1904, 1907." The last time Göll counted (in 1945), he had amassed a collection of 8,283 postcards in 231 albums;

unfortunately most of these are dispersed in the picture collection of the archive that received Franz's papers.[44] Another great project was the preparation of daily weather reports in which he noted temperature, wind direction, barometric pressure, and cloud cover. A now-lost register of films frustrated the compulsive Franz when he did not know precisely how to classify a drama with comedy scenes.[45] "I regret again and again," he commented, "not to have been able to catch everything in order to preserve it in the archives of posterity."[46]

But the zeal to collect always overrode the determination to classify and the desire to control. This is key to understanding Franz Göll's productivity, his graphomania. There was an extremely restless quality to Göll's autodidactic pursuits, as he admitted in 1950: "I have the sense that my knowledge is not a stationary property, but rather has an ambulatory character. My knowledge behaves like a drawn rubber curtain whose resilience reveals a spacious room behind. It is not knowledge methodically gained or firmly held, but something haphazardly, even randomly piled up that bumps, picks fights, and is at war with itself, decays, and crumbles to make way for new stockpiles." This diary entry is a good example of Göll's powers of observation and his sharp self-scrutiny, as well as of his awkwardly precise, strangely eloquent German.[47] But the inconstancy that Franz reproached in himself was the basis of new insight. For Franz, truth was more a method than a destination: "Even when you have graduated from the schools of life, sampled the most diverse circumstances, and suppose that you know yourself," Göll asked, "is that really so? Already the grown man finds that his childhood is actually quite strange to him; he has long grown out of it. The truth about a person is not a formation fixed for all time, but transforms itself over time and is really only fastened in outline."[48] Franz considered knowledge dynamic and contingent, as two aphorisms—his own—confirm. "The more you know," Göll asserted as a twenty-one-year-old in 1920, "the more often you will let what you know be contradicted by what you come to know." And near the end of his life, in 1974, in the middle of his critical inquiries into the origins of Christianity, he concluded: "For the philosopher, nothing is self-evident."[49]

Göll was fascinated by the possibility of probing beyond the limits of what was known, and he designed his reading program to contemplate "the dark side of the moon."[50] One of Göll's heroes was the sixteenth-century astronomer Nicolaus Copernicus, who dared to contemplate things that were not directly sensible, postulating a heliocentric universe in which human life on earth was no longer at the center. Following Copernicus, Göll considered what contemporaries did not know. In his scientific notebooks, for example, the eighteen-year-old reader excerpted the musings of the famous Berliner, "Urania-Meyer," M. Wilhelm Meyer, the director of the city's popular lecture series at the Urania Hall, who wondered whether "anyone could say something against the claim that atoms form the planetary spheres of their own cosmic scale and are inhabited, just as our earth is, by intelligent, comprehending creatures for whom particles of a grain of sand constitute the faraway stars of their universe." Meyer asked, "Should the ability of endless nature to produce have limits precisely where our narrow capacity to perceive comes to an end?"[51] It was this question that prompted Franz to experiment with the occult in the years after World War I, when he joined the Johanni-Bund and later the Society for Research into Psychology and the Occult. "There are people who boast of seeing things that others simply cannot apprehend," he noted; was such clairvoyance extraordinary sightfulness or just fantasy? (Such questions preoccupied even the eminent novelist Thomas Mann, who asked: if $E = mc^2$, why should we not be able to conjure the dead?)[52] Because the caterpillar knew nothing of the butterfly it would become, Göll was inclined to agree with Meyer about the probable existence of unknown lives: "The world does not end where the limits of perception are drawn around our senses," he insisted again in 1933.[53]

Although Göll's reading program veered toward the middle-brow, with well-thumbed, now largely forgotten novelists such as Paul Heyse and Ernst Zahn and the great popularizers from Wilhelm Bölsche to

Isaac Asimov and Erich von Däniken in the lead, the reading diaries contain some surprises: the philosopher Karl Löwith, poets such as Rainer Maria Rilke and Mikhail Lermontov, and the novelists Gustave Flaubert, Hermann Hesse, George Eliot, and J. D. Salinger. However, Göll put his own darker cast on the Darwinists he gobbled up. If Bölsche celebrated the developing bounds of human solidarity in his most famous book, *Love-Life in Nature* (1898–1900), Göll emphasized hostilities in the state of nature. In the very first book Göll picked up at Schöneberg's library, *War and Peace in the Ant Colony* (1908), Karl Sajo put the emphasis on "peace," praising ant colonies for "having finally really succeeded in banning the struggle for existence from their societies—the struggle for existence that remains the raging source of most of our own distress and misery." Ultimately, Sajo was sure that humans, whose brain was, after all, "a million times bigger than a small ant's," would construct improved social organizations.[54] By contrast, Franz used the imagery of ant colonies to condemn mass society, putting the stress on "war."[55] He returned again and again to a completely obscure book, *About Us People (Über uns Menschen),* published in Leipzig in 1908 by one S. Philipp—but it was "the deepest impression that any book has ever made on me"—and to one scene in which Philipp described social relations with reference to a horrendous spectacle in the Berlin zoo: "It was a hideous, grim sight . . . Suddenly one bird leaped up, hacking away at another and chasing him from his perch, then a third did the same with yet another so that there was a nonending duel. And one bird, who had been chased and fled, and cowered for a while, suddenly leaped up and himself started hacking at another, who was forced to flee. It was sickening." The state of hostilities in the zoo resonated deeply with Franz Göll because it portrayed the overwhelmingly difficult struggle for existence to which he felt he had been extradited. It matched his "attitude toward my environment."[56] With Philipp's *Über uns Menschen,* Franz Göll began to prepare his own syllabus.

Göll's readings also included a great deal of literature. By the turn of the twentieth century, more and more people read novels, but they did so not to be instructed by exemplary models of behavior but to recognize their own idiosyncratic selves in the characters. In novels Göll recognized his "self to himself," as Seigel puts it.[57] Even second-rate novels provided empathetic transcripts of his struggle in society, often bringing forgotten incidents from his childhood back to memory. Reading Selma Lagerlöf's *Another Piece of Life to Live* or Fritz Marti's *Prelude to Life,* he observed how "his being was often reflected in part or whole by the character of a novel."[58] However, Franz also came to realize that the lives of the characters he read about often followed trajectories more coherent than his own. This was the case because, in an insightful comment on Goethe's autobiography, *Poetry and Truth,* retrospective reflection "dispenses with the fire of youth, the agonizing doubts, the spiritual upheavals, the engagement with life and its values." The result was "a life whose resolution appears as the purpose, a portrait without animation, verse without poetry, winter without snow."[59] Göll prized more transitive forms of reading and writing. Indeed, Göll quickly recognized the fictional quality of literary resolutions. Paul Heyse's characters, for example, "stay stuck in the depths, in gloom," whereas Ernst Zahn's "struggle to reach the summit, the light."[60] Even so, Göll's main explanation for the discrepancy between life and fiction was psychological: Göll believed that he was constitutionally unable to pick himself up as others had. Moreover, he lacked the "patrons, sponsors, advisers, friends" that biographies showed famous men had relied on.[61]

In the end it was not the successful characters who intrigued Franz, but the failures. In his notebooks he excerpted Friedrich Hebbel on shyness, Marti on awkwardness with girls, Zahn on loneliness, Wilhelm von Polenz on dysfunctional families, and Adam Karrillon on troubles at school. Göll's favorite novel was Walther Staudacher's *Lonesome Way,* a book almost as obscure as Philipp's *About Us People.* Published in 1938, it portrays an impoverished Berlin schoolboy who loses his father in the war, struggles as a working-class child in an elite high school, missteps playing with a jazz band in the Metropolbar, and, once he is completely alone, abandons the city. Franz read the unhappy story of Bertel Kramer three times in 1941 and 1942 and again in 1949, 1955, 1973, and 1979. He identified closely with Bertel: he was "an uncorrupted example of humanity, who completely unselfconsciously confers his naïveté onto the world and who, shocked, confused, and disappointed, must discover that his set of values is not recognized in everyday life."[62] Franz recognized his unsuitability to make his own way or to promote himself. Both Bertel and Franz risked failure in life because neither was nor wanted to be a *Kampfnatur,* a fighter.

Franz entered the library enthralled and emerged from it more interested, but also more skeptical about how books produced resolution and authority. This awareness helped him reach his own conclusions and discover his own intimate characters on the world stage. As Göll noted, quoting his intellectual herald Philipp, "to be skeptical means to observe, nothing more."[63] Unlike Berlin's other famous Franz, Döblin's Biberkopf, Göll did not pass on the jingles and fashions of consumer society. Nor did he accept uncritically the expert knowledge of twentieth-century science. He was not completely fearless or immune to convention, particularly when it came to ideas about women. Nonetheless, Göll fashioned his own syllabus and aimed to observe coolly and disinterestedly, as he believed Copernicus had. In this regard, the autodidactic diarist resembled Menocchio, the sixteenth-century Italian miller whose "tangle of ideas and fantasies" drawn from a wide range of classic and subversive texts Carlo Ginzburg reconstructed from the transcripts of his trial for heresy in his classic study *The Cheese and the Worms.*[64] Although Franz never confronted a twentieth-century version of the Inquisition, not even under the Nazis, he, like Menocchio, studied books for their discrepancies, false conclusions, and the quarrels they picked with what passed for objective reality. As an autodidact, he was a figure familiar to the twentieth century, someone usually low born who read both obsessively and eclectically in order to puncture what passed as familiar and self-evident. And as an autodidact, a philosopher-clerk if not a worker-poet, Franz combined often-astonishing insight with insistently held, self-guiding formulas. Making individual claims about social knowledge appeared to Franz to be a lonely task, but it was probably widely shared in an age of contested authority.[65]

However, Franz lacked Menocchio's unwavering confidence in the face of opposition, and also his ribaldry. The more squeamish Franz was dogged with a sense of failure, and his reading and writing focused on why this was the case. In his autobiographical writings Franz makes a case for his insufficient self. If scientific readings first accompanied his premonition of genius, they later served as resources to explain his inabilities and incapacities. It was this search for taking stock of failure that provided fuel for his ongoing reading program and diary project. By the 1930s Franz had immersed himself in psychology and psychoanalysis in order to make his case more persuasively. Both the ability to make a case by energetically studying history, psychology, biology, and sociology and the inclination to see himself as a distinctive but explicable case study turned out to be a fundamental part of twentieth-century life. One way to read the diary is to understand it as a continuous transcript of his compulsive study of his battered self. This injured sense of self is both the premise and the product of his autobiographical writings. Göll's diary thus shares many of the melancholy characteristics of other modern diarists who, in fact, cite each other's lachrymose reflections: Göll cited the diaries of Goethe, Hebbel, and Henri-Frédérick Amiel; Kafka cited Goethe; Pessoa cited Amiel; W. N. P. Barbellion cited Maurice de Guérin and Marie Bashkirtseff; and so on. "Doors of chance into the rooms of experience" is how Arthur Inman described reading the diaries of Pepys, Rousseau, and Tolstoy.[66] In a more delusional and circumscribed fashion, and using less scientifically inflected language, the Saxon judge Daniel Paul Schreber (1842–1911) wrote his own case report based on his psychiatric confinement at Flechsig's Asylum in Leipzig between 1894 and 1902, *Memoirs of My Nervous Illness* (1903), an early study that Freud subsequently deployed as a telling example of homosexual panic.[67] Göll stands out, however, for making his self-scrutiny a lifetime project and the foundation of his broader intellectual pursuits. He foregrounded his symptoms as indicative of his physical body, his mental character, his personal circumstances, and his social milieu.

Göll did not pursue the diary to discipline or police himself or to make himself more normal, but to account for why he was different. In many ways his relentless theorization of himself made him think that he was more messed up than he really was. The business of medicalizing the soul was itself traumatizing.[68] Göll's efforts at self-analysis began when he explored the lonely, stoic role of someone called to greatness, as the fortune-teller had suggested in 1916. He read widely in the "solitary suns" of genius, excerpting the famous Otto Weininger, as well as the forgotten Heinrich Lhotzky and Rudolf Penzig, each of whom attempted to explain why the genius had trouble with women, thought of himself as sick, and appeared to be a complete outsider.[69] But it was not so much the suspicion that he was a genius as it was the realization that he could find no "confirmation" of being one that really propelled Göll's efforts at self-examination.[70] He considered sociological explanations in which the destruction of social milieus and the emergence of mass society had left the individual economically insecure and psychologically ill equipped to promote himself. Although he held on to his identity as "Franz von Göll," what frightened him was not the loss of distinction as a nobleman but the demands of modernity on the individual who by his own effort had to find a place in society without the support of social structures. He found social interactions in the workplace difficult; he often had dreams about losing his way in the bureaucratic and technological mazes of the big city. He also saw the problems his mother experienced coping with schedules, deadlines, and other aspects of modernity's temporal regime. Work, the streetcar, shopping— all involved increasingly extensive negotiations for both mother and son. The horror of the massification or the proletarianization of society, what Göll called "naked life," was that it exposed his inadequacies to mount the struggle for existence. This is precisely what contemporary scholars have identified as the challenge of living in a posttraditional "risk society."[71] In just a few years Franz Göll found himself cast from, in Roy Baumeister's words, the genial solitude of "Thoreau's cottage" into the bewildering alienation of "Kafka's castle."[72]

In both places, the cottage and the castle, Göll insisted on the distinction of being different. But in "Kafka's castle" Göll saw his inadequacies in the light of the abilities of others, the majority (of schoolchildren or work colleagues) who had been able to find their way, whereas in "Thoreau's cottage" Göll had been the special genius, the others an ordinary mass, a view that no longer held. The discrepancy between the self and society prompted Göll to undertake a more sustained analysis of his genetic endowment and psychological condition. Göll's investment in sociobiology and psychology in the 1920s and 1930s was immense; he filled scientific notebooks with long excerpts from works of Oswald Bumke, Arthur Kronfeld, and Ernst Kretschmer, among others. This trio was an odd assortment: rector of the University of Munich, Bumke was an avid opponent of Freud and a committed Nazi who was forced into retirement after 1945; Kronfeld was a left-leaning psychologist at the Charité hospital in Berlin who went into exile in 1933 before committing suicide in the imperiled Soviet Union in October 1941; and Kretschmer, longtime director of the psychiatric clinic at the University of Marburg, had once worked with Kronfeld but made his peace with the Nazis and continued research after the war. In the years after World War I, Europeans increasingly described themselves and explained their personal problems in medical terms. Indeed, picking up works on psychology and thinking about the self in psychological terms was unprecedented, a mark of twentieth-century life; more and more contemporaries parsed everyday culture with Sigmund Freud's words ("superego," "narcissism," and eventually even "Freudian"). "Symptoms" were recognized and regarded as symptomatic—of sexual pasts, of sociological presents, and of other dilemmas. New territories of the unconscious and the irrational were annexed to understandings of the self. In 1927 Göll went so far as to prepare for his case study of himself a "medical dictionary," in which he listed the "foreign words, forms of expression, conceptions, technical terms" he gleaned from his scientific readings. A sample: "adrenalin," "epiphysis," "hypertrophic," "infantilism," "necrosis," "spasmodic," and "trauma."[73] But it was Kretschmer, something of a guru in Germany and the United States in the 1920s, who provided Göll with the most resonant words and the most touching case studies.

Ernst Kretschmer was popular in the Weimar years because his physiognomic investigations seemed to describe the social pathologies of the young republic. In his most influential book, *Physique and Character*, first published in 1921, Kretschmer used (in an utterly unrepresentative way) detailed photographs of psychotic male patients to distinguish among constitutional types: the leptosome or asthenic, in which Göll recognized himself, was thin and effeminate in physique, which contrasted with the "broad shoulders" and "firm abdomen" of the more developed athletic and the medium-sized, stocky pyknic types. None of these was inherently superior to the others, Kretschmer argued, but the build of the body affected the condition of the mind. Asthenic individuals, in particular, were more prone to schizophrenia, which developed out of a three-way combination of genetic dispositions, social circumstances, and eventful experiences. In many ways Franz's diary followed Kretschmer's method as the diarist described his cumbersome asthenic parents, detailed his inhibitions in the workplace, and reported on painful incidents from his childhood and apprentice years that left him speechless and terrified. Reading Kretschmer's symptomatology of the schizophrenic, Göll must have felt that he was perusing his own case study. In his 1927 study *Delusions of Reference*, Kretschmer described patients whose feelings of inadequacy, combined with high ethical standards, left them "powerless" and "defenseless" in the "struggle for life." Shy and awkward, they felt particularly vulnerable in society, exposed like a "peeled egg," in Bumke's words, and frightened of the shameful humiliations they might experience in their daily interactions.[74]

Although Göll was more apt to seal his fate biologically by adopting Kretschmer's asthenic type, Kretschmer himself stressed the role of difficult social situations, which Göll cited in his notebooks and which must have recalled his feelings of misdirected, unrecognized genius.

Kretschmer contended that "unmarried, employed girls," "single, over-burdened farm lads," and "striving autodidacts" (like Göll) found themselves particularly vulnerable to humiliation because they experienced dramatic contrasts between their own ambitions and the more confining expectations society invariably imposed. What "society demands from older girls living alone," the psychologist explained, is "a continuous and unnatural tightening of their ethical sense of self, the most firm suppression of any erotic femininity, an overdrawn virtuousness, which it later reproaches her for as primness. . . . She finds herself cast permanently as a kind of minor, her private life is publicly supervised, she is paid poorly for her efforts, and, without social support, is open to all sorts of high-handed and unfriendly behavior."[75] Such individuals oscillated between a kind of autistic withdrawal into their shells and a high-minded "unworldly idealism" and "boundless metaphysical speculations." Kretschmer seemed to be looking right at Göll when he described the schizophrenic's prolonged puberty, sexual attraction to but intellectual contempt for women, and disposition "to restlessly give names and dates, to number and schematize, to make abstract, to build systems no matter what."[76] Kretschmer also introduced Göll to a range of fellow literary schizophrenics from Friedrich Hölderlin to August Strindberg, who quickly appeared on Göll's reading list. Other medical case studies, such as those collected in Karl Birnbaum's *Psychopathological Documents* (1920), taught Göll about the propensity of melancholiacs to keep diaries as records of their endless struggles with the outside world.[77]

Kretschmer aided Göll enormously in his understanding of his self, propelling Franz's reading and making his observations more astute, precise, and scientific. "In the process of exploring my self more comprehensively," Franz wrote in 1956, he was able to diagnose himself at once as an "asthenic, phobic, schizothymic." "Among the characteristic features of this kind of personality would undoubtedly be its own isolation from the surrounding world. These subjects know little about how to deal with themselves and their surroundings; they do not understand how to derive personal benefits from their social relations and do not put much value on their effectiveness. Moreover, these subjects possess little inclination or ability to initiate or maintain contacts with the rest of the world, either because their interests are so remote and obsessive, or because they are completely unable, as a result of their inner emptiness, to make a personal effort."[78] The work of diagnosis fueled Franz's graphomania as he established his "medical dictionary," widened his reading program, discovered and excerpted more and more case studies, and delved into his past in both the diary and the memoirs, which were written between 1941 and 1948 in 123 installments inside the diary. Composed during the war, alternating with entries commenting on Germany's battles and detailing Allied bombing attacks on Berlin, and completed in the tough postwar years, the memoirs covered his life up to 1945. Readings in literature, biology, and psychology, the scientific notebooks, and autobiographical genres such as the diary and the memoir all helped Göll make his case.

Franz also meticulously cross-referenced diary entries, repeatedly going over old ground while directing readers to pertinent entries: "(Compare this section with the diary entries from 12. II. 1916, 28. II. 1916, 30. VII. 1933, 19. V. 1934, 28. VII. 1934, 11. XI. 1934, 15. XI. 1934)."[79] Only slowly, in the 1950s and 1960s, did the formative years of the diarist, the miscarried genius of 1916, and the young man's struggles to earn a living in the 1920s relax their hold on Franz's writing. Even so, the self-referenced influence of the period of the Third Reich and World War II remained strong throughout the post-1945 years. Franz's scientific commentaries in 1981 still referred to arguments developed in 1924.[80] Cross-referencing made Franz's case more extensive and firmly anchored in time and more accessible to future readers. It reveals the extent to which Franz's life was intertwined with the task of making his case to himself and to us.

The entire autobiographical project—the records, the classification schemes, the readers' aids—revealed that Franz Göll's primary task was the accurate and extensive documentation of his life; it was the main accomplishment of his eighty-five years. It took considerable time and money. After World War I, photo albums constituted the largest single recurring discretionary expense in Göll's household economy. Magazine subscriptions, postcards, and notebooks added up as well. Employed in 1919 as a clerk earning a modest 150 marks a month, Göll spent 90 marks on a camera and 30 more for a tripod. (Franz continued to spend 150 to 200 marks a year on his "photo hobby," including a projector and screen in the 1960s and 1970s.)[81] When World War II finally came to an end, Franz thanked "divine will" that he and his mother had survived the "difficult times" without harm, and, he added, "the 200 albums of my postcard collection, which is cultural-historically extremely valuable, also survived completely intact." The albums and diaries had been locked in an "iron cabinet" at work or stored in crates in the basement for safekeeping. "When I laid the cornerstone in 1915," Franz summarized, "I had absolutely no idea what great importance this collection would have for the future, even if it was sometimes an odd hobbyhorse to ride."[82]

Many years later, in 1954, Göll looked back on his autobiographical project with remarkable coldness. "I used to take my self very seriously: my diaries, my collections, my readings, my poems, and, not last, my self. Today I have to admit: it would have been important to have acquired a trade, to have become a man, and to have founded a family. To have learned stenography and typing, business accounting, or a craft would have been more useful than composing poetry, keeping frogs, and collecting useless gewgaws. How wrong I saw life, how little sense for practical things I had. Nothing I did ever bore any fruit; it was all an idle wasting of time. All my activity was a flight from life, a retreat from reality, a game of hide-and-seek with myself."[83] But the restless commentary of which this morose diary entry is a part was his apprenticeship, his art. Perhaps closer to the mark is a still-critical but more telling account of the fantastic structure that Göll's graphomaniac pursuits erected. "Only a small, unadorned frame encloses my life, similar to a tiny stage, on which grandly conceived pieces with many active protagonists cannot be played," Franz commented in 1947. "For the most part, I stand on this miniature stage alone, lost in self-reflection, conducting monologues, poring over books, trying to get at the secrets behind the stage sets that are composed mostly of bookshelves, between which a few narrow shafts lead into the darkness, a stage on which the entrances take place without any applause, a game for myself, not an endeavor, but a self-absorbed pastime that takes childlike delight in the insights gained, an example of a hermit's existence, poor in action and deed, but rich in inner experience."[84] It was on this interior stage and proscenium with its handmade mirrors and windows that Göll probed the fragments of his self and the legacies of Germany's and the world's history. He thought the whole instrument of his self-inspection small, even indulgent and insignificant, but he acknowledged as he did so that he had built the theater himself. It was the setting for his self-realization.

2

Franz Göll's Multiple Selves

Franz Göll installed the interior stage on which he explored his life and the world around him, but the central protagonist on stage switched roles depending on the mode of his self-study. Scholars have long regarded the task of autobiography as one of shaping and constructing the self, an assignment in which the narration of memory provides a sense of individual distinction and a measure of personal stability. Autobiography makes a story of life.[1] But it is quite unusual for historians to have an array of ego documents for a single individual in which each genre choreographs the writerly self in a different way. Here multiple selves are vividly on display. Franz Göll's voluminous papers include the diary that the sixteen-year-old began in 1916 and continued for almost seventy years until his death in 1984; the memoir that Göll wrote inside the diary over the years 1941 to 1948, covering his life and family up to 1945; and household account books, in which he noted daily purchases for the years 1919 to 1927, precisely the period of postwar intellectual ferment, spiraling inflation, and the sharp economic recession that followed. Taken together, the diary, the memoir, and the account books reveal alternative modes of self-representation. They choreograph different selves, the existence of which destabilizes the authority of any single autobiographical text but enriches the corpus as a whole. What has to be recognized as Göll's graphomania composed a vast archive, in which the determination to narrate, classify, and monitor left its mark on the autobiographical production, but in which the zeal to find new perspectives and acquire new material created revisionist and even contradictory versions. The inspiration of the graphomaniac was to gain control, which his voracious method always threatened to undo.

The three autobiographical genres indicate the histories available to the chronicler and the witness, a series of differences rooted in motivation and genre, not experience or eventfulness. Göll's selves also underscore the different identities with which Germans experimented over the course of the twentieth century. The diary discloses Göll's lachrymose preoccupation with his physical and psychic degeneration, which he played out against the background of what he perceived to be an aggressive mass society. However, both the account books and the memoirs reveal a different register of engagement. The daily expenses show that Göll was an avid consumer of a new lifestyle: he shopped, took vacations, and went to dozens of plays and hundreds of films in the unsettled years after Germany's November 1918 revolution. Written in the 1940s, during and after World War II, the memoirs confirm Göll's pursuit of a new, consumer-oriented lifestyle in the 1920s and 1930s, but do so with a nostalgic cast in which Franz the historian both cherished and mourned the Weimar Republic. The degenerate diarist expressed many of the psychological scars of the "new world" of postwar Germany's Weimar Republic and outlined at least one path individuals took to get to the Third Reich. The consuming accountant, by contrast, revealed the opportunities Germans grabbed at during the early years of the Republic, as well as the sense of betrayal they felt when economic hard times returned. A third German position comes into view in the installments of the nostalgic memoirist who stepped back to take the measure of the social and political changes between the two wars, as well as the life journey of the autobiographer. Three Germans, each one named Franz Göll, and the Germanys they introduced combined in such a way as to break down the authority of any single history of the twentieth century. They reveal fragments and alternatives, existing side by side.

The Diaries

The diary (but not the memoirs embedded in the diary) unfolded as seventeen-year-old Franz Göll began to question his ability to realize his dreams. Despite the quick career change that the fortune-teller had foreseen at the beginning of 1916 and his ambitions to become a zoologist or a poet, Franz left the teacher's academy only to work as a low-paid clerk at the German Women's Fund for Children of War and then as a statistician for the Reich Coal Distribution Office, both agencies across from each other on Wichmannstrasse in western Berlin. His entries explored why and how the "autosuggestion to be genius" had not been confirmed in fact. In love with Klara, Franz wrote poems but seemed more interested in furtively following her down the streets and behind the curtains of her backyard tenement. "Hauptstrasse, Akazienstrasse, Belziger Strasse, and back to Eisenacher Strasse"—it was a terrific "adventure in love" just to watch her.[2] It was not long before "I examined our relationship from various angles and withdrew," a conclusion in which observation and reflection allied with retreat from activity to form the basic motive of the diary.[3]

Franz used the diary to examine remorselessly his lack of willpower and his inability to get ahead. He constantly observed himself and compared himself with others. "With her lively constitution and temperamental manner, she is the total opposite of me, the quiet, secretive brooder," he wrote in one of his first entries when a cousin came to visit.

The autobiographies he liked to read sometimes comforted him because the protagonists shared his misfortunes, but just as often they offered contrasting examples of how individuals achieved success despite early failures. "After a fall, an energetic, strong-willed, purposeful, self-confident personality will get back up and recover," Franz explained. But the problem was that Franz was not able to accomplish this rehabilitation and remained almost completely engrossed in the memory of his initial failure. The nostalgic tone of many of the diary entries in which Franz sprinkled stories from his childhood was really a recollection of his uncanny, awkward relations with the rest of the world written in anticipation of a sweetness he never tasted. In the first year of writing the diary, Franz related a dozen incidents documenting the solitary, *linkisch* (bumbling) boy. His favorite toys, he remembered, were wooden clothespins; he played horsey and, because he was alone, whipped himself; he felt the movement of ghosts in his room; he found it trying to look pleased at Christmas—Franz Göll could wait to open his presents.[4] Diary entries first wistfully introduced the prize and then abruptly withdrew it: "It was maybe eight or ten years ago," seventeen-year-old Franz recalled with all the embroidery of a mislaid wistfulness. "Every year, a restaurant owner in the area organized a harvest festival at the end of summer. The little garden was decorated with lanterns and garlands. Paper hats, torches, and sashes painted with figures in grotesque or exaggerated grimaces were for sale. It was always a lively pell-mell, full of surprises that pitched the frolicsome mood to new heights. One of these was the 'candy shower,' which took place in this way: the restaurateur dumped out a bag full of wrapped candies from the second-story window. While all the other children were busy picking up the candies, pushing and hitting each other as they did so, I just stood upright in the middle of the confusion. Without wanting to get hit, I surreptitiously stooped down to pick up one or the other piece lying around me that had been overseen by the others. As a result, my booty was very small."[5] Although his memories were packaged in childhood sentimentality, they actually revolved around the absence of innocence and his frustration with himself. In an aphorism, the diarist acknowledged: "The truth makes for a poor companion."[6]

Subsequent diary entries indicated how Franz continued to misstep as a young professional. A colleague at work once asked Franz "to fetch him three cigars for 45 pfennigs. At the tobacconist, I asked for what was wanted verbatim. With the greatest of care, the salesman thereupon wrapped up three thick cigars with labels around the middle and demanded 1.35 marks. I must have realized immediately that there had been a misunderstanding, but I lacked the quick retort. I consoled myself by telling myself that I had completed the transaction exactly as asked. Although my colleague was flabbergasted, he settled for the cigars, saying only that I could have figured that he did not smoke 45-pfennig cigars but wanted three at 15 pfennigs for 45 pfennigs total." This is one of three maladroit incidents recounted one after the other in a 1953 diary entry that serves as a perfect illustration of Ernst Kretschmer's case studies of schizophrenics who experienced great difficulty adjusting themselves to social situations.[7]

From the very beginning, Franz noted how difficult it was for him to function in society. Most of the time he came across as "withdrawn, cold, inhibited, and at a loss for words" because acquaintances in the neighborhood and colleagues at work "had what I considered to be an abhorrent way of interacting. What they did was to ensure the display of their own personality at the expense of others, fleecing others with random remarks or otherwise taking advantage through intrigues and ulterior motives."[8] "Community," he explained nearly twenty years later, in 1938, "engenders infighting, a battle for recognition, equal status, and domination. To endure this battle, which is often a nasty, covert guerrilla warfare fought out behind the scenes, one has to possess a certain physical and mental assertiveness. Because I did not have this, I was usually at a disadvantage." Franz never deviated from this explanation. His incapacity to act, to be the agent of his own desire, to make "propaganda" for himself (a telling 1930s word he adopted), and altogether his inadequate "motility," a term he also used repeatedly, left Franz paralyzed. If others remade themselves as Dale Carnegie advised in his best-selling self-help books, *How to Win Friends and Influence People* (1937) and *How to Stop Worrying and Start Living* (1944), Franz was stuck in the past. "I cannot get out of my past." the diarist admitted. "Sometimes I feel that my actual life for myself has not even begun yet, as if I still have to overcome the past (biological heredity)." The grip of the past was evoked by incidents from his childhood to which Franz still felt tethered.

But the diary did not just record Franz's passivity; it was itself the product and confirmation of his restraint. "What I want to do is simply to account for how I, on the basis of my constitution, am attuned to the environment, how the environment acts on me, and what reactions this activity produces."[9] Franz continued to search for answers, seeking out the fortune-teller, experimenting with occultist groups, and going to self-styled psychologists, such as Rudolf Diekmann, to whom he introduced himself in the Society for Research and Enlightenment in early 1918, but all these endeavors ended without result. Diary entries in the form of hard-luck aphorisms summarized his incapacities: "Who cannot as a master to life propose, will simply be disposed of as a tool"; "Whoever cannot make claims on life, will only get a 'naked life,' and whoever is too modest, no one will miss."[10] As he expressed it in 1949, "Life seems to me more like a dream, from which we, according to fate, are suddenly ripped."[11] One more example, a poem:[12]

Small in risks,
Big in failure,
That is my nature,
the judgment of fate.

Franz's unsettled employment history backed his feeling of homelessness. With the stabilization of the German currency at the end of 1923, the government dissolved the Reich Coal Distribution Office, throwing Franz out of work. In a frantic search for a new position, he found that prospective employers did not even respond to his inquiries, despite the enclosure of return postage. At the end of February 1924 he accepted a position as a traveling salesman for "J. Hansen Chocolate Wholesalers (Bln.-Schöneberg, Feurigstr. 39)," "a line of work for which I considered myself completely unsuited. My quiet existence resists this uncertain, agitated, fast-paced occupation." Day after day Göll shuttled between stores and restaurants, selling chocolate bars, candy drops, and *Katzenzungen* to earn a measly 5 percent commission: 1.66 marks on 28 February, 0.66 on 5 March, 3.62 on 14 March.[13] After three weeks he had made so little money and gathered so much stress that he quit. Eventually he found a position as a temporary package handler at the post office on Luckenwalder Strasse, near Gleisdreieck in Kreuzberg, but the job hardly relieved the suspicion that his life had come to a halt. "Who are you, what can you do, what can you offer?" Göll asked himself, "and I have to admit: 'Nothing.'"[14] At the end of 1924 Franz looked back: "Even if financial hardship affected the first years after my father's death, back then there were still some rays of hope to illuminate my confidence, but today?! I feel shipwrecked, stranded, swept up by waves on some foreign shore, exposed to all the inclemencies of the weather." "Money trouble, illness, no career, no future!"[15] By the end of 1925 Franz's shift at the post office had been reduced to six hours a day, at which point he broke off writing the diary altogether.

Two-and-one-half years later, the diary resumed with Franz in a secure position in the print shop at Julius Springer Publishers on Linkstrasse near Potsdamer Platz. He remained at Springer, to this day a prestigious scientific publishing house, until the end of the war, winning promotions and achieving financial stability. Even so, he felt completely uninvolved in the big changes that had taken place in his life. He regarded the new position as the result more of "coincidence than methodical effort." There was nothing about Springer to disrupt the lachrymose narrative Franz had constructed for himself. "Up to now in my life, I have never weighed more than 100 pounds or earned more than 200 marks," he reflected at the end of 1933, "a very modest performance on both counts." (His income, 2,600 marks a year, was just below the average for white-collar employees but 60 percent more than the average for workers.) Göll's life continued to appear as a "yawning emptiness."[16] As far as Franz Göll was concerned, the reason was the familiar one: "For example, it never occurred to me to restructure or influence my surroundings to follow personal ends and goals."[17] "Careerwise, in love, as versifier, as scientific researcher, as a 'politician,' . . . I have never picked out a goal," he explained in 1936; "I tremble at the thought of going on the offensive . . . I am just not a shaper. I cannot master my own destiny."[18]

"When I follow back the path of my professional career," Franz wrote in 1951, after he had quit Springer, had worked for several years as an ordinary laborer hauling away ruins of the war-wrecked city, and then in 1947 had found employment as a night watchman at a lumber yard on the Sachsendamm, "the harshest truth is the fact that my professional positions have just been episodes. There is no career path of advancement and a final success. If I take my school days as zero, the upward curve of career probation at the Fund for Children rose only slightly and continued its lackluster ascent, interrupted by short-term, ever more modest spikes. After the Coal Distribution days, which ended on an inglorious note, the curve fell back to zero. Then followed the post office episode, completely professionally irrelevant because it was just a transition. Then the days at Springer that offered a chance at advancement and could have become a permanent post. But even here my lack of self-confidence kept the curve flat and dragged down any significant upward movement. Only in my capacity as department head did I begin to free myself internally, and the curve reached its highest point. When I quietly, furtively left Springer after the catastrophe of 1945, the curve descended once again because there was nothing left that had any professional or permanent value."[19] Again and again Franz missed feeling part of an enveloping, meaningful life narrative.

Whereas other people saw themselves as active agents in their lives, Franz perceived himself to be the object of events over which he had no control and that he encountered as threats. And whereas others advanced in their careers and progressed in their lives, Franz saw only a string of episodes. The only thing that had changed was that "in the meantime I am older and have become a person without a future who, at the same time, does not have a 'past.'"[20] By his own testimony, Franz was unable to make use of his experiences, apply them to new situations, and thereby gain some control over his life. Well into his adulthood, he still felt himself to be a child. Indeed, he continued to live with his mother in the Rossbachstrasse apartment they shared until her hospitalization in 1952; Franz never moved out of his childhood home and died there in 1984. "Childhood is not a closed-off period of life that lies behind me," he wrote in 1938. Ten years later, near the age of fifty, he felt as though his life had not yet even begun: "I am still the young man," out of joint with time, "at once child, adolescent, and adult." He believed that he had not passed definitively from one stage of life to another and therefore was "never completely a child, a young boy, or a young man," remaining an incomplete, indistinct creature who was "hard to fathom." Because he had not "worked through" or "overcome" the different parts of his life, "all the fragments, remnants, push themselves forward as ballast."[21]

Franz tried to understand how the past was managed with the striking image of a developed film. "Spiritually healthy people," he explained in 1958, "clean themselves, so to speak; they make a final reckoning and make themselves available for new impressions, new experiences, new thoughts and ideas. It is not that the past is erased, but it is overcome and preserved in the form of a completed roll of film." On the other hand, unstable introverts, among whom he counted himself, "plague themselves with inhibitions, cannot let go of the past, and do not give themselves room for something new. For them, the past is always the living present rather than a developed and archived film." What they do is "experiment with the past, reexamine situations again and again in a new light, from a new perspective, dissecting, analyzing, finding new angles; the present rests completely in the shadow of the past."[22] This nervous activity characterized the "extra, bystander," the "observer," the roles that

Franz Göll self-consciously assumed in his diaries. Everything remained an episode, inconclusive, undeveloped, meddlesome. As a result, "all my entries are somehow tied to myself; the reflections tend to be mostly egocentric." "Like a gerbil chasing its tail on a treadmill, my intellectual efforts race around in a circle. The irrational aim of all this motion is to find myself."[23] The diary was the most direct medium by which Göll collected and held fast the incidents of the past and thereby observed and played out his lack of mastery. Cross-referenced entries directed readers to the old childhood recollections from 1916 and the melancholic reflections of the unfulfilled genius, "the quiet, secretive brooder," the extra, the half man, half child. If Franz's diary was addressed to a still-unformed, future self, the endeavor was a disappointment.

Franz Göll projected onto others the fully developed sense of selfhood in which an active subject attained mastery over the past, made deliberate decisions, and moved decisively from one goal to the other, but this projection disguised a more interesting, if unintended, acknowledgment of the lack of control that people in general may well have felt about their lives. Franz dramatized and personalized inadequacies that were hardly unique to him, as the psychologists he read repeatedly affirmed.[24] "Even the luckiest of the lives," concluded one study in the 1960s, "had its full share of difficulty and private despair"; what Freud referred to as the "psychopathology of everyday life" is "always with us."[25] Göll's own sense of insufficiency thus allowed him to undertake a critique of assertive individualism whereby people objectified situations and others around themselves to achieve their own advantage. Moreover, his inability to inhabit the position of master made Franz unavailable to the Nazis, whose claims to racial superiority and justifications for war and empire he rejected almost from the very beginning of the Third Reich. "Even if my work remains a mere fragment," he reflected in July 1949, "I am proud that the train of my thoughts, opinions, and views has never succumbed to time-bound dogmatism and never stood in the service of terror or coercion."[26] Unable and unwilling to seek advantage for himself in society, he also found that women appreciated what they took to be his modesty and courtesy. And even as Franz lamented being burdened with the ballast of the past, which he continuously shoved around with him, he also came to appreciate the creativity of experimenting with the images of the past rather than developing or archiving them. He felt condemned to run around in circles, but he achieved insights into his self from which he believed most people refrained. "I really lead a double life," he explained to his imaginary readers on his fifty-ninth birthday in February 1958: "In the real world, I am the bumbling, inconspicuous, harmless 'young man,' who has remained without significance. Only in my illusory world do all events concentrate themselves into a transfiguring symphony, a mystical understanding. And this is and will remain my life purpose."[27]

What accounted for his incapacity? Over the seventy-year course of his diary, Göll deployed two master metaphors to explain his personality and character. In the 1930s and 1940s, very much in the spirit of the time, he undertook biological assessments of his family in order to explore his depleted genetic endowment. Later, in the 1950s, Göll followed up psychological and psychoanalytic models that had been current in the years after World War I. In the years 1919 to 1923, as a young man, Franz was also fascinated with the occult, attending lectures, subscribing to the magazine *Psyche,* and reading widely. At one point he even came to the tentative conclusion that "the confusing, extreme, and contradictory" aspects of his "life and being" might be explained by the alignment of "two oppositions D 8 4/S and Ψ 8/λ" and "two quadratures ($\Theta\square$ D/A and $\Phi\square$ D/A)" on the day he was born in 1899.[28] But Göll ultimately found that heredity more exactly accounted for both his passive nature and the phlegmatic character of his parents.

Like psychology, heredity was one of the popular sciences that ordinary people translated into their personal lives. Across Europe autodidacts followed the lead of scientists in mulling over neo-Darwinian propositions about genetic heritage, fruitful marriages, and degenerate lifeways. Even Thomas Mann developed these themes in his famous early twentieth-century novels *Buddenbrooks* and *The Magic Mountain.* In the year after his father's death, in the midst of his infatuation with Klara, Franz attended a lecture by a Reinhold Gerling, a prominent "life reformer" addressing the Society for Research and Enlightenment on the topic "What Do Prospective Marriage Partners Need to Know about Heredity? (Is There Heredity?—Why Do So Many Sick Never Get Better?—The Inheritance of Medical Predispositions, Talents, Character Traits—Dying Breeds—The Inheritance of Tuberculosis, Madness, Nervous Afflictions, Cancer, Gout, Obesity, etc.—The Prevention of Damage)." These topics were pressing issues during the war, which had, after all, jeopardized the overall biological health of the nation; marriage rates declined while childhood mortality shot up. Franz was "more disappointed than satisfied" by the lecture but remained biocurious. The next month he heard Gerling speak about "proper choices for marriage (girls you should not marry; men who are not allowed to marry; the single child; signs of infantile behavior; the causes of marital disappointment; temperaments that do not match)."[29] The war, consumer culture, and popular science all made professional advice such as Gerling's profitable business. However, it was only when the Nazis were in power after 1933 that Franz undertook comprehensive genetic evaluations of himself and his relatives.

Because Göll focused on weakness rather than strength, the racial doctrine of the Nazis, who distinguished allegedly superior "Aryans" from other, allegedly lesser races, barely registered in his reflections. Although he, like almost all other Germans, had to prepare an "Aryan" table of ancestors in the Third Reich, he was less interested in confirming his racial bona fides than in tracking down particular pathologies in his family. Göll was keenly interested in the inheritance of biological weaknesses over the generations, but as a result, he ended up working with the same genetic propositions that undergirded Nazi laws mandating the sterilization of "unworthy" life—indeed, he wondered whether he was "unworthy." At the end of July 1933, just two weeks after the Ministry of the Interior published the Law for the Prevention of

Hereditarily Diseased Offspring on 14 July 1933, some six months after Hitler had come to power, Göll took a long look at the "enfeebled mental constitution" of his mother's family, the Liskows:[30]

> Mother's father was a mental weakling, someone who was not able to get what he wanted. As long as life flows uninterruptedly, there are no problems for such mental asthenics. But as soon as someone with a sthenic mental constitution butts in, the trouble starts. My grandfather's undoing came in the form of his son-in-law, the husband of his younger daughter, my Uncle Carl Amboss. This person knew how to run around my grandfather, to string him along in order to achieve what was to his advantage. Too lazy to support himself and his family, my uncle let my grandfather support him. After failing, despite support, in all manner of professions (cook, dentist, barber, meat inspector), he threw in his lot and was able to get my grandfather to sign over his business to him. In this way, without putting in a penny, my uncle received a house with a grocery store and garden . . . Thereafter, my grandfather, who was already a widower, lived in his own house as a barely tolerated tenant . . . My grandfather let himself be robbed of his rights instead of taking his son-in-law and his family on as tenants in order to keep some sort of leverage. This shortsighted course of action, combined with his asthenic paralysis of will, this giving in to the encroachments of the outside world without any struggle, is typical for my grandfather's family.

Moreover, as he embroidered on the case study, "in family biological terms, it is worth noting that my grandfather married relatively late in life (at thirty-six years of age?), while his brother died as a bachelor. Another brother who emigrated to America was also said to have lived as a bachelor. The marriage of his sister Marie (Frau Hentze) remained childless." The whole line of Liskows was dying out. This was in contrast to the pushy, determined Ambosses, the family his mother's sister married into, who in one form or other appeared repeatedly in Franz's accounts. They stood in for the rowdy schoolboys in Schöneberg whom

Franz disliked as a child and later for the ambitious work colleagues at Springer from whom he shrank in fear and dislike.

The division of human types into pseudoscientific categories, in this case the belligerent "sthenics" and the weak-willed "asthenics," was typical for Franz, who not only saw social interactions as the sum of a relentless struggle for advantage but also embellished his diary entries with a vocabulary gleaned from a wide variety of books and magazines so as to give his conclusions intellectual veracity. Franz was familiar with the hygienic literature that sprouted around the themes of love and marriage after the turn of the century; he read naturalist novels about milieu and inheritance, such as Zola's *The Belly of Paris* and *Nana,* and he had a passing acquaintance with Nazi tracts—Göring, Hitler, Rosenberg. But his scrupulous biological analyses owed the most to psychiatrists such as Ernst Kretschmer who constructed elaborate physiognomic readings of German society.

In July 1934 Franz prepared an even more detailed "hereditary biological study" of his uncle's family, the Ambosses:[31]

The family produced seven children, of whom one, a girl, died in infancy. In their physical and mental constitution, three of the remaining children (Martin, Gertrud, Kurt) show the influence of the Ambosses, two (Helmut and Margarete†) have a streak of Liskow in them, and one child (Rudolf) is a mixed type (physically = Liskow, mentally = Amboss).

The sthenic effect of the Ambosses is evident in the fact that Martin and Rudolf have made themselves economically independent (each renting or owning a tavern); Gertrud has made a magnificent match considering (Mrs. Captain Matthes), and Kurt is trying hard to make something of himself professionally. The other two children clearly show that they have inherited the weak mental streak of the Liskows. Helmut, who as a child suffered in silence, trained as a baker but is still only an assistant, that is, a wage earner without the prospects to make himself independent anytime soon. Mentally too weak to effectively resist the reality of the ongoing demands of life, Margarete committed suicide. Her motive: a broken heart.

By Franz's reckoning, the "spiritual-mental structure" of his mother was all Liskow: "Naïve, sweet tempered, tender hearted, somewhat sluggish, bumbling, and awkward in interactions with people, unassured, frightened, and inhibited in public, nervous and weak spirited in private." His father was not very different. The elder Franz Göll "had a small, compact frame, physically in good nutritional condition, but with a flabby constitution—otherwise without remarkable features. From a spiritual-mental perspective, he had a ponderous nature, something of the solitary eccentric who never really enjoyed life, was easily defeated, lacked a sense of assertion, was ready to give way, socially awkward, always seemed shy in every situation, inhibited in showing or expressing his feelings, self-conscious, quite uncommunicative, lacking in energy, naïvely sweet tempered, receptive only in a limited way."[32]

Again and again the diarist came to the conclusion that as caregivers, "my parents were grossly neglectful in every way."[33] They took little interest in Franz and provided him with few resources. He never sat on the lap of his mother or father; he was nothing but *Luft,* hot air.[34] His parents conducted a loveless marriage in which husband and wife increasingly kept to themselves; for a time Franz even slept between his estranged parents.[35] As a result, Franz believed that the "autosuggestion" that he was a genius served as a strong resistance or counterweight to the obstacles he encountered at home. He even supposed that he had discovered a natural law of "resistance-accommodation" to explain his self-willed suppression of his upbringing. Thus, Franz left room for compensatory psychological mobilization that could overcome biological inheritance. But the entire "hereditary biological study" of his family continuously echoed his miserable assessment of himself. He clearly felt the heavy weight of his mother's melancholy Liskow relatives in his body and the lack of the more offensive nature that characterized the more aggressive Ambosses. However much he appreciated the cultivation of his autonomy, to which the whole diary project is testimony, Franz regarded himself primarily in terms of his family's decline. "Already for generations, the signs of degeneracy have been observable in our family," he commented in 1936; "the offensive nature is suppressed; indeed, we have already evacuated our defensive positions and find ourselves in retreat. Where this will lead, whether and when it will come to a stop, only time will tell. Perhaps it will end with complete dissolution, final renunciation, unconditional surrender, an unceremonious extinction." Franz's imagery was completely entangled with ideas of the ongoing struggle for existence. "I am the last of the line," he concluded; after that, "decay, ruin, and rubble."[36]

Göll was quite clear about his conviction that the "social stratification of a people represents not an artificial but rather a natural process of selection; in the individual case, a personal fate determined by the unity of the human in nature."[37] This was a general rule that he believed ordered the universe. Göll explained at the beginning of 1929, "Just as the individual person is forced to remain in a particular sphere of life (generally speaking) and one race subjugates another (in the most drastic case whites over blacks), so it is everywhere in the universe. There, the same laws apply in the end. The earth compels the moon to orbit it, the sun, the earth." As a result, there was little the state could do to alleviate social misery. Göll considered "strikes, demonstrations," and other revolts "passive rearing-ups," not signs of collective strength or resistance; "even the giant struggles in vain against his bulk, the midget against his diminutiveness, and the cripple will never become a whole person."[38] Evidently, Göll explained his inability to move forward with static explanations drawn from biology. Given his plight in society, he was not unsympathetic to suffering, to the injured and dead on the field of battle, or to Cäsar, the farm dog whose mistreatment by his Amboss cousins Franz detailed in the diary, but he consistently translated his frustrations into general laws that would explain his incapacities.

However, there was a logical flaw in Göll's argument for biological destiny. His own family provided an example of the onset of "a general weariness of life," so that the "spiritual-mental structure suffers damage" in ways that made it possible to imagine the "giant" turning into a cripple after all.[39] Moreover, his theory of "resistance-accommodation," in which he overcame the "mama's boy" to realize his autonomy in 1916, and his appreciation generally of the role of the genius and the superman to transform life indicated the possibility of innovation.[40] But by the 1930s Göll's observations had become more melancholy, more drawn to iteration than to innovation and to degeneration rather than to regeneration. Springer had provided Franz with modest financial security but had not changed his pessimistic outlook on life.

With Germany's defeat in World War II and the end of the Nazis' biopolitical regime, Franz's confidence in genetic evaluations receded. Ten years later a broad, politically rather mixed reading in psychology and psychoanalysis (C. G. Jung, the Freudian Otto Rank, revisionists such as Karen Horney, and Igor Caruso, a problematic Nazi-era psychologist, as well as Ernst von Aster and Wilfried Daum) provided him with revamped categories for self-analysis.[41] Of course, heredity and psychology were not mutually exclusive methodologies to explain character, but Göll's biological studies tended to see people such as his mother and father as passive receptacles, whereas his psychological assessments probed deeper into the tangle of phobias and distortions that made up individual personality. Once again he considered the Liskows, this time the sister of his mother's father: "For example, when it was not allowed to open a single window in the house of Frau Maria Hentze . . . I would interpret the manners of feeling in the following way. This representative of the Liskows regards anyone who contravenes her rules as her enemy who is set on harming or destroying her. It would be an attack on her person." His grandfather Hermann—who under a psychological lens suddenly gets a name—also "considered everything that disrupted his dull, contemplative peace to be a 'hostile' action." As for his mother, "Any umindful word or gesture she regarded with suspicion, distorting all sorts of jokes into their opposite." Franz concluded: "I totally suffer under this egocentric complex"; "I always suspect that I am creating resentment and displeasure around me, misjudging matters, making a fool of myself, or making myself unpopular."[42] Franz continued to find biological relationships relevant as he proceeded from grandfather to mother to himself, but his focus shifted to the individual and to potentially reformable traits. At the same time, Franz's general pessimism gave way to a more fine-tuned understanding of the complex individuality of each and every person.

In 1956 Franz began to write down his dreams, which he realized were a "source of making one aware of what is hidden in the unconscious or subconscious."[43] It is not clear whether his psychoanalytic studies made him more aware of his dreams or just more apt to write them down. Most of the dreams revealed the anxiety of the individual who had been required to fulfill an unfamiliar task or to reach an unknown destination. Many involved metropolitan amenities that needed practice to negotiate: train stations, subways, department stores. They recall the shocks of early modernity that Franz Kafka (with streetcars, gates, and walls) and Ernst Jünger (with elevators and stairs leading nowhere) worked out in dreams as well.[44] Franz recorded "a polymorphic dream" on 25 January 1957:[45]

I found myself on the street. There must have been quite a commotion because everything appeared to be "disheveled." I entered a department store but did not use the main entrance and instead climbed up a ladder on the scaffolding, turning and shifting so as not to get myself dirty. At the top of the ladder was another ladder over to which I had to balance myself. Then I proceeded along a corridor next to the windows, and as I did I ruffled the drapes, which an employee then silently straightened back out. Next, I looked for the exits and simply used a mast down which I unhurriedly slid. There was still lots of commotion on the street. People with eating utensils rushed about. Although they apparently were very hungry, they all appeared chubby and plump. Then I went ice-skating down the street. Because I did not feel completely confident, I only took half steps, but I had fun.

Particularly interesting are the dreams that Göll designated as "Springer dreams," which he had on and off well into the 1970s:[46]

> I was given the task of picking something up as quickly as possible, but I did not have an idea of what object I was supposed to get. I wandered the unfamiliar streets aimlessly, searching in vain for a point of orientation. Finally, I spontaneously entered a bookstore in order to figure out the object. Everyone was working diligently, and no one noticed me. Because it was getting late, I was expected back soon, so I ran back outside in the unfamiliar precincts. Completely by coincidence, I found the Springer House, stormed up the steps, and entered a department in which people were busily working. Among the unfamiliar faces I saw colleagues, but no one recognized me. I felt completely redundant and went back down the stairs. Everything seemed amiss, and it was only out of a sense of duty that I, who had returned empty-handed, looked for my superior. But I found neither him nor the exit.

These were twentieth-century dreams of coordination rather resistance to power.

"Remarkably, these Springer dreams," Franz commented, "which come to me after long intervals, all took the same course. In all of them I rushed about searching spasmodically, in vain, through workplaces, across half-lit floors, over secluded courtyards, not seen or recognized by anyone, only to find myself suddenly outside." In many respects the dreams recapitulated the stories Franz introduced at the beginning of the diary of the socially awkward, insecure adolescent frightened of ghosts. They dramatized Franz's incapacities exactly as the early diary entries had.

The Household Account Books

If the household account books were all that were left of Göll's legacy, an entirely different person would take shape in the mind's eye. They are remarkable documents because they register Franz's daily expenses from the beginning of 1919 through the great German inflation in 1922–1923 to the end of 1927 and the period of financial stabilization. In two respects they confirm the man whom the diaries introduce. First, they indicate Franz's zeal to collect postcards, to pursue photography as a hobby, and to maintain his aquarium and birdhouses. Newspapers, magazines, and food for the animals were routine expenses. Second, the household books reveal the deep rupture that the loss of Franz's job at the Reich Coal Distribution Office left behind at the end of 1923. Even when he regained some financial stability with a position at Springer Publishers in 1926, Franz and his mother had little money and drastically cut back on the forays they had taken into the city immediately after the war. For the rest of Franz's life, 1924 figured as a catastrophic year of crisis. But it is the differences between the self constructed in the diaries and the self whose consumption and movements the household books reveal that jump into view. There is little sign in the accumulation of daily expenses of the withdrawn "fancier of an autistic way of life," or of someone who saw himself "living in a charming cottage with a small garden and stables."[47] Berlin after World War I was loud, sharp edged, and bursting with energy; businesses flamboyantly advertised themselves as "House of Soap, House of Fruit, Paper House, Sport House, Stocking House." As a consumer, Franz moved through the big city with dexterity, taking advantage of the goods it offered, the spectacles it staged, and the lifestyles it enabled.[48]

The daily expenses that Franz registered beginning in 1919, when he was twenty years old, showed the young man outfitting himself for middle-class adult life. The frame was simple: the tenement building at Rossbachstrasse 1 was electrified in 1920, so it was no longer necessary to purchase city gas (piped in from Schöneberg's famous Gasometer) for cooking and light, but for many years it lacked a bathroom; Franz bought coal briquettes to heat his rooms until the apartment was outfitted with central heating in 1979. Part of Franz's weekly routine was to visit the public baths and also a barber to get a haircut and a shave— Franz purchased tickets for twenty visits at 7.50 marks. He bought hair

oils and hair tonics. "Tooth powder with peppermint" gave way to
Chlorodont toothpaste in November 1921.[49] But as a statistician at the
Coal Distribution Office, Franz assumed the status of middle-class
employee, however modestly he was paid. This meant proper dress:
overcoat, boots, and suits, as well as all the gear around the neck: de-
tachable bow ties, paper collars and then permanent but still-detachable
ones, which required collar buttons, and finally ties as fashion shifted
throughout the temperamental 1920s. Heads required hats, including
nine fedoras that Franz purchased between 1919 and 1926; hands received gloves—Franz bought at least four pairs, although he might have
lost some—and feet were outfitted with boots that needed to be regularly waxed, resoled, and repaired. A suit of clothes was expensive: in
September 1920 it cost Franz 560 marks to buy a new suit and have another altered (by contrast, a book sold for about 2 marks). Suspenders,
and eventually hangers for the trousers, cuff links for the sleeves, and
garters for the socks completed the middle-class outfit in 1920s Berlin.
In addition, there were small discretionary touches: the "etui" for comb
and mirror, the walking stick, the watch with an "illuminated dial," the
pipe and tobacco bought in May 1920, the cigarettes first purchased in
April 1921, the cigars, the dickey, the two linen shirts picked up (perhaps
on sale) for 8,000 inflationary marks on 13 January 1923, and the nine
fedoras or *Filzhütte*.

If, when Franz Göll was growing up in the 1910s, he thought that his
family lacked "a sense of style" because it had no valuable "art objects
(pictures, vases, figurines)" to interrupt "our uniform, slow-moving family life," he made up for it in the 1920s.[50] For his mother's birthday he
often bought pictures, including one depicting "Goethe's garden house"
painted by "M. Schmock"—probably an embellishment of one of the
town of Weimar's characteristic postcards.[51] It was perhaps patriotic inspiration at the height of the hyperinflation that moved Franz to buy a
framed portrait of Frederick the Great in August 1923 for 1.6 million
marks, exactly the cost of eight pounds of pears. New furniture arrived
as well, a wicker chair in December 1919 and an upright clock the follow-

ing October. As was fitting for any proud Berlin family, Franz Göll kept flowers for house and balcony, buying seeds, soil, and fertilizer every spring and otherwise following the instructions of a how-to book, *Caring for Flowers at Home.*[52] Franz also bought sheet music to play the piano, which the memoirs revealed his parents had already bought in 1910.[53]

Franz's "Springer dreams" revealed a man pushed and prodded into big-city traffic, uncertain about how to reach a destination or to find his way back, but the household books indicated that Franz took public transportation almost every day, usually the streetcar, but also buses, the subway, and the elevated (now the Stadtbahn). This urban movement took place in the years before 1927, when the Berlin Transport Association created a unified transportation system and a single flat ticket price. Franz spent weekends taking trains, ferries, or steamboats into the countryside surrounding Berlin. We see Franz constantly on the move, browsing, breezing, buying newspapers and his beloved postcards, which he often selected by the dozen, picking up a pound of apples, plums, or cherries from a fruit cart on the corner, drinking a glass of beer or a *Weisse mit,* Berlin's favorite sour beer with raspberry syrup, stopping at a café for coffee, lemonade, or a bottle of "boa-bie," grabbing some chocolate or a roll of mints at a *Tabak,* and bringing home to his mother a slice of "honey cake" or "gingerbread" from a bakery he had passed by.[54] In the roiled year 1923, when French troops occupied the Ruhr and German finances spun out of control as workers in the district called a general strike, political activists often approached Franz, who donated 1,000 marks—at the time, about the price of ten cigars—to the Ruhr Relief Fund on 15 February and again on 21 and 26 February, 20 and 28 March, 28 April, 8 and 18 May, 25 June, 11, 16, 21, and 30 July, and 15 August, by which time inflation had boosted his regular contribution to 20,000 marks.

The eight-hour day and the forty-hour week, among the great achievements of the German Revolution in 1918, left bachelors like Franz Göll with considerable free time. There is little mention of going to the movies in the diary, but Franz went frequently, well above the average for Germans in the 1920s. In 1919 he went to the cinema 19 times, about once every three weeks; in 1920 he saw 21 films; by 1923 the number was 28. There were times in November 1923 when Franz went to the movies almost every day. The crisis in Franz's life, when he worked in the post office, employment that was incompatible with his calling as a man of learning, a writer of poems and manifestos, was accompanied by much more moviegoing—38 cinema visits in 1925 and an astonishing 74 in 1926. (The Weimar-era diaries of Victor Klemperer, a professor of literature in Dresden, confirm that this pace was not unheard-of; every day nearly 2 million Germans went to the movies.)[55] Unfortunately the film diary Göll kept has gone missing. Franz also attended symphony concerts three or four times a year and went frequently to the theater, enjoying Leon Jessel's operetta *The Girl Detective* at the Central Theater at the end of December 1921, Eugene Brieux's drama *The Red Robe* in the Lessing Theater in January 1922, and Alfred Lorentz's comedy *Moonshine Lady* at the Walhalla in February 1922. Over the course of 1922 he attended more serious plays as well: Bjørnstjerne Bjørnson's *Beyond Human Power* and Gerhard Hauptmann's *Rats* at the left-leaning Volksbühne on Bülowplatz, *Death of Danton* at the Grosses Schauspielhaus on Friedrichstrasse, and Shaw's *Widowers' Houses* at the Neues Volkstheater on Köpenickerstrasse, which catered to a working-class audience. With his visits to the Volksbühne and the Grosses Schauspielhaus, and their repertoire of Expressionist and engagé dramas, Franz took in the most innovative productions of German theater, an extraordinary cultural circuit that his childhood experiences did not anticipate and his diary did not record.

Franz scampered around Berlin, undertaking expeditions to the Cathedral, the Altes Museum, and the Schloss. On 24 June 1919 he climbed up the Victory Column. He went to the aquarium to see the exhibition on walruses and to Lunapark, where he amused himself three times in May 1921. He attended talks at the Urania and saw educational films at the Treptow Observatory. Fifty pfennigs allowed him to look at Saturn through a telescope in May 1919. A keen interest in the occult lured Franz to lectures by astrologists and new "life reformers" Karl Brandler-Pracht, Leonhard Stark, and Peryt Shou. Franz joined the mystical Johanni-Bund in August 1919 and the Society for Research into Psychology and the Occult in November, and also the Friends of the Treptower Planetarium. Except for Franz's dabbles in the occult, none of this busy urban activity, which added up to two or three events every week, registered in the diary.

All of this was more than restless diversion. The household books indicated that Franz avidly pursued his hobbies, photography and especially his reptile and fish aquarium. Between 1917 and 1938 the diaries made no mention of the aquarium, but the household books indicated a regular routine in which Franz bought water fleas, frogs (at 3 marks each), snails, and salamanders and a weekly supply of lettuce for his turtle. Aided by a subscription to the *Blätter für Aquarium und Terrarienkunde,* he built his aquarium himself, as the purchase of a glass cutter confirmed, and added sand and rock and provided food. Historians sometimes forget that Weimar Berlin, the battleground of the Republic in the tumultuous 1920s, was a place where one could buy goldfish or the small net, a *Käscher,* to scoop them up in (an aquarium with goldfish is visible when Franz Biberkopf seeks out Minna in her apartment in Rainer Fassbinder's 1980 film *Berlin Alexanderplatz*). We also know that Franz had a remarkable talent for taming birds, which flocked to the birdhouses he kept stocked with seeds that he bought by the pound. At the end of October 1920 he purchased a little finch. Around the same time Franz pursued a new passion in meteorology. He bought a barometer for a precious 85 marks, half a dozen thermometers, and graph paper along with a how-to book, *Our Weather,* in order to keep a daily weather log.

Aside from providing a few dates in the early 1920s, the diarist did not report on the vacations he enjoyed. This is a surprising omission because vacations remained luxury excursions even after World War I, which is why the National Socialists deliberately offered holidays through their Strength through Joy program as a way to integrate workers and "the little man" into the national people's community they claimed to represent in the years after 1933. As late as 1934 the majority of workers at Siemens in Berlin, some 28,500 out of 42,000, most of whom certainly earned more than Franz did in the Reich Coal Distribution Office, had never been on a holiday trip beyond the forests and lakes ringing the city.[56] In other words, at the beginning of the twentieth century, most Berliners had never seen the ocean or the mountains that railroads had placed within striking distance. As indulgences in which vacationers paid a premium for the room and board they had already purchased at home and pursued their own whims without regard to obligations to family, vacations exemplified the new choices available to contemporary consumers. Franz left his mother alone and stayed clear of his relatives in Kladow in order to pamper himself. Lying beyond the circuits of visits exchanged among family members, holidays were unambiguous and expensive declarations of autonomy and selfhood. Indeed, the Nazis' Strength through Joy program was popular because it created for the individual a sense of value and entitlement in which the regime appealed to the dreams of each and every (racially acceptable) German rather than to particular interests of class and status. Franz wrote extensively about his vacations, discussing the Strength through Joy trips he took in the 1930s in his memoirs and the holidays he enjoyed in the 1960s and 1970s in his postwar diaries, but the first indications of his travels around Germany appeared in the household books in the early 1920s.

Franz's trips were planned as special excursions. For his July 1920 holiday, he purchased trail maps and a guidebook, outfitted himself with a new fedora hat (85 marks) and suitcase (55 marks), and enjoyed the services of innkeepers who provided him with coffee, beer, and "buttered bread w/ham." When he returned after three days (from what the memoirs confirmed was the Spreewald, a charming destination barely beyond the suburbs of Berlin), he purchased a book on Homer's *Odyssey,* perhaps in preparation for greater adventures in the future, and a tree frog to continue at home the study of nature his vacation had enabled.[57] Armed with new guidebooks, he traveled to Mecklenburg a year later. Even in 1923, as Germany spiraled into financial chaos, Franz confidently purchased a rucksack and a walking stick and traveled by "mailbus" at the end of May.[58]

The travel guides that Franz bought were much more than simply aids to the exploration of the countryside. They sat on the shelf alongside other helpmates such as *Concert Key for Laymen, Caring for Flowers at Home,* or *Our Weather,* how-to books that indicated the extent to which Franz guided his life into what he considered new and uncharted territories. Reaching beyond what he learned at home or at school, Franz was intent on gaining mastery over a distinctly personal lifestyle, which he continually embroidered and improved. The guides indicated Franz's ability to make choices in an increasingly consumer-oriented economy. If the clean break and big chance had eluded him in 1916, he was nevertheless able to fashion a kind of mastery over his life a few years later. Guidebooks provided the rails to his cherished autonomy.

Historians often depict Germany's postrevolutionary and inflationary years as dark, severe, and difficult. The household books certainly registered the impact of the inflation, and they did so in extraordinary detail because Franz noted almost every daily expense, except for the groceries his mother purchased. Already in August 1922, change was no longer counted in pfennigs; soon expenses were rounded off in hundreds (November 1922), then thousands (March 1923), and finally millions (October 1923) of marks. At the height of the inflation, in November 1923, Franz bought cuff links for 14 million marks, a tie for 39 million, and, a few days later, a dollar currency-conversion chart for 360 million. But for Franz, who had seen a life of misery after his father's death, the early years of the Weimar Republic, including the worst years of the inflation, represented a period of exploration and acquisition. Franz was not rich, but as a state employee, he enjoyed a modicum of discretionary income and took advantage of regular inflation-era cost-of-living adjustments to his income, enough to add to his postcard collection, buy books, visit the theater and cinema, accessorize his wardrobe, and embark on annual vacations. He continued to attend occult lectures, take coffee and cake on Saturday afternoons, and enjoy a steamer expedition on Sundays. Franz the patriot donated inflationary marks to the Ruhr Relief Fund and acquired a framed picture of Frederick the Great. The evidence from the household books indicates that Franz had adjusted himself quite well to the economic opportunities that the new republic offered workers and employees and to the cultural experiments it offered consumers. In the years of the inflation, Franz achieved by his own efforts a high degree of refinement.

If the household books reveal how well Franz surfed the swells of the inflation, they indicated as well how hard the economic recession of the stabilization hit small employees. The end of the inflation in 1924 was accompanied by a serious credit crisis that left many small business owners and farmers bankrupt and white-collar employees and low-level bureaucrats such as Göll without jobs. Franz's daily budgets revealed the harsh new economies. He continued to go to the movies but curtailed most other discretionary expenses. Whereas in the early 1920s he had always given his mother generous birthday gifts, in 1924 he laid out only a few marks. New Year's concerts gave way to more modest celebrations with pancakes and punch. There were no more vacations, at least until a visit to Neupinnow in 1929. Instead of fedoras, linen shirts, and cuff links, Franz acquired a workman's blue smock and a workman's cap, items that confirmed his new, somewhat shameful proletarian identity as a post office worker. The thrifty week was interrupted by an occasional morsel of chocolate (50 pfennigs), a bite of wurst (two pair for 50 pfennigs), a glass of beer (15 pfennigs), or a cup of coffee (25 pfennigs). There were larger expenses as well: week after week, Franz continued to escape to the movies (about 1 mark a show in neighborhood theaters), and in 1925 he tried his luck at the horse races. He bought a racing journal (30 pfennigs) and placed 1-mark bets on Jester, Armature, Rose Bowl, Cold Front, and finally Colberg—names that revealed a lot about Germany in the year 1925—but despite a few wins at short odds, he lost more than he won, and after a week he gave up the risk.[59] His scrupulous household accounting ended in May 1927, about midway between the end of the diary in December 1925 and its resumption in August 1928. On the whole, the stabilization stands in contrast to the inflation; Franz endured a straitened, penny-pinching existence without being able to afford the styles of life he had enjoyed in the early 1920s (his mother also stopped working regularly at the end of 1922). But the more dramatic contrast is between the mobility registered in the household books and the immobility Franz performed in the diary entries.

The Memoirs

In the middle of World War II, in January 1941, after Germany's victories in western Europe but before the invasion of the Soviet Union, Franz Göll set out to write his memoirs. He interrupted his diary entries to provide long retrospective accounts of his childhood and his years as a young man. Running for as many as fifteen or twenty pages, his autobiographical installments, over 120 in all over the course of the years 1941 to 1948, contained some of Göll's longest essays. The memoir was an exercise of sustained reflection and writing, constituting somewhat less than one-fifth of the total number of words in the diary. At the outset Franz declared that the diary he had kept for a quarter of a century lacked "overarching connections." "Life, in terms of an autobiography," he explained, "means that one does not just provide simple descriptive accounts of events but also a portrait that elucidates, explains, and justifies the particular course of life." By writing an autobiography, he would be able to put aside a purely "egocentric disposition" and see himself both as the "subject and object" of his environment. "We probably all see ourselves as soloists, but in fact we are usually just poor, bungling accompanists waiting for the right signals from the conductor's baton."[60] In this respect the autobiography elaborated themes already introduced in the diary: Göll's feeling of helplessness and his desire to examine the reasons for his passivity and inactivity. At the same time, however, the reflective nature of the memoirs allowed Göll to construct his life according to a self-invented developmental schema in which the child grew into the schoolboy and the schoolboy into a young man. He traced his early apprenticeship in the social, political, and professional world. Moreover, Göll the memoirist paid much more attention to the historical context of his life in the first half of the twentieth century. During the final battle for Berlin in 1945, he provided long, elegiac descriptions of Berlin as it once had been. In his memoirs, in contrast to his diaries, Franz Göll revealed a much more confident authorial presence both by inhabiting the role of historian and by describing a much fuller life, which the diaries, with their obsessive concentration on Franz's maladies, had withheld. The memoirs calibrated the self to historical time.

As a self-conscious historical observer, Franz the memoirist gave a robust account of his life and times. He deliberately eschewed the episodic or ruminative organization of the diaries. As he testified, autobiography required context and narrative in a way in which diaries did not. But the historical moment of 1941 also drew out Franz's autobiographical self. Over the course of the 1930s, working in the print shop at Springer, Franz had achieved financial security and professional self-reliance. Although he sometimes contested the confidence he had gained, promotions and raises allowed him to look back on the past from a certain distance and height. As late as 1936 his mother still bought groceries on credit from neighborhood retailers; Franz would return home from vacation to empty cupboards. At one point Franz wrested control from her to manage the household economy: "I have been able to put a firm foundation under the erratic and lax household economy of my mother and have transformed what had been a provisional household inventory into a stable one." By 1939, "since the takeover," Franz secured "almost always a surplus as a reserve at the end of the month." With a monthly income of 225 marks, he managed to save 100 marks by the end of the year, 300 by the end of 1940, and 770 marks at the end of 1942. Except for the first difficult years after World War II, Göll continued to accumulate what at the end of his life had become a substantial nest egg, over 100,000 marks in 1983.[61] At least financially, forty-year-old Franz was no longer living day-to-day but had broken with the past and planned for the future. Philippe Lejeune comments that "autobiography meant growing up"; growing up also enabled autobiography.[62]

Nineteen forty-one did not just mark a measure of personal success. The onset of the war, even more than the rise to power of the Nazis, had created a deep divide between Franz's life before and after. There is no mention of the political circumstances that might have motivated the retrospective work of the memoirist. However, the present intruded on the autobiographical text in the dramatic form of the break that the Nazis, the war, and the destruction of the Third Reich had made with earlier events that the memoirist subsequently "developed" into the past. Another diarist who wrote a memoir during the war was Victor Klemperer, whom the Nazis considered to be racially Jewish. Klemperer began his *Curriculum vitae* in the winter of 1939, before the war but in reaction to onrushing events: "I try to think of nothing contemporary." The writer "buried" himself in remembrances of his childhood that were frankly nostalgic and as settled as only the recollected "world of yesterday" could be. Klemperer's memoirs traced out a personal and historical itinerary that did not lead directly to his situation in the Third Reich.[63] Like Göll's, Klemperer's text dramatized the noninevitability of the wartime present. Thus Franz's acquisition of financial security and personal stability by 1939, as well as his perception of drastic historical discontinuity after 1939, authorized the retrospective authority of the memoirist.

The memoirs open much as the diary had, with detailed descriptions of Franz's parents, but for the first time they are introduced in a conventional biographical manner with names and dates. His father Franz was born an illegitimate child in 1864 (and died in 1915); his father's mother later married Hermann Karsch, an electrician in Berlin, both of whom ignored the child, who was sent off to live with his mother's sister, Olga Heckert, in Löbau. Eventually settling down in Berlin as a typesetter at Günther and Sons, printers in Berlin-Schöneberg, Franz's father was "by nature small and stockily built, made a somewhat scrunched-up impression in his later years, accented by so-called flabby jowls. His senses had developed normally, hair was light blond, eyes gray, and you immediately noticed his conspicuously thin arms." "What was lacking was a fresh, hale, brisk countenance; instead, his whole body expressed languor and a lack of energy. In the best years of a man he became quite decrepit and had fallen into a state of exhaustion."[64] Born in 1874 (she died in 1954), Göll's mother, Anna Liskow, was not very different: "With an asthenic physique, she gave the impression of being underdeveloped"— this is all Kretschmer's vocabulary. "A certain unworldliness combined with a rural-naïve perspective on this. Disinclined to learn or to adapt, simple minded, no special talents, no sense for productive effort and work—these were her most prominent characteristics."[65]

The negative influence of his parents on Franz was overwhelming. "As a result of our tardiness we always came too late," Franz remembered. "It was only around lunchtime that my mother was dressed ready to go shopping. If she went to market on the designated days, she had to rush, and the best stuff had already been sold."[66] His parents never went out, visited the theater, or took a trip. When the family took weekend expeditions to Grunewald, Schlachtensee, or Wannsee, "we never got out of the house until late afternoon, despite our best efforts." "The entire treat of a Sunday excursion consisted of sitting in an outdoor cafe near the train station, and we would have sat there until the return journey if they had not given in to my badgering and finally gotten up to walk. My parents did not even hold a lively conversation; they just sat across from each other in silence."[67]

Even the one grandparent Franz knew well, Hermann Liskow, his mother's father (1834–1920), rarely came to visit, and when he did, he arrived empty-handed, although he lived in the countryside and could easily have brought along, Franz thought, "a small basket with fruit, or a chicken, a duck, or fresh eggs." When Hermann was finally moved by good weather to take a walk with little Franz, "then he went down Hauptstrasse with me. But I found these walks boring; Grandfather just looked stubbornly ahead, never even stopping in front of a show window, because," Franz remembered the lines, "'with their displays they just want to take the money from our pockets.' On the village square there was a small playground and a kiosk for drinks. If I was thirsty and asked for a glass of cherry juice, my Grandfather would reply: 'Child, then let us quickly go home, turn on the faucet, and have all the water we want for free.' It was already a big deal if he gave 2 pfennigs for a Gummibär, which would also have to last for several days. All the way, he did not say a word to me, did not point out anything, and simply left me to plod alongside."[68]

The memoirs confirmed what the diaries had already chronicled. Franz was a solitary, sickly child. He continually felt himself to be a "failure," an underdeveloped "misfit" *(Kümmerform)*, an inferiority complex his mother only reinforced by agreeing with company, "Yes, well, he is and always will be a little palebill *[Blaßschnabel]*."[69] The (attentively cross-referenced) childhood memories, the teasing at school, the painful Christmas spirit at home, and the awkward social situations are familiar. Recollections of the schoolboy's inability to get his arms out of his heavy winter coat, which meant that his mother had to help him dress and undress before and again after school (Schöneberg's Gemeindeschule IV on Kolonnenstrasse)—and as Göll's favorite novelist Walther Staudacher observed, "If you are brought to school by your mother, you only count half"—or of the terrible steamboat outing when Franz opened his lunch to find that the bottle of raspberry juice had not been corked properly, soaking his sandwich and spattering his clothes, echoed the childhood tribulations recorded by the diarist.[70] And as in the diaries, Franz neatly captured his sense of underdevelopment with startling imagery. The more he tried on his "spiritual wings," the more the world around him seemed to fall by the wayside. The memoirist realized that he was alone before "he had found himself."[71]

What Franz added were more physical details that retrospection put into clearer focus: "And so it came about that to relieve my internal tensions I developed bad manners and physical tics, picking at my fingernails and toenails and at my ears."[72] "Characteristic for my life," he summarized himself, "is the fact that I have never mastered situations. That is why even my recollections of incidents that are usually associated with good cheer, a merry mood, frolicsome joviality, and games and tricks are always drunk with a cup of bitterness."[73] At first glance, the memoirist and the diarist resemble each other closely.

On second glance, however, the deliberate memory work of the memoirs introduced new features that the diarist's preoccupation with his eccentricities had obscured. The very composition of the memoirs served to propel Franz from one stage of life to the next. He organized the autobiographical installments into five chapters, "My Parents," "My Childhood," "My Private Life as a Schoolboy," "As a Young Man," and "The Man," all of which provided evidence of Franz's awkwardness in social situations and his sense of inferiority. Still, the movement from one stage to another, as he recounted growing up, indicated that Franz finally had mastered situations. The transition in 1916 from his school days to his life "as a young man" required him to adapt to the professional world of the Fund for Children. "The work assigned to me was not difficult," he conceded, "so despite my own expectations, I found my place quickly. What was significantly harder for me was to fit into the company of adults. Until then, I really had not had any independent interactions with adults. I was not yet sufficiently open, adaptable, or polished for my surroundings. My reserved nature cornered me in a variety of ways." Even so, Franz was able to adapt. Franz was also free to pursue his interests after work, which had not been the case when he studied at the finishing school: "I rushed home and immersed myself in my own studies, which I regarded to be my principal task."[74]

In similar fashion, Franz's employment at Springer in 1926 not only marked the transition from "the young man" to "the man" but also

culminated his efforts finally to get a position as a white-collar employee. Whereas the diary account emphasized the play of coincidence,
the memoirs registered the success of Franz's endeavors to find something better than work at the post office. At Springer, "once again, it
was not the work as such that I found particularly difficult, but the people with their personal attitudes, special interests, and self-importance."
Nonetheless, "slowly I gained my self-confidence" and also the trust of
his supervisor, "Comrade Helterhof": "After work, we often smoked a
cigar together, drank a draft of beer and on special family occasions, I
was invited over to the Helterhofs."[75] Moreover, the memoirs pointed
out that both at the Reich Coal Distribution Office in 1919 and at Springer
twenty years later Franz was promoted to department head. In his new
capacity he organized a Christmas party for his employees in 1941. He
trimmed a tree and gave his first public speech, in which he outlined the
gravity of the war to express the desire for peace before handing out
small presents and earning the gratitude of his colleagues—as he himself acknowledged, Franz had been in tip-top form.[76] If the diaries reflected on how little he weighed and how little he earned, the memoirs
indicated growing professional responsibility and financial security. All
the self-doubts of the diaries were replayed in the memoirs, but they
were framed by a developmental logic in which Franz did grow up.

Simply by virtue of explaining himself in the context of his times, a
new way of thinking about the present day, Franz the memoirist played
down his eccentricities. The narrative style persistently folded the singular self into larger, more general patterns. "The little being survived
the danger years of infancy," Franz noted, "and grew into a small child.
I probably behaved like all other small children, even if, on account of
my weak constitution, I probably did not act as impulsively." The memoirist replaced the solitary child of the diaries who played horsey by himself with the pal and "two somewhat older kids from the same building
who played horsey with me," something that delighted Franz.[77] "Of
course, I did not shy away from the typical games on the street," the

memoirist reported about the normal child. Indeed, Franz spent "many happy hours playing together" with "Fritz Stoepper, Kurt Ackermann, Walter Mattutat," friends the diary never introduced.[78]

Even moments of crisis, when Franz sought out a fortune-teller to give him advice after his father died, were cast in a broader social context by the memoirist: "Now predicting the future, telling fortunes, was a booming business during the war. Especially war wives and war widows wanted to find out about their personal destiny in the coming years, and the method employed, whether with cards, coffee grounds, or horoscopes, did not really matter. The war with its horrors, suffering, and deprivations had lasted too long to rely on reason and rationality. People were tired of the nerve-racking waiting and wanted finally to have some 'certainty' about the outcome and end of this world conflagration. Old prophecies were 'unearthed,' and ominous coincidences were 'illuminated' with numerology."[79] Franz had assigned himself the duty to be an exact social observer (and, writing in 1943 about 1916, he expressed an unmistakable protest against war). As well, the diarist's shameful years as a post office worker from 1924 to 1926 were retold in a lighthearted feuilletonistic fashion that reinserted the memoirist into the rhythms of the city. "At that time, horse traffic still prevailed at the post office," he recounted. "As dusk fell, innumerable consignments arrived from the main post offices around Berlin, blocking for a time the large courtyard. After a great deal of pulling on the reins and pushing and shoving the wagons to the loading docks, the exhausted, nervous post horses could enjoy a half hour of rest. On the docks the packages piled higher and higher before being carried off and sorted in fenced-off compartments." "The post was a predominantly male line of work," Franz added, "and the occasional salty phrase could be heard," but the memoirist had to admit "that I was always treated with respect and courtesy, despite the comradely 'Du' form."[80] To relate the story of his life and times in context meant that the exploration of the "times" reconfigured the narration of the "life" as a less solitary and more integrated existence.

What distinguished the memoirs from the diaries was Franz's depiction of himself as an independent, resourceful young man. Franz's capacity as a social observer signaled growing self-confidence in discernment and judgment. Indeed, Franz linked his independence with his journeys of exploration. It was when Franz had achieved "a certain sovereign independence . . . that I made pilgrimages under a starlit sky to the precincts of the metropolis, to Tempelhof with its newly laid-out garden colonies and forlorn parkways."[81] Like many big-city flaneurs from Victor Hugo to Franz Hessel, Göll sought the suburban edges that juxtaposed old and new in jumbled zones of capitalist real-estate development. "Here, where the contradiction of city and countryside came into contact with each other, where the first solitary tenement buildings had been erected and the gaps filled out with garden colonies and open fields and meadows, where urban gardeners pumped the levers of the well in even measure to water their flower and vegetable beds, where neighbors gossiped at the garden gate and the cat, with eyes squeezed tight, trustingly caressed its mistress's feet, where the dull thump of rackets hitting tennis balls echoed and the lively measures of a small band in a suburban café drifted over in delicate scraps, where evening melted the real world into a silhouette of dream and life and desire and beauty— here I felt my soul dissolve and harmoniously resonate with the infinite."[82] It was to catch the ephemeral and the transitory aspects of the city and to find a "route" into his remembered past that Franz began to collect postcards. Franz later maintained that the charm of Berlin could not be captured in metropolitan panoramas, only in postcard-sized evocations. "The born and bred Berliner stands to his hometown," Franz explained, "much in the same manner of feeling as a man to his pure loved one. *Heimat* is actually just a locally bounded precinct of a neighborhood in which he spent his youth. Within these borders, the cords of memory attach themselves to idyllic squares and to more or less happy or sorrowful experiences . . . Berliners express this attitude when they say that they are at home in Wedding, or in Moabit, or in the 'Plumpe,'" Berlin's football team BSC Hertha's old stadium at Gesundbrunnen, or

in Franz's own "Schöneberger 'Island.'"[83] Göll's memory fastened itself to local places, an illustration of Nietzsche's caressed antiquarian
history.[84]

Along with the postcards, the memoirs attempted to hold on to familiar places to which Göll felt connected. If Göll's diary and especially his
"Springer dreams" described Franz's confrontation with an unfamiliar,
vertiginous geography, the memoirs located him in intimate, if changing, neighborhoods. He thereby abandoned the subjectivity of the lost
boy to assume the authoritative role of informed historian. The very nos-
talgia in which Franz indulged integrated him into commonly held experiences of Berlin. What he produced in his memoirs was social history,
not individual pathology.

Take Franz's apartment in Schöneberg's Rossbachstrasse, which in
his diaries he felt lacked a "sense of style" and which he even described
as a dreadful pile of his mother's junk. In the memoirs, by contrast,
Franz's "father's house" was typically old fashioned, but hardly eccentri-
cally out of place: "Our apartment was consistent with the furnishings
and accoutrements of the style and taste of the lower middle classes current at the time. The furniture with unavoidable shell-like carvings, outfitted with columns and so-called *Puppen,* overflowing with cheap knick-
knacks, the window treatment consisting of long *Stores* and even longer
Seitenschals made out of dark fabric that no light could penetrate."[85]
Whereas the diaries repeatedly insisted on Göll's exceptionality, the memoirs invoked exemplarity in order to make Franz's historical and histori-
cizing perspective accessible.

At the very end of World War II, in March and April 1945, as the air
raids of the Allies gave way to the artillery fire of advancing Soviet
troops, Franz mustered extraordinary detail to portray the long-lost
Berlin of the 1920s. The memoirs dedicated about one in fourteen pages
to this fascinating survey. By the time of the endgame of World War II,
Franz's memoirs had advanced into the dramatic, revolutionary years
of the Weimar Republic, which he evoked in terms of "the spirit of the
times," a contrast to the somewhat timeless portrait he had drawn of

old Schöneberg and of the cobblestoned streets, village church, and rural ambience surrounding his childhood. In contrast to the melancholy diary entries of the 1920s, Göll wrote vividly twenty years later about Weimar Berlin and his encounters with the modern city. The memoirs finally brought Franz Göll to life. He reviewed the tumultuous social life after the war: the movies, cafés, and dance halls, the vulgarity and shamelessness of entertainers, and also the refreshing freedom from prewar prudery. "A fresh wind" provided "a strong feeling of life." He escorted readers to the *Zelten,* the beer gardens on the edge of the Tiergarten, which resembled a veritable "meat market." This was a period, he reflected, when people declared that "my body belongs to me" and explored lesbian and homosexual relationships. He went on to sketch a striking scene in an amusement park: the "unavoidable food stalls, where you could get sandwiches, *Bockwurst, Röstwurstel,* dill pickles, finger food, and potato pancakes for 10 or 15 pfennigs—a blind man could have found his way simply by following the penetrating smell of cheap cooking oil." And "of course, every carnival had the beloved attractions: carousels, shooting stands, and airborne rides. During the peak hours of such a carnival there were nonstop crushing, jostling, hooting, cackling, tinkling, and shrieking. Then suddenly the noise of a shrill, tinny-sounding ringing of a vigorously shaken bell accompanied by loud beckoning-bleating 'Aha' shouts drowned everything out."[86] He also recorded scandals and affairs, for example, the sensational disappearance and resurfacing of the Russian "Princess Tatjana" or the marriage of the former kaiser's sister to a "no-gooder dressed up as a rake with the name of Subkow" in "the blind panic of being left on the shelf" (a story Döblin places in *Berlin Alexanderplatz* as well); the fad of elixirs and vitamins; and the almost endearing characters of the hyperinflation: "The nouveaux riches, so-called *Raffkes* in the vernacular, who had previously been ragpickers and junkmen."[87] After twenty years, recollection provided a loud, colorful, basically wistful reconstruction that was entirely missing from Göll's reflections at the time. In the diary Göll had crafted his lonely self with psychological reflections that relied on the scarcity of experience. Entries brooded and inhibited the exposure of events. By contrast, Franz wrote up his memoirs as a historical text with a wide readership in mind. As a historian, he often began his Weimar chronicles with the introductory explanatory phrase "it was the time when." In 1944 and 1945 Göll interrupted the memoirs to comment on the war raging around him, but the battles did not intrude on the text except to seal off more securely the pre-Nazi past over which Göll assumed a protective stewardship.

Both the diary, with its more self-centered focus on Göll's unhappy lot, and the memoirs, with their broader social historical perspective, worked familiar clichés of the Weimar Republic. The first text depicted Weimar as a treacherous, inhospitable ground that would become familiar to readers of Hans Fallada's best-selling 1932 novel about Depression-era Berlin, *Little Man, What Now?*[88] Years later, in the memoirs, however, Franz turned Berlin into the scene of carnival, in which transgression instead of deprivation and diversionary metropolitan spectacle rather than self-absorbed scrutiny prevailed. The diaries created a bridge to National Socialism, across which one way out of the economic and political impasse could be found according to the maxim "everything for the whole" instead of "everything for the individual," which Göll identified with the failed Weimar Republic.[89] By contrast, Göll's memoirs shut Weimar off from Nazism, reanimating the Golden Twenties while acknowledging the period's irretrievability. The epochal breaks represented by 1933, when the Nazis came to power, and 1945, when Germany lay in ruins, enabled Franz to historicize the period of the Weimar Republic. The memoirs also confirmed what the contemporary household accounts had revealed about Franz. Whereas the diarist was repetitive, solitary, and homebound, the memoirist moved around Berlin, wandered its streets, and delighted in the refreshing innovations of postwar urban culture.

Making note of the walking stick or the guidebooks Franz had purchased, the household books provided clues about the trips Franz took across Germany. These out-of-the-ordinary expeditions, the very definition of holiday, absorbed considerable space in the memoirs, although they were ignored by the diarist. Franz's recollections of his vacations spilled over pages, and he very attentively described the new settings he explored. Nearly one in five pages (a total of 82 out of 442) in the memoirs was given over to the vacations Franz took on his own between 1920 and 1923 and again between 1929 and 1931, when his finances had improved, and those he took under the Nazi Strength through Joy program between 1934 and 1939. As he put it in 1948, looking back on 1937, "This time around, the Taunus and the Rhine"; holidays constituted "what for me is the greatest occasion of the year."[90] Simply the ability to move around the country had become an important marker of lifestyle. Vacations represented the fulfillment of a good life.

The attentive descriptions in the memoirs conveyed the delight the Berliner took in exploring the mountains, seaside, and rural outposts of Germany, which until the 1920s had been generally inaccessible to most city people. Franz's trips were relatively modest affairs, with private lodgings in second-rate resorts in which he did not always have access to all the amenities available to other vacationers. Nonetheless, under the Strength through Joy program in the 1930s, Franz enjoyed holidays that stretched as long as ten days. Like any vacationer, he found that freedom from the routines of the workday was perhaps the greatest joy. It was luxury just to lie around: "The best are the hours in the morning—awakening without worries or cares, coffee outside, and the peaceful beginning of the day's program. Quietly taking in my surroundings, losing my thoughts simply by staring at the blue sky, languorously abandoning myself while sunbathing, the relaxing snuggle of an afternoon nap in the deckchair, and other small comforts filled the happy hours." Seeing the sights was entertaining as well, bringing to life romantic scenes the day-tripper had otherwise only read about in books. On the road in Neuruppin in 1929, for example, Franz "strolled through the country, visited the surrounding small villages with their strange-sounding names like Sargleben, Hühnerland, and Hühnerwasser, and undertook more ambitious excursions to Boberow, Grabow, and Ludwigslust. In the smaller hamlets, the 'locals' stared at me as if I were a complete stranger. It was really quite exciting when I came upon the 'populated' towns of Grabow and Ludwigslust." At the end of "an enjoyable day, it was already dark when I took the path through the forest back to Neupinnow. This path through the enchanted nighttime forest was totally romantic, a living 'Freischütz' theme."[91] Both the ironic distance vis-à-vis the exotic locals and the literary reference to Carl Maria von Weber's popular opera revealed Franz to be a knowing, capable traveler able to translate the sights he had seen to a wider, imaginary audience.

It was also on holiday that Franz tested his physical abilities. So long the *Kümmerform,* awkward and underdeveloped, Franz experienced empowering moments of self-discovery completely at odds with the diarist's portrayal of himself as a weakling. Franz's July 1930 hike through the Silesian "Riesengebirge" in southeastern Germany was a "test of my skills," a big step after flat Neuruppin the year before. Despite the rain, he began to climb: "Soon I stood in awe before the powerful, audaciously soaring rise, like a warrior who stands against the threatening dangers with his protective shield." Göll's clichés should not obscure what he had accomplished for himself. Franz continued the journey with "a shudder of joy at life," muted only by "a quiet fear of the unknown." "When I arrived in Bad Schwarzbach" and "looked up at the heights," Franz did so "confidently trusting in my own strength." The next day he reached the summit of the Schneekoppe at 1,605 meters: "I was astonished at the formidable distances that could be laid behind in the thin mountain air without exertion. I had not counted on being able to accomplish such a hike."[92]

By the time Franz joined a Strength through Joy trip to the Bayerischer Wald, on the border with Czechoslovakia, in 1935, he counted himself among the "top group" of climbers who gathered at five "in the fresh-cold morning" to ascend with "rustic step" the Arbergipfel (1,456 meters). However, this time Göll was no longer alone, as had been the case in Silesia, but had become an intimate part of a group; "we" replaced

"I" as the prevailing pronoun of the narrative. In Strength through Joy vacations, Franz combined group hikes with touristic spectacles such as fireworks, campfires, and displays of folk dancing and local costume all designed by the Nazi tour organizers to strengthen the affinities of the group and deepen an appreciation of the physical and social contours of the nation. The group became part of Franz's experience and gave him a greater sense of integration and belonging, something the diarist always steadfastly denied feeling. On the last evening "a Bavarian band provided musical entertainment at the party. With yodelers, jokes, and roughhousing, Bavaria's dry good humor prevailed. This too was a unique tourist experience and provided plenty of stuff for conversation at lunchtime for the next few days."[93] Three years later, in 1938, Franz traveled to the Sächsischer Schweiz, where he "found really nice contact with the other travelers as never before; I gratefully appreciated how easily and uninhibitedly I was able to insert myself into the social interactions. Not simply tolerated, I was actually flirting. So the days flew by in high spirits with companionable company."[94]

In the end, Franz's vacations presented him with an opportunity to overcome the solitary self depicted intimately in the diaries. "I was always a small wage earner and had to concern myself with the economic upkeep of our household," Göll commented as he summed up his holiday experiences. "Moreover, I had a secret shyness about living around strange people, something I overcame only late." Nonetheless, he came to recognize his "phobic fear" as "a 'stupid' illusion" that, once dismantled, allowed him, "against expectations, to see a bit of the world: the countryside of Mark Brandenburg, the sea, the low mountain midlands. I caught a glimpse of the high mountains, got to know a different big city with a proud national history [Frankfurt], beheld the German Reich's river of destiny [the Rhine], wandered across Germany's borderlands, and finally possessed for myself a picture of a classic medieval city [Rothenburg ob der Tauber]. To be sure, it is only a limited selection of what our mother earth has to offer its people, but given my modest demands, I am satisfied and thankful to have been granted these provisions for the road."[95] Except for once stepping into Czechoslovakia in 1934 and a trip to Holland in 1973, Franz never left Germany.

Franz Göll's Selves

Read in juxtaposition to one another, the diary, the household books, and the memoirs reveal startlingly different versions of Franz Göll. In the diary Göll undertook a severe investigation of himself to the point that he mocked his routines of self-absorption and deprecated the construction of the interior stage on which he conducted his reflections. His deployment of the vocabulary of transparency, thanks to his original metaphors, was incisive, but the self he fashioned could be contradicted by his other autobiographical texts. The household books reveal a mobile, engaged subject, and the memoirs, which were written from the shifting but compressed vantage points of the years 1941–1948, expose a more satisfied, confident, and integrated individual than the diaries ever portrayed. If the diaries undertook the study of Franz as a biological and psychological subject, they ended up construing him as an object, passive, tossed about by coincidences, and unable to frame episodes into a life. And although the memoirs opened with a strong argument for the role of the environment in bringing the subject to realize itself as an object of outside forces, they finally strengthened Franz's subjectivity and his mobility (and motility), even if the diary's melancholic themes echoed in the memoir project.

To some extent, the discrepancies can be explained by the financial and professional security Franz had found when he began to write his memoirs in 1941. The difficult moments in his life, the crisis of the genius in 1916 and the terror of unemployment in 1924, had been overcome. They could be regarded from a distance and could be placed in an overarching autobiographical narrative. But this explanation is insufficient because the (upbeat) household accounts were contemporaneous with many of the (melancholic) diary entries in the 1920s, and diary entries in the late 1940s continued to develop the self-lacerating themes that the contemporaneous memoirs of 1941–1948 had revised or settled. In the end, neither autobiographical genre is truer than the other, even when regarded from the point of view of chronology. In 1921 Franz the diarist contradicted Franz the accountant just as much as Franz the memoirist contradicted Franz the diarist in 1948. The diary was written in a speculative, exploratory mode in which Franz rigorously examined himself, his intimate social relations, and his professional anxieties. By contrast, the memoir was the work of a social historian whose task of setting the scene required sturdier framing and more authoritative judgment. In the one, Franz repeatedly fell down; in the other, he picked himself back up.

Both the diary and the memoir were carefully crafted in the sense that both relied on widely circulated templates of modern life: suspicions about biological degeneracy, psychological vulnerability, and hard economic struggle in the case of the diary, and nostalgic depictions of a quieter, more peaceful life "before" and feuilletonistic evocations of the Golden Twenties in the case of the memoirs. However, the fact that the memoirs were largely written in a period of political upheaval, from the middle of World War II right up to the period before the stabilization of the West German currency, needs to be kept in view. From the vantage point of the years 1941–1948, the remembered past of Wilhelmine Schöneberg or Weimar Berlin seemed far away, untouchable, wonderful. These places were available for historicization and periodization, and they attracted a nostalgic gaze directed backward from an unpredictable present. Franz was right to think of the diaries as a huge piling of the past into the present, an almost unbearable burden he kept pushing forward. The memoirs, by contrast, were an attempt to leap in front of the pile and see if the experiences could be sorted out in narrative and developed into a finished film after all. For that reason there were no holidays or Strength through Joy trips in the diaries, whereas the memoirs repeatedly presented the photo albums of the Weimar Republic and the Bayerischer Wald.

Some final comments: The autobiographical genres under review, especially the diary and the memoirs, were highly performative. They were governed by psychological and historical or narrational aims that distorted any sense of immediacy. The diaries revealed little about what Franz did, just as the memoirs resisted the continuing anguish that Franz felt. Together, the texts provide a fascinating composition of the self-construction of a psychological sensibility and a twentieth-century lifestyle; alone, they are highly suspect historical sources. If historians had only the diary, Franz would misleadingly introduce them to an eccentric recluse; if historians had only the memoirs, they would misunderstand why Franz began his autobiographical project in the first place. The account books establish a kind of middle ground, confirming the spirit of the memoirs for the early 1920s while authenticating the lachrymose failure of the diarist in the later 1920s. But the chronology that results is not faithful either to the time frame of the diary entries, which are unhappy even in 1921, when we know that Franz was in Lunapark, or to the production of the memoir, in which the satisfactions of 1921 are the product of the vantage point of the disastrous wartime 1940s. What is more, each genre produces a multidimensional effect: the diary entries are cross-referenced and self-reflective, the memoirs move about in time and space and jump from the first person to the third person, and the account books pour out details. However, each genre reports on the one-dimensionality or flatness of the others. Without one or the other, both the strongly performative aspect of the texts and the contradictory, though robust, self of the author would be lost.

What all three genres share is perspective on the disintegration of enclosed social and class milieus. The preoccupation with degeneracy in the diaries indexed the arrival of a competitive, mobile mass society in which Göll no longer felt a secure place. Entries repeatedly emphasized Göll's lack of stability and control; Göll's own physical and psychic state, one in which the individual was no longer an autonomous subject, corresponded to his perception of a gathering war of all against all in the conditions of advanced capitalism. But it is precisely the dissolution of encompassing milieus that Göll the accountant and Göll the memoirist explored and cherished. The man in the fedora hat made his own way, browsing through self-help books and fashioning a lifestyle.[96] Indeed, even the observation post constituted by the diaries was made possible only by repudiating the narrow confines of his parents' life. Nineteen eighteen remained a decisive break, one that both challenged Göll's sense of security and propelled him to model new worlds and to inhabit a variety of twentieth-century German sensibilities as degenerate, consumer, and nostalgic.

3

Physical Intimacies

Franz Göll's entire autobiographical project was deeply entwined with his relations with women. The diaries open in 1916 with Franz's astonishment at his feelings of love for Klara Wasko, who structures the way he thinks about himself as a lover well into the 1950s. Klara and the diary go hand in hand as Franz sets out to discover himself. The diaries also return repeatedly and obsessively to the figure of Franz's mother, whose overbearing presence in his life is reported in detail in the entries and whose family, the Liskows, was the object of Göll's biological inquiries in the 1930s. The sheer acts of writing a diary, of testing novel ideas, and of commenting on new books expressed Franz's attempt to repel in himself the "mama's boy" *(Muttersöhnchen)* and to make space for himself in the confinement of the small household that he and his mother shared. However, the diaries also renounce his relationships with women; not only did Göll regard writing as a male act of creativity from which women were excluded, but the intimate diaries persistently withhold information about women and sex that the more "public" memoirs reveal. The diarist's anguished self relied on the careful excision of a range of objects the memoirist showed interest in and an array of verbs that he in fact had mastered. If the diaries introduce the bookish genius whose self-contained world would not make room for the lover, a self-styled trade-off between creativity and sex that Göll adopted from Otto Weininger, the memoirs offer glimpses of the lover, who could abandon his self-made enclosure.

Sex is everywhere in Göll's autobiographical writings, which comment at length on the sexual revolution of the twentieth century, particularly the openness with which Europeans explored sexuality and assumed new gender roles in the years after World War I. Göll's diary entries analyze the natural history of sexual attraction but also worry about the powerful role of women as sexual creatures. The diaries make an intellectual case for the threat that women posed and the caution men had to assume. By contrast, the memoirs are more frolicsome. They introduce Franz as a sexual tourist, lover, and more agreeable observer of the sexual scenes of the 1920s. Desire, repulsion, and renunciation all combine as standard themes in Franz's poems, which show the young man pushing forward and pulling back during the tempestuous moments of his love affairs. Ultimately, the accounts Franz told about himself were inadequate to represent the experiences he had. The diaries hone a story line of renunciation, while the memoirs tell stories; the former fabricate an autobiographical design of the tortured artist, while the latter survey new possibilities.

Anna

The single most powerful figure in Franz's life was his mother Anna, née Liskow (1874–1954), who was present every day in the small precincts of the apartment on Rossbachstrasse until Franz was well into his fifties. In his view, her impact was invasive because her frightened responses to the world transferred to him in a process of direct, almost physical absorption. Franz tried to resist her in order to claim his autonomy, but he also knew that he was very much her product. The ongoing replay of the mother's difficult birth of the son contrasted sharply with what he learned about her own childhood, which only deepened the mystery of her character and overwhelming influence on Franz. "My mother apparently lived a childishly happy youth," he commented with surprise. "From when I can remember, she frequently and happily told stories about the days of her childhood." That she had been "a saucy ice-skater" who loved to dance and surround herself with "a circle of girl-friends" made his mother's childhood unrecognizable to the mother's child.[1] There was no way to reconcile Anna as a girl with either the difficult, poorly prepared woman Franz saw sitting in front of him or the mother of his weak, anxious self.

In his memoirs Franz observed, "My mother is a very anxious person. Everywhere she senses disaster, is spooked, or has forebodings." The example Franz introduced to illustrate her anxiety revealed the trouble many migrants from rural Germany—in her case Kladow, across the Havel River from Berlin—had when contending with the complexities of urban life. His account placed her exactly where his "Springer dreams" had tossed him: in the middle of the network of trains and schedules, arrivals and departures. "When we were at the station waiting for a train," Franz explained, "my mother was already noticeably excited, which only got worse: 'Will we be able to get on? Will the third-class wagons stop here? I just wish we were already on board'—she just blabbered on in this state of anxiety. Because she always held me fitfully by the hand, her agitation carried over to me. When the train pulled into the station, she yanked me this way and that, and only in the last moment did we finally make it into a compartment."[2]

Franz also enlisted more specific reasons to explain his mother's nervousness. As a child she had been spooked; a bolt of lightning had knocked her unconscious when she was outside playing with friends. In another incident, "My mother let herself be taken across the Havel with the Sacrow ferry. As soon as the ferry was in the middle of the river, it was lightly rammed by a barge and pushed sideways. It spun around several times," giving Anna a scare. But, Franz added, "This trepidation of my mother communicated itself suggestively to me, because I possess a certain predestination for states of anxiety."[3] Franz's reading among the psychologists undoubtedly informed him that even very minor traumas such as a cut to the finger could induce hysterical fits, as Jean-Marie Charcot discovered among his Parisian patients; Freud himself was frightened of train travel.[4] Anna Liskow was not a natural child of the city, but also not a completely unusual case.

His mother's loveless marriage to Franz von Göll, combined with the death of her first daughter Gretchen (whom Franz did not remember) and the difficult birth of Franz himself in 1899, aggravated her nervousness. A combination of dependency and disappointment marked her life. Not interested in men after the death of her husband in 1915, the widow focused all her love and attention on Franz, whom she both infantilized and relied on to the point of suffocation; Franz experienced "this too much" as "a harmful burden." "From the very beginning, the immaturity of my mother was at the center of my life." "I was never able," he concluded when he was already fifty years old, "to cut the umbilical cord."[5] At the same time, his mother interpreted his persistent attempts to release himself from her "apron strings" as "rejection," which led to quarrels and intermittent "estrangement" and "separation." Franz understood quite well that his mother saw her son's alleged betrayal in the light of her disappointment with her husband, an ongoing record that convinced Anna that she had been "cheated" out of her "happiness." The result was that she responded to the world around her with "mulish misinterpretations, misconceptions," and "revenge fantasies."[6]

"Even the most trivial matter was like a spark on a pile of explosives," Franz continued in his case study; "she apparently was always on the alert."[7] There were many incidents with the shoes, the keys, the oven, and the neighbors, but the memoirs gave pride of place to a Sunday outing to Schmöckwitz's lakeside in the summer of 1928. Franz had wanted to take his mother someplace other than her childhood home in Kladow, so off they went to the Berlin suburb. Once again the action took place along the streetcar lines in and out of the city. The journey proceeded harmoniously until, as they were preparing to go home in the late afternoon, a streetcar accident up the line near Grünau stranded day-trippers farther down in Schmöckwitz. As soon as people figured out what had happened, they began to make their way to the nearby Stadtbahn station in Eichwalde. This was not a long detour: a Google Maps search reveals that the traveler would take Adlergestell out of town and turn left on Godbersenstrasse and left again on Bahnhofstrasse to the S-Bahn station, a total of 2.7 kilometers, a thirty-minute walk. However, Franz's mother considered this alternative to be a "total imposition." "You want to have us be attacked by bandits in the dark," she protested; "I am not going one step farther even if I have to stand here and wait for the streetcar until morning." So they waited past dark until an overfilled streetcar finally arrived. "My mother was pushed into the car, while I remained standing on the back platform." At the accident site they disembarked to transfer to a streetcar waiting on the other side. "My mother went all the way into the front of the car and found a seat, while I remained as usual on the back platform." Lots of passengers got off at Grünau, the next stop, and as Franz looked into the car when it drove on, he no longer saw his mother. He quickly got off and ran back to Grünau but could not find her. "Because I was well acquainted with her unworldly and confusedly impulsive behavior in such unexpected situations, I was overwhelmed with worry. Why did she not just follow logic and stay at the streetcar stop? What is more, my mother did not have money or a key with her; she never takes these things along when we go out together." Franz searched high and low without finding Anna and, once it was completely dark, went home hoping to find her waiting at the door. He waited in the apartment. "Every minute stretched into an eternity," and "any noise from the already emptied streets startled me."

Finally, Franz's mother arrived home after having begged the street-car fare from passengers and asking strangers again and again for directions to Rossbachstrasse. Filled with suspicion, she accused Franz of arranging the whole mishap in order to get rid of her and live alone. "It was as if I had encountered a clap of thunder." The next day she maintained her "absurd allegations" despite Franz's "truthful and logical explanations." "She had other evidence that I was out to kill her. Thus one evening I deliberately left on the gas valve in the kitchen (although the main valve was shut). Moreover, I had subscribed to a particular magazine to procure information on accident and life insurance. For months she locked herself in her room at night and refused to be talked out of her iron-clad opinion." It was a long time before the tension at home cleared.[8]

Anna's illnesses made her increasingly dependent on Franz. Her feet swelled up, her legs cramped, and she suffered headaches and lower back pains. In 1934, when Anna was sixty, a small stroke left her partially crippled on her left side. She was all but housebound after the amputation of several toes during the extremely cold winter of 1946–47; without those toes she had difficulty walking, which led to a fall and a broken leg. By the late summer of 1952 Anna could no longer take care of herself, and Franz moved her to a rest home, where she seemed to be comfortable and at peace and where she enjoyed her eightieth birthday, for which the district mayor of Charlottenburg sent his congratulations. When she died on 27 October 1954, Franz was pleased that in her last years she had become more "even tempered." Even so, he considered, her life as a whole was "dominated more by renunciation, suffering, disappointment, and a poorly disguised sense of having been wronged"; "all that was left were 'the crumbs that fell from the rich man's table,'" a balance not very different from the one the diarist had often drawn for himself. But the parallel, like mother, like son, was more complicated. Franz portrayed his mother as someone who was not a "go-getter," but her role in his life was so outsized that he feared that he would find his mother in the women he met. As a result, he drew back in reaction to cultivate himself in the solitary spaces of his own design.[9]

Klara

Without a doubt, the most important love interest in Franz's life was Klara Wasko, the girl with the "brown braids," the "small red jacket," and "a little black cap." It was his love for her, or rather his infatuation with her, since he never got to know her, that Franz poured into his early poetic efforts. Restless in both his literal and figurative attempts to leave home after his father died, Franz followed Klara around the streets of Schöneberg. His detective trips up and down Hauptstrasse to catch a glimpse of Klara eventually extended beyond the wetlands of Tempelhof, across the precincts of Berlin, and finally to his holiday destinations all around Germany. Klara stood at the beginning of his effort to gain independence. Franz also imagined Klara as his "bride" at the very moment when the fortune-teller predicted for him a new career and suggested to him his call to greatness. In the winter of 1915–16, right after the death of his father, Franz felt that the bride, poetry, and genius were all within his grasp. But quickly his poems testified to the unattainability of the objects of his desire, which was the starting point of the diary. Franz's self-knowledge was strongly related to what he realized he could not and would not be able to have.

In his early diary entries Franz introduced his love for Klara in the present tense: "I caught a glimpse of Klara, my girl, my bride. She is my 'better half,' as the fortune-teller indicated. The girl has blond hair, blue eyes, she is after my taste, and I love her." Klara was a part of the future life he had no reason to believe he would not possess. He believed that he and Klara spoke to one another with "the secret language of glances."[10] The challenge that remained was to meet her, to put himself in her universe, as he wrote in his 1915 poem "Riddle":[11]

Who strolls through the streets
In a small red jacket
and wears on her head
a little black cap?

Who roams through the streets
and follows the red jacket
searching, to run across it,
the little black cap?

So how to hit upon,
The right solution;
And also for my boldness
I ask for forgiveness.

Nothing had happened, but everything would. "When will I kiss you /
For the first time, my child?" he asked in "Premonition of Love," written
in January 1916. "It has not yet arrived / the beautiful time of spring.
But when the spring is here . . . then I will kiss you for the first time / on
your red mouth."[12] A few weeks later, however, the poet displaced his
love into a dream; as such, it seemed to slip away as Franz grew more
aware that serendipity would not bring Klara to him—"through the
streets, I have to hurry"—but that his shyness had kept him from going
to her. In "Blessed Dream," dated 27 April 1916, Franz recounted:[13]

You appeared in my dream
And smiled at me;
we went arm in arm
gently up the Kreuzberg.

I talked to you, child,
fluently, thoughtfully;
I do not even know how,
but I also laughed.

At a quiet place,
we sat ourselves down,

and looked at each other knowingly,
every sense cheered.

What happened to us after that,
I never found out;
at that I woke up
and was like one newly born.

Franz no longer sensed his "boldness" but dreamed to conjure it up. Gradually Franz imagined the treasure to be not love for Klara but the memory of his adolescent feelings: "No doubt, I have left you, / my first love, you; / but I have not forgotten you / of that you can be sure."[14] As the diaries reported, in May 1916, "I examined our relationship from various angles and withdrew."[15] At this crucial turning point, Franz assumed the role of the observer partly out of feelings of shyness and awkwardness, the inability to say the right thing at the right time, and partly also as an aesthetic choice, one that was entirely consistent with what he saw as his task as poet and with his penchant for wandering the fields and streets and nights of Berlin. When he wondered whether he should finish his work or look for Klara, "go to her" or "stay at home," he stayed. Following the quirky philosopher Otto Weininger, whose studies Franz was busily excerpting in his scientific notebooks in September 1916, he had chosen genius over women; Weininger considered the two incompatible. The realization of the one demanded the renunciation of the other, and because, in Weininger's view, every single person oscillated between female and male states of being, with no single "empirical individual" adhering to the ideal type, the achievement of renunciation involved effort, which the writing of the diary monitored. "There is perhaps a deep ethical reason" that "important men have always loved prostitutes" and preferred "the vixen" (*Weib;* a tough translation), Göll cited from Weininger's wildly misogynistic but widely influential 1903 book, *Sex and Character*—Kafka, Freud, Robert Musil, Ludwig Wittgenstein, and Arthur Koestler, like Göll, all had their "W" phase.[16] At the same time, Weininger, who in

1903 famously committed suicide at the age of twenty-three in the
Vienna lodgings in which Beethoven had died some seventy-five years
earlier, made Göll tolerant of the homosexual parts residing in every
"empirical individual."

At one point Franz reflected that his surprise at the force of his feelings for Klara had the effect of freezing his idea of love. Because he
never interacted with Klara or gained recognition from her, his love
remained abstract, untested, and rigid. However, nothing else ever approached these original feelings, which both disappointment and inex-
perience trapped in an inaccessible shell. Was not love the mark of a
"high degree of optimism?" he wondered in 1917. He did not want to let
go of his love for Klara, but he also guaranteed that it would never
be realized by making sure that "the colorful soap bubble" of his "un-
approachable saint," his "idol," could never be "burst." He did not dare,
he finally figured out nearly twenty years later, in 1934, "to tear off the
veil and look into the eyes of the flesh-and-blood person that was my
love, that is, to see *das Weib*." Göll toyed with the idea that the maintenance of the illusion of saintliness was a sign of cultural advancement,
an enriching idolization because concealment introduced ambiguity. It
was not literal minded. But the consequence of this exaltation was that
it cast a shadow over all other lovers, who could not approach Klara's phantom. On the other side of the illusion was physical attraction, "marriage
for sex" or prostitution, which Franz considered quite soberly, but which
he neatly distinguished from his idea of love. Franz admitted that he
overcame his feelings of inferiority only when he did not have to uphold
the idol and could encounter "the naked reality," "the person," "*das
Weib*."[17] Thus Franz's image of Klara at once introduced and withheld
the idea of sex. For the rest of his life, Franz would be attracted to women
and acknowledge their attraction to him, but his idolization of femi-
nine virtue both kept him from approaching appealing acquaintances
such as Klara with any confidence and confirmed their unworthiness
when more intimate relations were established. Franz never forgave women
for appealing to him.

At one point during his fantasy "marriage" to Klara, Franz remembered that as a young boy he had spied on girls in the stairwell of his apartment building; the cellar was right below the front entrance, so a "secret observatory" of boys, armed with "opera glasses, mirrors, rods, and squirt guns," managed to peek up the skirts at the white panties of girls, whom the boys then chased away with their squirt guns, providing an "experimental" conclusion to "our 'natural scientific' observations."[18] However, in this case the technologies of observation doubled as defensive weapons (rods and guns) deployed to preclude an encounter, to keep the girls away. Whether in the stairwell or looking up at the windows of Klara's courtyard apartment, Franz Göll frequently put himself behind the looking glass. He seemed to be caught endlessly between the fantasy worlds of poems and panties.

But there was more to Franz's sexuality than the division of labor between the idolization of the princess and the carnality of the whore. When Franz reported on himself, rather than on the status of his love, he often described his episode with Klara as a great shock. In 1923 he referred to "a seizure of feeling," which he was determined to resist with "due intellectual consideration."[19] More than ten years later he explained that "for me, my first love was such an overwhelming, internally disturbing event that I did not realize how much in danger I was of being completely thrown for a loop."[20] In 1943 he confirmed once more that "what for others is the normal course of development, which they grow into, was for me a break that convulsed my self." None of this shock was adequately understood in Franz's frequent references to his lack of skillfulness. It was undoubtedly true that Franz, shy and awkward, did not know how to undertake "the harmless-joking flirtation, free and easy give-and-take, carefree boasting and brawling, in short, all the handiwork of the playing fields of youth."[21] But the shock of Klara was described not as omission or failure, but rather as an unsettling presence. Franz may well have been overwhelmed by unfamiliar, perhaps masochistic sexual fantasies, which threatened to return him to his mother.

Franz's adolescence and Klara's presence coincided with a sexual revolution that loosened relations among men and women after World War I. There are numerous clues that Franz explored this new sexual terrain just at the moment he was dreaming of Klara. In 1916 he attended lectures on marriage and heredity; a few weeks later the expectant husband had turned into an intrigued lover-to-be who learned about "eroticism and dance" from a certain Gustav Keil and about "love" from Herr Mahler.[22] Franz also purchased books on sexuality, including Otto Emsmann's *A Healthy Sex Life!* and a whole series of prescriptive aids by Reinhold Gerling—*Boy or Girl?, Girls You Should Not Marry, What Do Men Need to Know about Girls?, Why Do Men Hurt Girls and Girls Hurt Men?,* and *What Do Men Need to Know about Marriage before Marrying?*—literature that was clearly addressed to men, as were the male fantasies Franz acquired: Leopold von Sacher-Masoch's *Venus in Furs,* Émile Zola's *Nana,* Hans Ostwald's *Ladies of the Night,* and Eugen Dühren's study of the Marquis de Sade.[23] Evidently requiring a close reading, each one of these texts was purchased by Franz and formed a part of his personal library. Reading about the animal world, as well as human sexuality, Franz may have been astonished at the range of choices available and the excitement associated with various sexual identities and practices. What Franz took away from all this, in a December 1919 diary entry titled "Sexual Psychology," was that "life does not have a particular norm as its basis, certainly not one determined by people"; "sexual perversities," he went on to report, "are much more widespread than one generally assumes." The example that follows is telling because it takes up male sexuality, whereas Franz usually spoke about female sexuality: "When a man strokes, squeezes, even torments and bites the beloved girl, these can be taken as indications of a certain disposition toward sadism. An unconscious attraction to lesbianism or homosexuality might be revealed when a girl shows off her legs, her skirts, or her whole body to her female friends, or when a man regales himself with his half-naked body (sport, boxing) and exercises. Kissing a letter might be considered a latent tendency to fetishism." All this was not abnormal,

Franz insisted, relying on Weininger, but rather part of life, "a rhythmic back-and-forth, like ebb and flow." However, without quite taking away the robust sexuality he had put into view, he added that "our ethical superiority rests on the fortification of our moral power to resist excessive fluctuations."[24] It appears that Franz was confronting his own fantasies: not just the depth of feelings, but the diverse forms in which such feelings manifested themselves, often in a mixture of sadism and masochism. Franz Göll argued for the healthfulness of desires such as his, but he resisted them and was frightened by them.

As a result, Göll did not report on his sexuality in any detail; he certainly did not carry his commitment to be "honest, honest, honest" as far as the obsessive Boston diarist Arthur Inman (1895–1963), Göll's near contemporary, who regretted having listened to his father's "talk about how masturbation landed people in the madhouse" and described his loss of virginity when Alma "inserted me into her . . . tickle box," but then realized, "I seem to satisfy but am not myself satisfied."[25]

A reading of Franz's sexuality in which masochist tendencies threatened to return him to mother figures and thus to his mother may be going too far, but the evidence suggests that he feared his mother's oversized maternal role. Franz never flinched from acknowledging human sexuality. He despised the prudery of the prewar years. However, the amplitude of both male and female sexuality that Franz explored at least theoretically narrowed to an almost exclusive focus on female sexuality, which he believed expressed itself in strong maternal desires. "A girl is more specifically girl than a man is man," he maintained already in 1920. "A man is completely satisfied to sleep with a girl," he explained, always keeping in place the asymmetry man/girl, "but beyond that, the girl possesses greater sexual sensations and feelings that find their release in motherhood. Hence the 'cry' for a baby. That is why the girl feels misused and jeopardized in marriage, while the man (the husband) tries out of egoism to avoid getting her pregnant."[26] Göll embroidered his insights more than thirty years later: "For men, the sexual sphere is really just an erotic accessory, an enjoyment to which he abandons himself from time to time." As a result, "Only in rare cases do men speak openly about intimate matters with one another." By contrast, "For women, motherhood is a calling and a duty that they strive for and are fulfilled by," whereas men consider fatherhood "a necessary evil." What testified to the more intense sexual identity of women was that "they trust each other quite freely with their intimate circumstances, desires, needs, and illnesses and demonstrate an accompanying earnestness when discussing these matters." Even "young girls thirteen to fifteen years old," he noted, taking up the thread in 1953, discussed "their hopes for the future on these matters in a very serious way."[27] In sum, "The manner in which women appear is almost completely tailored and adjusted to the erotic (hairdo, attire, perfume, etc.)."[28]

The disparity between the deep sexuality of women and its surface manifestations in men (in contrast to his report about fetishes from the year 1919) was evident as well in Franz's analysis of women's struggle for emancipation. In the twentieth century, he maintained, women had grown, whereas men had not. Göll held his 1925 assessment of the liberation of women for the rest of his life: "As a result of the world war, the *Weib* stepped out of her passive role in life and became active. Since then she has been a strong rival of men in professional life. There is hardly an occupation that is totally closed to the *Weib*." Economic freedom also meant personal freedom: contemporary women "go out with whom they want, where they want, and return home when they want. If a boyfriend has the stupid idea to talk about love and marriage seriously, he is laughed at and put on ice. When the *Weib* gets older, she simply marries a man in a secure position." Of course, all this contradicted Göll's analysis of female sexuality. Nonetheless, he predicted, "The time will soon come when there will be a men's liberation movement."[29] Twenty years later, gender trouble was still "contrary to custom": "It began with socialist leveling, the emancipation of women, and the right to strike" and was

aggravated by Nazism with its "May Day celebrations and folkishness."
As a result, "women wear the pants; men dress up in adolescent fads."[30]
"Ultimately" the lot of men would be the fate already illustrated in the
animal kingdom: "To be a mere semen provider."[31] The problem with
women was not simply Franz's inadequacy. Franz persistently gendered
the challenges of modernity; women stood for the breakdown of milieu,
the insecurities of work, and the unsettling freedoms of individual
choice. Without sturdy supportive structures, men regressed into boys;
on this point Franz was consistent.

The personal conclusion that Franz drew is illuminating but slightly
displaced: "If the turn of phrase pointedly refers to the child in the
man, this does not apply to the woman, for women do not experience
regressions into childhood. Rather, it is more the case that there is already the future woman and mother in the girl. The mature *Weib* looks
quite consciously for the father of her children, whereas the man usually feels trapped."[32] Again and again Franz looked at women and saw
his own mother, and the childlike behavior he observed in men was
both the infantilizing product of and the means to resist the forceful-
ness of the maternal figure. Female sexuality threatened the precious
autonomy Franz had secured. Franz's idolization of Klara allowed him
to displace his sexual fantasies, which he never completely rejected, although he did not cultivate them in a long-term relationship. Even as
he intermittently pursued sex and love, he regarded both as fundamental threats to his independence and well-being.

Addressed to himself, a poem from the year 1941, when he was attracted to a somewhat older woman at Springer, Alice Büsscher, with
whom the topic of marriage apparently came up before he ultimately
ended the relationship, brought many of Franz's fears and desires to the
surface. The title of the poem, "Eine Stellungnahme," is literally a statement of resistance, of holding ground:

A Statement
Do not let yourself go soft,

Boy, be prudent,
for the state of marriage
you still have plenty of time.

Do not let yourself be misled,
Boy, stay hard;
Today you love Klara
And tomorrow Hildegard.

Do not let yourself be bartered,
Boy, stay a hero;
Everything in marriage
revolves only around money.

Do not let yourself be beguiled,
Boy, only a half smile,
When she asks: "My darling,
how do you like my hair?"

Do not let yourself be tempted,
Boy, stay cool,
When she gushes about
marriage, love, and feelings.

Do not let yourself be seduced,
Boy, just be smart,
for the wiles of women,
you know all too well.

Do not let yourself be intoxicated,
Boy, pay attention,
even on a walk,
when her knees rub lightly.

Do not let yourself be entranced,
Boy, stay sober,
when she draws you near, breathing:
"Schatz, do not be so shy."

Do not let yourself be duped,
Boy, stay firm,
when she talks about marriage
and her "warm nest."

Just do not let yourself be caught,
Boy, do not be lazy;
with "sweetie," "baby," "dearest"
she is just buttering you up.

Do not let yourself be persuaded,
Boy, this latest attempt;
If you cannot shake her anymore,
then drive with her to Bedlam.

Let yourself be well-advised,
Boy, just stay alert,
Stand them all up
to stay a single man.

In this dense case sexuality was the weapon of female predators who imperiled the "boy" by threatening to return him to the "warm nest."[33]

In his reports Franz repeatedly renounced women, either by exaggerating his failures and dramatizing his passivity or by clinging to his ideas of woman as princess and of himself as self-sacrificing genius. Only here and there do texts expose his more active role in relations with women. After Klara, whom he fleetingly glimpsed in walks around the neighborhood, Franz worked in the Reich Coal Distribution Office, where he was surrounded by young women who were his age (most young men were at the front). "Although in accordance with my being, I held myself reserved and passive," he reported cautiously in the memoirs, "it could not be avoided when working together to talk about private matters every now and then." One coworker, in particular, Margarete Schuster, "a 'misunderstood' blond, who thought she saw in me, the quiet, withdrawn youngster, a 'like-minded kindred spirit,'" took Franz on as her confidant, the *Posten* or "little colonel," to whom she poured out her "disappointments with life."[34] However, by choosing Franz instead of a same-sex companion, she introduced rather than displaced sexual rivalry. She had taken the "active role." But Franz, at least in his poems, was more interested than he let on.[35] He imagined what transpired during the love affairs she told him about: "Where did he first kiss you . . . Where did he first find pleasure?" "Did you give yourself to him completely / in wild high spirits? . . . Did he totally possess you?"[36] Evidently the Reich Coal Distribution Office on Wichmannstrasse was the site of quite frank discussions. Perhaps Franz was bewildered by how far Margarete, only a year older than he was, had gone, but he also wanted to try, wanted more "courage to sin." "You have such an adorable little mouth, / so delightful, so small for kissing," he wrote in the privacy of his poetry; "Oh, just lend it to me for an hour."[37] At least in his fantasies Franz was more than a "confidant." Still, he insisted that this was "erotic flirtation," not love.[38]

The memoirs introduced another coworker at the Reichsstelle, Margarete Landwehr, "a young girl, blond, with gray-blue eyes, well formed, in short, a very appealing sight." "Unskilled in the area of courting," Franz waited a long time before exchanging pleasantries with her. In 1923, when his attraction shifted to her younger sister, Else or, soon enough, Elschen, a tarter, more "statuesque, true Germanic type," Franz once again felt unable "to court" or to summon the "will to act." "I always feel like I am standing in front of a carousel in which others circle past me on their merry rides, while I look on forlorn without taking part."[39] In fact, however, the account books indicated that Franz went out with Elschen at least twice.[40] Exactly what happened to the relationship is not clear, but whether he renounced her or she rejected him, Franz had not simply lingered on the sidelines.

A few weeks later, Franz's cousin, seventeen-year-old Margarete Amboss, the daughter of his mother's sister in Kladow, came to visit. He was immediately interested in her sexually: "It was her physical lusciousness that entrapped me," wrote the diarist; "intellectually I am not attracted to her."[41] But the memoirs were more generous, describing "a flourishing young girl, completely unaffected and with an alluring charm." They also related a budding affair with "stolen squeezes to the hand and eventually . . . secret kisses."[42] But despite, or perhaps because of, his erotic attraction, Franz broke up with her, arguing that he could not afford the marriage that apparently had become a topic of open discussion and indicating interests that he "estimated" higher than "love and marriage." Once again he acted out Otto Weininger's playbook in which the genius trumped the girl. For Göll, as for Weininger, the pursuit of sovereignty demanded a strict gender differentiation. This act of renunciation did not keep Franz from continuing to fantasize about "my Gretelchen": "Girl, you little blond / beguiled the youngster's heart / take heed of his pleas / heal his lovesickness."[43] Again and again Franz followed his erotic attractions, but only up to the point where he felt threatened by a real relationship. Franz's problem was not that he watched from the sidelines; it was that the lover wanted to return to the sidelines and take pleasure, as he put it in his good-bye letter to Gretchen, in recollecting in later years "many an unhappy episode." Franz's passivity was the end result of his erotically charged steps forward and his subsequent self-imposed retreat. That Margarete Amboss committed suicide at the age of twenty-five in June 1931, after the parents of the dentist with whom she had fallen in love refused to sanction marriage between the two lovers, suggested to Franz a "disposition to fixed ideas" among the Liskows that in turn could only have recalled his stubborn, inflexible mother.[44]

Eva

Most of Franz's relationships developed at work, Margarete Schuster and Margarete and Else Landwehr at the Coal Distribution Office and Alice Büsscher and Brigitte Otterstein at Springer. But in 1930 he met Hildegard Meissner in the quintessential metropolitan setting of the movie theater. However, the only reason we know about Hildegard (born in 1902) and then her friend Eva Wulkow (born in 1899) and their adventures together with Franz in the big city is that Franz recollected them in his memoirs; the diaries are entirely silent about both Hildegard and Eva except for an otherwise bewildering entry from August 1948 in which Franz reported that he had bumped into Hildegard's old friend, a woman named Mührke, who updated him on the old group: Hildegard had married in 1943 and moved to Euskirchen, across Germany near Bonn; Mührke did not know anything about Eva, but Eva's sister, Irmchen, had divorced her husband and now lived in Thüringen.[45] So Franz, the solitary diarist, had been part of a group.

At the movie theater Hildegard Meissner "sat next to me. Her nervous fidgeting had an irritating effect on me. She seemed to have noticed my displeasure, apologized for her behavior, which she blamed on rattled nerves, and entangled me in a conversation during intermissions." As in many of his accounts, the woman played the active role, but somehow Franz made a good impression on her. She asked him out for coffee, and they later agreed on a date. The encounter left Franz dismayed, which means that he must have been attracted to her. But he left only this single account: "Like a storm on the surface of the water, waves were breaking, tossing, surging—I found myself in a state of painful agitation." When he wrote to cancel the date, she wrote back pleading with him to keep it, because she claimed "to have liked me right from the start." They settled on a friendship in which he told her not to cherish any "false hopes" and she offered to help out with expenditures. However, there must have been more, because Hildegard, by Franz's admission, showed off her "conquest" to friends and family, and he himself labeled her unambiguously in photographs as "my girlfriend." A poem, "To Hilde," revealed a relationship that was not passionate, but also not reserved: "I thought of you / when in the morning I awoke; / I thought of you / when in the night I lay awake; / I thought of you / in places dear to the heart; / and think of you / in a thousand words of love."[46] Moreover, Franz's photo album shows many happy moments with Hildegard on the beach and in the forests around Berlin. One photo shows Hildegard hiding behind a tree, playing with Franz, and vamping as Mieze had with her own Franz (Biberkopf) in Rainer Werner Fassbinder's 1980 adaptation of Döblin's *Berlin Alexanderplatz.*[47]

According to Franz's description, "Frl. Hildegard Meissner was a delicate *Persönchen* with a somewhat Jewish aspect about her, dark haired, dark eyes, and in comportment and dress a bit slack, that is, not spruced up. What was irritating about her was her perpetual physical restlessness, her nervous twitches, spasmodic movements, the lack of any physical composure." Because she married in 1943, when the racial laws of the Third Reich applied and German Jews had been largely deported and murdered, Hildegard could not have been either Jewish or half Jewish, but in any case "she knew how to put her character in the best light and to play the elegant lady." It was with Hilde and her friend Eva that Franz first explored "dance halls" and "fancy cafés," a world "that speculated on and was attuned to the stimulation and pleasure of the senses."[48]

In the company of "slack" Hilde and sexy Eva, Franz went clubbing: "On a lark the three of us once visited the ladies' club 'Dorian Gray' on Bülowstrasse. At first, when I arrived with my escorts, I caused a sensation because I was a man. But soon enough the special attention we had been paid wore off, and we sat quite unceremoniously in the middle of this world of women who amused themselves in their own way. I was rather astonished to see so many conspicuously regal types among these decadently voracious [*triebenarteten*] women. The behavior was completely decent and had nothing scandalous about it . . . Because no one knew exactly what was up with me, the child of what sort of nature I was, I ended up the center of well-inclined attention and, to my surprise, could attract a few secretly steamy glances. We found this milieu to be a lot of fun, and it was an interesting thrill to obtain insight into this peculiar sensual world of love." The club scene was also an affirmation of the shifting sexuality Weininger had reported on in every "empirical individual"; Franz had not peeked across some impenetrable divide, but had discovered sexuality's plotted points on an open-ended continuum.

Franz, Hilde, and Eva also sought out Dorian Gray's counterpart in the male sphere: "Café Hollandez" in "the notorious *Bülowbogen*." As voyeuristic sex tourists, Göll's company was well informed. At Café Hollandez, "a meeting place for homosexuals," "it was naturally my lady escorts who attracted lively attention. The place was packed. For the most part, we saw impressive characters, dressed to the nines, decked out in delicate bracelets, gold necklaces, and other jewelry . . . The men danced with one another, smoked, and had lively discussions, without acting in any way offensively." Always the naturalist, Franz took the sexual diversity he observed in stride.[49] What is more, in spite of all the evidence assembled by the melancholic diarist, the memoirist reported having a lot of fun.

Franz broke up with Hildegard in the summer of 1931 as a result, as he put it, of "mutual weariness." It was the "first proper friendship with a girl," Franz admitted, but he continued to resist a closer relationship and withheld information about his feelings. For someone so alert to his physical shortcomings, it was surprising that Franz wrote contemptuously of his satisfaction at being free of this *Zappelliese*, or "nervous Nelly." It was a mean-spirited remark with racial overtones. A day later he met, "as if by coincidence," Hilde's friend Eva. Franz had in fact chosen one girl over another; aware of Eva's "sex appeal," he described "my new girlfriend" as "a dark blond, blue-eyed, Aryan type, very skinny with world-weary facial features"—incidentally, Franz deployed this racialized vocabulary of "Jewish aspect" and "Aryan type" while writing this part of the memoirs in 1947, more than two years after the end of the Third Reich. Once again, Franz made the distinction between an affair of the heart, which this was not, and an eroticized relationship, in which he indulged to "pass the time." But Eva was not so easily contained by Franz's physical description. He referred to her as "Eve's daughter" whose sense of adventure eventually led her to neglect Franz and seek out other men. It was Franz who felt put out, rather than pulled in too closely, and in September 1932, after more than a year of going out, he broke up with Eva because she had cheated on him. Franz acted out of interest rather than disinterest, his classification of the affair as cool eroticism rather than hot love notwithstanding. His photo albums captioned the pictures of Eva, who is the subject of many striking and flamboyantly posed snapshots, with the beginning of the "official relationship, 3.8.31," and the end, the "final breakup, 31.10.32."[50] Eva was clearly a big part of Franz's life. It was Eva whom Franz asked about when he met Mührke at the end of the war.

What made Franz even more involved was that he probably lost his virginity with Eva. Unfortunately, he did not comment on this milestone, although Eva revealed to him that "as a lover" he was "too boring, too unenergetic, too naïve, and, for her, too ponderous," an assessment Franz registered without further comment.[51] Franz may also have had a sexual relationship with Alice Büsscher in the late 1930s. In any case Franz was not passive; he chose Eva over Hilde. He was not impotent but gained experience. He was not autistic but instead rather curious about sex and sexuality.

In his memoirs Göll reflected on Hilde and Eva and realized that without them "I felt untroubled, without worries, I was again master of myself. I had enough of women and knew from my own experience that I had no aptitude for this subject."[52] Even so, Franz occasionally felt lonely. When, in his fifties, he wondered whether he should reply to a marriage advertisement in the newspapers, Franz concluded that he was too old and too set in his ways.

But Franz did not completely withdraw. In 1958 the diarist reported on a flirt he had engaged in with a waitress. "The whole drama—it consisted of only one act—took place in a restaurant on Kolonnenstrasse," near home. She was "a nice, friendly blond, whose comely womanly being in both form and attitude I took immediately to heart." A small man, Franz liked bigger women. He surprised her with small jokes and pleasantries and soon advanced to her "favorite guest." "When I arrived and departed, we shook hands and I caressed her oh-so-soft arm." Then the moment came when Christel informed him that she had taken a position at La Poularde, a chicken barbeque on Wilmersdorfer Strasse, near Kurfürstendamm. His follow-up visit to her there, he reasoned, would entail certain obligations. As had happened many times, Franz told himself that he did not want to raise her hopes, but he acted in a way to deepen the relationship by asking her out. It was not Franz but Christel who refused because she already had a "steady boyfriend." "We shook hands one more time, said good-bye, and went our separate ways."[53] Years later Christel surprised him during his regular Saturday lunch in the refreshment room of Held's department store in Steglitz. In the meantime Christel had married and had tried her hand at running her own restaurant with her husband before returning to La Poularde, but because barbeques were no longer novel on the Kurfürstendamm, she had switched over to Held's. The following spring she and her husband accepted positions as waitress and steward on the cruise ship *Regina Maris,* the first passenger ship built in Germany after World War II, which confirmed that the postwar "economic miracle" now extended well beyond chicken barbeques on the "Ku-damm."[54]

But economic stability could not guarantee emotional contentment in postwar Germany. Although it was only a "short intermezzo" for Franz, a 1961 incident with Inge from the apartment building next door reveals the loneliness of a generation of women whose husbands, fiancés, or future partners had been killed in the war. In 1945 there were 169 women for every 100 men in Berlin, and this imbalance did not change appreciably. In Franz's hard-hit turn-of-the-century cohort, sixteen women gathered for the fiftieth anniversary of the Königen-Luise-Gedächtniskirche's 1913 confirmation class, but only five men showed up.[55] I count Inge Stamulla among these women who felt that they had become superfluous, but this is just a guess because Inge cannot speak for herself and I have only Göll's account. In any case, in the summer of 1960 Franz bumped into Inge, a neighbor who greeted him with "surprising friendliness," but because Inge had been running late that day, the two did not cross paths again. Then in February 1961 Franz was on his way to make a Sunday visit to an acquaintance convalescing in the hospital; while waiting at the streetcar stop, he was joined by Inge's father, who was also visiting a patient. Stamulla chatted about his interests, his collection of family documents, and his daughter's painting talent. An invitation to dinner quickly followed, and Franz found himself ringing the doorbell that very evening. According to the clipped sentences in Franz's diary account, he walked in the door, was addressed with the informal "Du," and then was embraced and kissed by Inge, who begged him "to offer her his name." An irritated Göll believed that he had been set up by father and daughter, but he was not sure whether he was the object of attention as an eligible bachelor or as a mysterious nobleman. He stayed for dinner but broke off all but "neighborly" relations with Inge in an awkward exchange of cards a few days later. Franz pretty much lost sight of Inge. Ten years later, however, Inge appeared at his door on New Year's Eve with a small present that she left with a "deep, sad, tear-rimmed glance." In 1975 "Inge Marschall" gave Franz a Christmas present. She did so again in 1976 and 1977. "It is as if she tends to a secret affection," he reflected at Easter 1977, but it was Franz Göll who appeared to be the lonely one without ties to cultivate.[56]

After his mother's death, the one constant presence in Franz's life was Brigitte Otterstein, who as a sixteen-year-old had been Franz's employee at Springer during the war years. "A fresh, lively, naturally carefree young girl," Brigitte drew men to her like a "magnet" (one Springer employee divorced his wife to make himself available), and although Franz was already over forty he developed a crush on her. But the relationship was more like a comradeship, and Brigitte was one of the few people who, by Franz's own admission, could pierce his armor of privacy and share his thoughts and hobbies—from her parent's garden in Mahlsdorf, she brought him "snails, larvae, bugs, and plants" for his aquarium.[57] "I had never encountered such an outgoing person; her openness and sincerity allowed me to bare my soul to her." Franz remained a close friend even after she married and had children.[58] The age difference evidently contained Franz's sexual desire. No longer caught between a woman as princess and as vamp, he was able to have a happy, fulfilling friendship.

However, comradeship was not love. Toward the end of his life Franz confided to his diary that he was happy never to have married, preferring life alone. He insisted that he had never been in love.[59]

Franz

Full of details about the weak, apathetic Liskow side of his family and the sickly disposition of his parents, Franz was alert to his physical well-being. He suffered from diphtheria, scarlet fever, and chicken pox as a child, stuttered in his adolescence, and developed migraines as an adult. Like Franz Kafka, who had passed through Europe's primary schools sixteen years earlier, Franz Göll hated gymnastics and swimming. The schoolboys' roughhousing *(Allotria)* intimidated him, and the focus on his body unnerved him. But Kafka, who once thought that he was too skinny to "preserve an inner fire," eventually mastered the situation and "stopped being ashamed of my body."[60] Weighing less than a hundred pounds, well below average, Franz Göll, however, always remained extremely conscious of being a small person in a society made up of larger people. He was ashamed all at once of his size, his sexual inertia, and his uncontained desires.

It was adventurous, then, for Franz to buy a bicycle, an "Alpenkönig," for 50 marks in 1933. When it came to "physically applying myself," Franz was determined not to flinch. Fifteen years later he remembered: "Of course, at first I had to pay my 'dues,' but as we became more familiar with each other, I turned out to be a jaunty Sunday cyclist . . . Without exaggerating, I can dispassionately draw attention to the fact that I usually managed to reach a speedy tempo, felt secure in the operation of the bicycle, and also responded alertly to dangers. You needed dexterity and confidence to bicycle in the busy traffic back then." "I really enjoyed it," he reported with a plainspokenness about pleasure that is rare in the diary, "and at first I could not believe that I was really sitting on a bicycle and riding out into the world."[61] Taming a sparrow had registered similar feelings of delight in the diary. Bicycling gave Franz a feeling of freedom and speed, but also confidence for having calibrated himself to metropolitan traffic, judging the movement of oncoming vehicles, fixing the angle of the wheels to cross streetcar tracks, and negotiating turns while riding. He had followed the advice of popular psychologists who, at the turn of the century in books such as *The Philosophy of the Bicycle* and *Nervousness and Bicycle-Riding,* encouraged cycling as a way to achieve self-confidence, gain moral courage, and reanimate the will.[62] In a key respect, then, Göll had mustered a kind of pride in his body. Franz experienced a similar feeling of accomplishment when he hiked in the Riesengebirge and the Alps. This physical exertion was in stark contrast to his mother, who curtailed family weekend expeditions, insisting that "ten horses will not carry me farther."[63] It is easy to underestimate the sense of power and accomplishment twentieth-century contemporaries felt when they learned to ride a bike or swim in the ocean or climb a mountain. Like tourism, sports had long remained an idiosyncratic habit or a gentleman's luxury, and only in Franz's generation did physical activity become a crucial expression of the confidence and potential of the self.

Along with his parents, Franz suffered from ulcers and other stomach problems. Sometimes he vomited on the way to work. He checked himself into the hospital after a particularly bad episode at the end of October 1953, when he worked as a watchman at the lumberyard in Steglitz. In more than ten pages Franz scrutinized in great clinical detail his nine-week stay at the Auguste-Viktoria Hospital in Berlin-Schöneberg; it was his first convalescence. After he checked in, his blood was typed (O positive), and Franz was given a blood transfusion (250 ccm). Over the next few days he continued to receive more transfusions, as well as "blood coagulation shots" and "sodium chloride injections." He was put on a regimen of cold milk. "For the time being, I still produced the unwanted black stools, which after about ten days turned a lighter color. After a microscopic examination revealed that there was no longer any blood in the stool, I could go over to a more solid diet. So now I received the so-called soft food fare [*Schleimkost*], which consisted of oatmeal

porridge and semolina pudding, mashed potatoes, milk, and apple sauce."
X-rays were also taken of his thorax, stomach, and intestines, a "ceremony"
that was completely new to him. As an amateur naturalist, the diarist
faithfully reproduced his medical statistics:

> Blood count: lowest red blood cell count 30, highest achieved 78
>   (normal around 80)
> Blood pressure: lowest reading 80/50, highest reading 125/80
> Blood sedimentation rate: worst reading 45/74, best reading 5/15
> Blood type: O rh positive
> Temperature and pulse oscillated around normal
> Weight: lowest 38 kilos, highest 45 kilos

Forty-five kilograms is just shy of 100 pounds; Franz was indeed a small
man.

Franz also left behind an unvarnished account of the daily hospital
routines, the small Christmas celebration his friends arranged (with
three bottles of wine), and the female nurses' unembarrassed treatment
of male bodies. In his ward Franz observed "a stomach that had to be
pumped as a result of an overdose, a centrifugation to separate out com-
ponents of stomach acid, the application of swaddling in a case of pneu-
monia, tube feeding through incisions, [and] body-roll therapy," as well
as death, about which he was quite unsentimental: "The living human
being is a person; a dead one is, by contrast, a case. You have feelings for
the living and show concern; with the dead this engagement ends abruptly.
The dead only 'live' in the memories of the bereaved."

One nurse in particular, Nurse Käthe, recalled the barely contained
sexuality of many of the women Franz described and their counterparts,
the passive men among whom Franz often included himself. "She sometimes lets go in a way that made the oldest grandpas blush. One day she
was feeding a recently admitted grandpa (apoplexy) porridge when she
saw that he was wearing dentures. She told him to give them to her.
When grandpa resisted, she took them out of his mouth with the words:
'Give it up already, Grandpa, otherwise you will swallow them and next

time I wipe your bottom you will end up biting my finger.' To measure the daily urine discharge, something that was usually dealt with pretty casually, she asked the ambulatory patients to estimate. For the fun of it, the patients gave her odd amounts—the first 426.5, another 443.75. The nurse guessed the game and, shaking with laughter, responded: 'If the next one gives me such a crazy number, I will tap him until a round number comes out.' Another patient complained about having 'no leverage.' Thereupon he received a catheter. Nurse Käthe had the night shift, and the next day the doctor asked the patient about the outcome. He confessed that there was little success. At once, Nurse Käthe broke in and very drily remarked: 'Now stop it, my dear; when I walked past your bed at night, I had to hold onto my skirt.'" Käthe played to Göll's erotic fantasies about stronger women, but more, her easygoing, objective manner appealed to Göll's sober, naturalistic portrayal of the world.[64]

The hospital stay was an adventure, a new location to describe at a time when Franz could not afford vacations. It ultimately confirmed his well-being. "Considering my schizophrenic peculiarity, I was at first concerned about a hospital stay," he explained, "but the experience taught me the opposite. Once I checked in, I was so completely cinched into the operations of this new domain that I never even had mental complications. I was simply just an invalid who did not have any problems to solve other than to get better again."[65]

Franz Göll was almost fifty-five when he checked out of the hospital, but he did not feel like a "Grandpa." He had the feeling that he had "finally brought his body under control."[66] Fifteen years later he still felt well. "I do not know if there is a specific feeling about growing old or how a seventy-one-year-old normally is expected to feel," he wrote in 1970; "as for myself, I do not feel my age and could just as well be forty, fifty—sixty, at most. I actually have a hard time imagining myself as old as seventy." A few years later, after more ulcers and a diagnosis of diabetes, Franz conceded that "the small adversities of age have set in and every now and then weigh on spirit and mind. For some time now, I have taken smaller steps. I swallow pills to help heart and circulation, I also swallow pills to avoid bronchial obstruction, and I get shots to keep the prostate from swelling"—"a small list of ailments." But his basic attitude was unflinching. He felt as he always had, as he had learned from Philipp's *About Us People* long ago: he was part of the rhythms and struggles of nature. "Old age approaches with leaps and bounds," he wrote in a poem transcribed into the diary in 1974, "And time, it is remorseless; / There is no use in pleading or appealing, / The path leads to eternity, / and if you ask yourself: how was life, / Was it gratifying for you? / Then you can only say, so it was / An exchange between day and night."[67] Franz, who had resumed his annual vacations in 1960, after returning to Springer, continued to travel through the year 1979, when he turned eighty. The diary itself broke off almost entirely in 1982 and 1983; the reading diary ended in 1980. Perhaps it was not a coincidence that Franz had purchased a color television (a Philips for 1,300 marks) a few years earlier.[68]

4

The Amateur Scientist

Working at the German Women's Fund for Children of War since May 1916, Franz earned only 75 marks a month. Even with modest cost-of-living supplements, this put him at the very bottom of the wage-earning scale in Germany. But there was enough money for Franz to buy materials to build an aquarium. At the end of the year the diarist reported that "I got aquarium glass for myself. The receptacle is 42 cm long, 27 cm wide, and measures 27 cm in height." "So many desires, hopes, plans, ideas, and expectations are tied up in this!" he added. But the work proceeded slowly because Franz wanted to divide the aquarium to include a terrarium so he could observe plants and small freshwater animals, as well as fish. He had to build a watertight divider, as well as a raised gauze-enclosed lid that could be opened and closed. "The construction of the framework is painstaking and time-consuming work," he admitted. The project "weighs down on me like a physical load" because

Franz dreamed of fashioning for himself "the life and movement of a piece of 'nature'" in "lively, bright colors."[1] This would allow him "to observe an environment with all its individual fates and its interactions and reactions." Because the aquarium remained relatively small—about the size of a big boot—Franz was continually disappointed in the results. His miniature was never as "colorful, diverse, and instructive" as he had expected.[2]

Like Wilhelm Bölsche's natural theology or Alfred Brehm's *Animal Life,* aquariums registered the growing popularity of natural history in everyday life. Amateur naturalists were walking around with collecting tins and butterfly nets at the beginning of the eighteenth century, but it was Philip Henry Gosse's descriptions of marine life in the 1850s that ushered in the aquarium craze that climbed into thousands of British parlors in a few short years.[3] Soon Emil Adolf Rossmässler introduced home aquariums, the "sea in a glass" or the "ocean on a table," as he called them, to German consumers, who quickly dominated the pet fish trade in Europe and the United States.[4] "German sailors collected fish from all over the world; German businesses established collection stations in Asia, Africa, and South America, and German ichthyologists organized expeditions to acquire new aquarium fishes and provided most of their scientific descriptions."[5] Hundreds of thousands of goldfish must have been swimming in glass bowls in Berlin alone. In Germany, as elsewhere, aquarist societies flourished and published their own magazines. Berliners founded the Triton Society in 1886, which entertained its two thousand members with regular meetings and lectures in the rooms of Zum Heidelberger, a bar on Friedrichstrasse, a "fish exchange," and Sunday family evenings "with dancing." How-to books followed on the success of Rossmässler's *Das Süsswasser-Aquarium,* which had appeared in four editions by 1880, and specialty stores such as Aquarium Falkenberg and Scholze & Pötzschke on Alexanderstrasse offered hobbyists in Berlin a wide array of fish and food.[6]

According to the writer Gerhard Nebel, the great appeal of the aquarium was that it allowed amateur naturalists to see the entire life cycle of fish living in their own world "from the moment they came into existence to their chases and battles, to love and the upbringing of the young, and finally to their deaths." It was a little like playing God. With care and sufficient supplies of plants and snails, aquarists could observe a functioning ecosystem, although many aquariums left the parlor as quickly as they had entered it, the result of "dead fish, murky water, and putrid plants." The abiding promise of the aquarium, however, was the opportunity to observe the intricate parts of nature, "the greatest show on earth."[7]

Franz was not as enterprising a naturalist as his fellow diarist and English contemporary, W. N. P. Barbellion (1889–1919), would become before dying of multiple sclerosis. Barbellion, a pseudonym for Bruce Frederick Cummings, read just as intensely as Göll, studying Darwin or John Lubbock's *Ants, Bees, and Wasps* until "the clock strikes midnight," and like Göll he was nagged by doubts about his ability to become a "great naturalist"—maybe it was just "a child's fantasy"—and also very self-aware, as the twenty-three-year-old's conclusions about his deteriorating body confirmed: "I am living on my immense initial momentum—while the machinery gradually slows up." But in his short life Barbellion proved more industrious, "egg-collecting," "bird-watching," and dissecting dogfish, sea urchins, and an eel, in which he "found what I believe to be the lymphatic heart in the tail beneath the vent."[8] Even so, Franz pursued modest zoological and botanical studies, taking expeditions to the "so-called Black Hole *[Blanke Hölle]*," undeveloped marshy land between Schöneberg and Tempelhof, and to his cousins' place in Kladow along the Havel River, "the Eldorado of my childhood dreams," to collect specimens.[9] In his reading in the winter of 1918, he followed on the heels of Hans and Harald, characters who took nature walks with their father, or he trailed behind Hans, Kurt, and Fritz, who were accompanied by "Dr. E," little fraternities that in his own life, with his sickly father and disinterested grandfather, he never enjoyed. Sitting alone in the Schöneberg library, Göll dutifully transcribed lessons about trees, plants, insects, and the seasons and even copied the animal tracks that Harald had sketched in his own notebook.[10]

Perhaps because he was "shy and reserved," which disadvantaged him in society, Franz developed the gift of taming birds, including the young sparrow he found on his balcony one summer. It hopped on his arms and shoulders and "happily chirped his 'ziep-ziep'"; "My joy was indescribable."[11] This gentle, tender empathy certainly distinguished him from his cousins, who drowned cats in the Havel and starved their dog Cäsar. Given his talents and his patience, it was not altogether fanciful for Franz to imagine himself as a zoologist; as a child, Konrad Lorenz, born in 1903, kept pet birds at his family's summer home in Altenburg, Austria, and his future collaborator, Niko Tinbergen, who was four years younger, built homemade aquariums in the backyard of his house in The Hague. But because they were born to stable, wealthier families, Lorenz and Tinbergen enjoyed resources Göll never had: they attended elite secondary schools that tracked them directly to university. By 1916 Franz's dream of becoming a zoologist already had something wistful about it. Nevertheless, he pursued his studies: day after day "I preferred to be alone, where I could keep busy immersing myself in my own thoughts."[12]

To cultivate his research, Franz sought guidance from a weekly periodical, *Blätter für Aquariums- und Terrarienkunde*, which had aided hobbyists since 1890, and from the growing shelf of books he acquired in the early 1920s: *The Freshwater Aquarium, The Terrarium, Introduction to the World of Small Animals in Our Waters, The Parlor Aquarium, Caring for Reptiles and Amphibians, Practical Care for a Terrarium, Walks through Nature (Meadows, Moors, and Heaths), The Butterfly Collector's Pocketbook,* and *Catechism for the Terrarium Enthusiasts,* among others.[13] The account books show Franz maintaining his aquarium; throughout the 1920s he purchased water fleas, water plants, and fish food, as well as caterpillars, turtles, salamanders, frogs, and snails. He also acquired sand and rocks to enhance his small patch of nature. Even during the war, in the 1940s, Brigitte Otterstein, the likable young woman who worked for him at Springer Publishers, supplied him with "snails, larvae, bugs, and plants" from her parents' garden, and Franz, in turn, "had to provide her with updates on the life and goings-on in the terrarium and had as well learned to put up with the good-hearted fun she made over my eccentricities."[14]

Franz studied the struggle for existence that the aquarium was designed to simulate more thoroughly in his reading program, which he had initiated in 1913 with Karl Sajo's *War and Peace in the Ant Colony* and continued in the 166 books on natural history he read in the following ten years; after literature, natural history was the autodidact's favorite subject, according to the "Statistics: Number of Books Read" he fastidiously prepared for the years 1913–1922.[15] Franz continued to read widely in geography, zoology, botany, and psychology in the years that followed. This was a period of widespread popular enlightenment in which ordinary people took an active interest in new discoveries, retailed the predictions of technological progress in popular mechanics, and attended lectures and exhibitions. In Europe and the United States citizens encountered a world that was being explored, mapped, and packaged for consumption with ever-greater resourcefulness. As a result, they increasingly calibrated their lives into deliberately cultivated, scientifically informed lifestyles, a remarkable twentieth-century identity based on self-improvement through preventive medicines, health fads, and sports. Utopian destinations such as the metaphorical "New World"—the name of a famous bar in Berlin's Hasenheide—worked themselves into expectations of life itineraries, which were built around the idea of progress. Self-help and self-knowledge constituted new technologies of being.

Like most amateur naturalists, Franz developed a structural-functionalist view of the world regulated by struggle and adaptation and delimited by physical form and capacity. This materialist perspective enabled him to translate the relationships he identified among species into the interpersonal interactions among individual people and the political and economic competition among nations or ethnic groups in such a way that the aquarium in his apartment in Rossbachstrasse served as a model for the neighborhood of Schöneberg's Rote Insel, the corporate setting at Springer Publishers, and global politics during World War II and the Cold War. Göll worked with a series of homologies in which local incidents could be interpreted as symptoms of larger processes. His method was inductive; he illuminated the general at the expense of the particular. As a result, he had a hard time when it came to drawing general conclusions about extraordinary events such as the wars of Adolf Hitler in the Third Reich, in which the absence of self-regulating limits and the persistence of surprise played a large role. Nonetheless, as a rule, Göll was inclined to interpret the resolutions of natural and political history according to larger developmental schemata.

What augmented Franz's functionalist perspective on the world was his zeal in trying to figure out how the world worked. The accumulation of knowledge was developmental rather than static; the collector ultimately outbid the classifier. Franz admitted that he was drawn to the "border regions" of science, "which have a special appeal for me, for it is primarily the borders that convey overall survey and general impression."[16] But this sightfulness and legibility remained provisional: "I have an irresistible urge to immerse myself in the secrets of this world and the psychological need to gather ever-new perspectives and transformations, and to make connections that for a few moments can be intuitively sensed but remain scientifically completely incomprehensible." It was at this border between knowledge and intuition that Franz felt creative and alive: "In such hallowed moments, my whole body trembles and vibrates, and I have to divert this internal excitement in physical activity by getting up and walking outdoors somewhere." "I wandered into the distance / into the wide-open field"—at this point the sober naturalist gave way to the exalted poet who concluded the diary entry:[17]

Stars twinkled
along the heavenly tent.

Wide awake, my spirit day-dreamed
About the stuff of eternity,
And in serious matters
I lost myself in time and space.

As my spirit dreamed away,
my mind at peace,
from high above—
I felt a gust of wind

With my thoughts, it pulled
me back to reality,
as the shapes of dream dispersed—
snow settled on the horizon.

In the skies, the moon seemed to wane
I froze in its shining light.
Everything was bare and white—
I went home all alone.

Astronomy provided Franz the scale with which to consider the limits of scientific knowledge. As a young man he regularly visited the observatory in Treptow. In his diary he recorded the appearance of the northern lights and the 1957 Arend-Rolland Comet, although he never mentioned the spectacle of Halley's Comet in May 1910, when hundreds of Berliners camped out overnight on the Kreuzberg to watch the nighttime blaze. Space travel also prompted Franz to consider forms of extraterrestrial life.[18] It was revolutionary astronomical discoveries about the constitution of the universe that indicated to Franz how tentative scientific knowledge was at any given moment; he held up Copernicus and Einstein as models of the adventurous spirit of scientific inquiry. Images such as the "dark side of the moon" not only suggested what was not yet known because proper scientific instruments were lacking but also the degree to which the very categories of scientific knowledge were tethered to what could be seen and apprehended.[19] The incomprehensible suggested the precincts of the unknown. In this regard Franz's persistent frustration with the size of his aquarium, which be believed to be too small to permit extensive observation, stood for the more general problem of observation, which was always limited by technologies of investigation and categories of analysis.

Astronomy helped Franz become alert to the elusive and even illusionary nature of the most authoritative statements scientists made about the natural world, which in turn pushed him to recognize limits to scientific knowledge, to understand the situation of the observer, and to celebrate the sheer multiplicity of possible perspectives on the world. Although Franz had a basically structural-functionalist view of nature, he never considered its contents or mechanisms to be entirely predictable or self-evident. He shuttled between more rigid and more open-ended lines of thinking that I will present in order, moving from "the state of being" to "innovation" to "truth and lies."

The State of Being

Franz's key insight was that human beings were part of nature, although the reliance on technology and "the predominance of the man-made" in modern life inhibited recognition of this fact. This was the foundational judgment of natural historians such as Darwin, Ernst Haeckel, and Wilhelm Bölsche, all of whom Franz cherished. He repeatedly compared men and women to animals, reducing the intellectual apparatuses of the species to their functional equivalents in the animal kingdom so that intelligence operated as a kind of highly developed sense or scent.[20] Each species, he explained, was endowed with "a specific basic character," a particular biologically predetermined mode of adaptation to the environment. Franz called on the testimony of those who worked closely with animals ("farmers, hunters, coachmen, gamekeepers, herders") to make the case that "species being" (*Artgebundenheit*) could be observed in the precise quality of its antagonisms against and concessions to the outside world, which Franz summed up as a self-regulating system of "resistance-accommodation." "Perseverance, attack, [and] pursuit" were positive manifestations of offensive behavior in conditions of security, while "flight, standing still, or gathering in numbers" constituted the manifestations of inhibition in conditions of insecurity. Franz went on to argue that for all their differences, human beings were also characterized by "the basic character of species being," in which "will" took over the role of predatory instincts and "reason" the role of governor to regulate the will when it was necessary to induce the effects of inhibition. Even the "pride of creation" was subordinated to its own "built-in regulatory system."[21]

Given the enormous variety of dangers and opportunities present in the state of nature, the range of potential adjustments to adapt and re-adapt was exceedingly large. "It is amazing," commented Franz, "how life in all the major time periods adapted to the prevailing conditions of the environment." The circumstances of "sickness, injury, misfortune, assault, hunger, thievery, natural catastrophe, murder, war, etc." required humans to engineer increasingly complicated accommodations. Franz's model of human sociability, therefore, admitted considerable psychological and cultural variation; human history was not the result of any internal drive to develop particular modes of social being or to move through developmental stages. Franz returned repeatedly to the problem of the individual and its ontology. He acknowledged that people endeavored to set themselves apart from others, and he explored the creative role of genius in history. But he put the emphasis on the reproduction of adaptive functions rather than on the creative generation of novel forms of life. To be sure, "We analyze as though 'life' followed an inherent process of diffusion," but it was misleading to think so without reference to the external challenges and stimuli that human beings always faced.[22] Even spectacular periods of civilization such as ancient Greece or imperial Rome had been misunderstood because most Greeks and Romans had inhabited their time mostly as consumers rather than creators of culture. The textbooks were wrong to exemplify them as the "Adonis of body and mind." Moreover, Franz argued, even the most flamboyant cultural forms proved to be transient, surface appearances in times of hardship. Their eclipse "left no doubt" that human beings were nothing more than animals. Like many contemporaries who grew up during World War I, saw firsthand its brutal effects among thousands of crippled war veterans on the city streets, and experienced the general strikes and mass assemblies of the revolutionary postwar years, Franz Göll had no trouble identifying human beings as "the most dangerous and bloodthirsty animals, as we see in war, in revolution, in the fanaticism of mobs and masses (herd), in the 'wild' rifleman, despot, and tyrant," but also in the role of "combatant and champion for personal and general purposes and aims."[23] Twentieth-century history brutally exposed the struggle for existence for Göll, as it did for many other contemporaries, from Freud to Hitler.

As a natural historian, Göll repeatedly submerged the particular into the generic either by invoking the inescapable circumstances of jeopardy in which all human beings found themselves or the overwhelming mass of people who returned to a state of nature when faced with danger. To make his case, he returned to the Zoological Garden, to the birdcages mentioned in Philipp's *About Us People,* or to the primate house, where "monkey troops of baboons or vervets" showed the same "greed, pugnaciousness, and panic" as "human troops."[24] Their behavior was ruthless but neither arbitrary nor incomprehensible. Seemingly validated by war and revolution, Göll's interpretive template was, of course, a product of its times; Darwin's older German-language popularizers, Ernst Haeckel and Wilhelm Bölsche, whom Franz knew well, had cultivated much more benign views of human development.

The compact model of the zoo was very portable, and Franz applied it to various social settings to explain individual as well as collective political behavior. In the 1920s and 1930s, when Franz experienced unemployment and other personal disappointments, and when he observed revolutionary uprisings, the struggles for economic advantages between labor and capital, and growing international tensions, his natural histories of human history turned especially rigid. Franz operated with a broad neo-Darwinian model of biological development in which higher forms of life had emerged: living organisms from chemical admixtures, animals from plants, and human beings from more developed mammals. Nonetheless, his descriptions of change remained locked in the static frame of constant struggle that he saw in the cages at the zoo. In his analysis of the ongoing rhythm of resistance to and accommodation of the material world, he tended to put the accent on accommodation. It was futile to struggle against the differences that the state of nature always reimposed in new forms. Despite constant movement, it was not possible to compensate for individual debility or structural inequality; biological destinies rendered social and political innovation useless. Because all human beings were endowed in different ways, Franz explained in 1929, it was not possible to legislate social misery out of existence. People were condemned to find the place in the pecking order to which they belonged: "Just as the individual person is forced to remain in a particular sphere of life (generally speaking), and one race subjugates another (in the most drastic case, whites over blacks), so it is everywhere in the universe. There the same rules apply in the end. The earth compels the moon to orbit it, the sun, the earth and the other planets, the major sun the minor suns, and so on (?!), all in the service of progress and higher development." "Demonstrations, strikes, and similar uprisings," he added for good measure, were "passive rearing-ups."[25] It was the specific role of religion more or less successfully to offer human beings consolation about their fate.

However, Franz did not offer a clear way to distinguish between active conquest, which was tied to species being, and fruitless protest, which contradicted it. Why did wars have utility, but strikes did not? Nor did Franz relate the successful, "if not always ethically recognized," resistance of particularly intelligent types, "the ruthless hotshot, the con man, the spy, the Jew, etc.," as he noted in a 1931 rant, to the overall process of "higher development."[26] Although Franz's model was by no means closed because he admitted the possibility of resistance and acknowledged his own family's degeneration, his main argument was to point out the overwhelming power of hierarchical relationships, which precluded social progress. It was as if he was explaining in scientific terms his own sorry state.

Franz's thinking was fixated on the animal kingdom and the distinctive character and role of the species that inhabited it. Highly influential books such as Alfred Brehm's *Animal Life* (first published in 1864–1868), or "the Brehm," as it was popularly known (so much so that it even makes an appearance in Döblin's *Berlin Alexanderplatz* to aid a discourse on chickens), had introduced animals to nineteenth-century readers in highly anthropomorphic ways. Brehm described their actions as "jealous or sad, devious or affectionate, reproachful or forgiving."[27] This sentimental rendition of animals in natural histories and visually compelling museum dioramas encouraged thinking about the activity of human beings, either individually or collectively in states and nations, in terms of a zoological species. For Göll, individuals might be predator or prey; depending on their capacities, they behaved like lions or like sheep. The politics of nations could also be modeled on the interactions of species. But Franz resisted thinking about other kinds of social behavior in the same way; he could recognize the efficacy of the individual's aggressive struggle for advantage, but he dismissed the collective action of workers or the oppressed. In his view, it was nonsense for a group of sheep to demand to be treated like lions.

At the level of the nation-state, Göll configured international relations in the 1930s and 1940s as a Darwinian struggle for scarce resources in which state actors were conceived as distinct species who mobilized their populations in the most effective way possible. "Nature always works through power and energy differentials," he explained; "In the same way, states (people) constitute fields of energy." "Depending on strength (population, social and ethnic unity and energy)," he continued, "a people fills out its living space more or less completely until this diffusion reaches the limits imposed by the counterpressure of bordering groups."[28] Franz accepted the self-evident subjectivity of the entity "Germany" or "the Germans," as well as the proposition that politics was the means to improve the circumstances of the collective subject. There was little room for accommodation or détente because world resources were scarce, circumstances that set the stage for a permanent state of emergency and required relentless expansion and struggle—just as he had seen in the zoo. Thus tough global competition explained Germany's war with Russia in 1941, as well as what Göll considered the Allies' exploitation of Germany and Japan after 1945.

Franz was quite frank in admitting that in politics "might," not "right," determined outcomes, but without "perception," a clear understanding of the situation at hand, "might" was insufficient. In other words, on the level of state action, the ability to recognize and translate the understanding that "might equals right" applied augmented state power.[29] This insight put Franz quite close to the position of the National Socialists, who argued that racial superiority manifested itself in the racial self-consciousness that energized the collective struggle for power. It also suggested an intriguing parallel between "the ruthless hotshot, the con man, the spy, the Jew," on the one hand, and the Nazis, who operated recklessly at the state level, on the other. Franz would in fact explore this parallel, but it also exposed some of the contradictions of his model. As a self-ascribed middle-class professional who talked and dressed the part, Franz was deeply invested in the notion of individual achievement. He had only scorn for what he regarded as the compensatory collective strike or the trade-union activity of less capable individuals who composed the laboring masses. When Franz faced his lack of success, he could see only hypertrophic forms, his own *Kümmerform* or the menacing shapes of schoolyard bullies, con men, and Jews, to explain the gap between expectation and result. He was a classic example of how prejudices of social class individualized the ugly politics of resentment.

At this point Franz hit the theoretical limits of his natural history of social relations because he could not (in 1929) accept con men or Jews as legitimate combatants, just as he would not accept (by 1939) the

Third Reich as a legitimate state actor. In the end Franz indicated that religion and other "humanlike superbeings"—that is, the gods—were the vessels in which humans gave "form and content to their increasingly problematic being."[30] Moreover, Franz could not explain why war rather than peace, as Wilhelm Bölsche had argued in *Love-Life in Nature,* was closer to the state of nature or why the destructive effects of war were less dysfunctional than the complacencies of peace. The biggest problem with Franz's model, however, was the fact that he insisted on development and innovation but did not indicate their origins or impulse. His notion of scarcity and his two-stroke model of resistance and accommodation kept things looking very much the same, even when matter was in constant motion. His analogies from the animal kingdom kept him thinking in zero-sum terms. Although Franz's natural histories served to explain his failures, they cast the rest of the world in implausibly rigid forms. Franz built an aquarium, potted his plants, and fed his turtle lettuce, but when the curious young man looked through the panes of glass, he saw his own melancholy self.

What Franz did not worry about in the 1920s and 1930s was death or the death of the human subject. Many of his contemporaries resisted the monist perspective of nineteenth-century figures such as Haeckel and Bölsche, who saw no larger divine or extranatural purpose of the continual fluctuation and development of the natural world. They expected the species to die out. Especially in the years after World War I, young people in Germany searched for more meaningful modes of being in the immortality of the nation or the "people." Anne Harrington explains that "the national humiliation, class fragmentation, and political polarization engendered by the loss of that war acted as a radicalizing force for many scientists involved in developing holistic reformulations of life and mind." The end of the universe, the dissipation of energy according to the second law of thermodynamics, and finally the disappearance of time itself, which Göll considered without sentiment in his scientific notebooks, greatly disturbed "holists," who, Harrington notes, searched for meaning in an overly rational and scientific age.

However, "monists" such as Göll accepted entropy. In this regard they constituted an older scientific generation whose contemplation of other worlds kept them from worrying unduly about the fate of this one.[31] Monism was a further reason that Göll was not immediately attracted to the growing might of right-wing politics in post–World War I Germany. He accepted the mechanics of nature and its lack of teleology. At least in the first ten years after World War I, Franz Göll did not feel the need to rehabilitate or save Germany.

Innovation

Franz grappled with the problem of innovation, but he did so at the level of personality, not world or natural history. It was the study of character and the problem of knowledge that led Franz to advance more open-ended hypotheses about the production of difference in the nature of being. At first, Franz counterposed the genius to the mass, somewhat self-servingly exploring the position of master observer and intrepid scientist that he had assumed for himself. But Franz also analyzed the constitution of character as such. He was most interested in how character assimilated changing stimuli in the environment and thereby reformulated and even defied the fundamental structure of species being. He explored the possibility of overcoming the fateful combination of milieu (Rossbachstrasse) and biology (the Liskows) that seemed to define his life decisively, and he explained how he made a "case" of himself. Finally, from an entirely different angle, Franz returned repeatedly to the state of self-consciousness that he believed distinguished human beings from all other natural life. He was fascinated by the extrasomatic adaptation to nature that culture represented and the degree to which knowledge was inextricably bound to the categories of its own analysis, setting limits to comprehension but, at the same time, creating and re-creating many marvelous perspectives on the universe.

The figure of the generic type—the exemplar, not the exception—dominated Franz's thought. Most people fell into the category of the mass, whose movements were predictable, standardized, and ultimately animal-like. Despite the cultural achievements of peacetime, the inescapable dangers of the natural and political world continuously exposed the fundamentally bestial quality of human society. Moreover, people generally preferred to live with comfortable illusions about their own identity and about the world around them rather than undertake the arduous task of examination and investigation. Franz's thought worked to enclose human beings in the animal cages that he so often held up as an illustration of the real state of social being. But Franz always peeled off an exception: the genius whom the mass did not recognize, who rallied the "inner courage" of a Copernicus, and who created new, almost unbearable knowledge beyond the limits imposed by received wisdom. Copernicus's projection of a heliocentric universe ripped apart assumptions that were both familiar and consoling. He shoved "what had been the all-important earth, the workplace of God's grace and love," into what for humans was the "incomprehensible remoteness of the universe." "Untethered to the fundamentals of tradition and faith," the earth became a "plaything of incalculable natural forces."[32] What made Copernicus a genius was his willingness to pursue knowledge for its own sake, to remake assumptions even as they unsettled and terrified those who were less strong.

Writing in his diary, and resolved to probe the limits and composition of his self and his relations with society, Göll initially believed that he had embarked on an intellectual journey that was in some sense comparable to Copernicus's. After all, the fortune-teller had confirmed his call to greatness. Göll was attracted to the idea of genius because it corresponded to his sense of self: his solitary journeys around Schöneberg, his drive to gain the knowledge he believed he had been denied by his spiritually impoverished upbringing at home, his resistance to the dogmatic, unquestioning education he received in the teachers' academy, and his lack of recognition by family and colleagues. "The genius lives only for genius and can only be completely understood by him," Franz insisted in 1916, at the outset of his scientific deliberations.[33] To account for his idiosyncrasy, he held the belief that society at large usually considered the genius abnormal, mistaking creativity for deviance or illness. As a young man, Franz regarded himself as a Nietzschean figure who sought "to escape the resting place of appearances" and who thereby "lifted himself above" his being: "The human being is something that must be overcome" ("der Mensch ist etwas, das überwunden werden muss"), which is a precise, though unacknowledged, quote from Nietzsche's *Thus Spoke Zarathustra,* a text Franz read in 1924, the same year he wrote the diary entry.[34]

But Franz set an unattainably high bar for himself when he counted himself among the innovators "who spread uncomprehended ideas and opinions, who resemble strange beings that go through life like comets, suddenly appearing, threatening along the firmament, and abruptly disappearing, recognizable only through their deeds."[35] Ultimately he switched gears to delve into his own personality to discover why he was such a "strange being" without actually being an intellectual comet. The "psychological confusion" of considering the "autosuggestion" of genius without being able to find any "confirmation" stayed with him all his life.[36] This sober reassessment also redirected his intellectual energies so that the more mature Franz Göll went on to explore the conflict between the snug world of appearances and the production of new knowledge. What eventually interested Göll was not the comet of genius itself, but the ways in which genius was interpreted. He turned away from the muscular figure of the genius who dared to know and instead made the category of genius a way to illuminate the struggles to achieve self-knowledge and to comprehend the inadequacy of knowledge itself. Along the way Göll dropped Nietzsche's "envisioned superman" only to arrive—apparently independently—at many of the philosopher's ideas about "truth and lies."[37]

In a series of diary entries in the 1950s, Franz cut genius down to size by disconnecting the person from the deed. Like a mother who has given birth to a child, he explained, the creator was often left exhausted and empty, sometimes permanently so. This was the case because "his work has no retroactive effect on him; it does not leave anything permanent behind." And once in the world, the creation resembled "a child growing up" "who distances himself more and more from his mother and estranges her." In other words, the genius was not necessarily reflected in the creative product, and the product revealed little about the genius. Citing the example of Schopenhauer, Franz asserted that the genius was not even apt to follow up in his own life the insights he had developed in his philosophy. Indeed, to make acquaintance with the genius was usually to be disappointed. It was sobering to dig beneath the *Aschenregen der Gloriole,* a striking image of the volcanic ash that had hardened into a nimbus, to excavate "human beings as they were and lived"; the legend of "Old Fritz" crumbled into a more "true-to-life portrait of King Frederick II." The prevailing formula here was Nietzsche's "human, all too human." Moreover, the creation itself did not constitute a self-evident value: "There are deeds whose effects last only a short time in spite of all the dust they kick up, and there are those that last centuries, although they prevailed over the forces opposing them only with difficulty."[38]

Making the distinction between the person and the deed, Franz drew two conclusions. First, he asserted that there was no such thing as a born genius. Genius did not constitute a "particular species of being," as he had once believed. Even if the creative person might appear mad or abnormal, similar deviations manifested themselves in any number of less creative individuals, something he took from his readings of Ernst Kretschmer. In any case the genius always relied on the accomplishments of others, as well as hard work, tenacity, "and luck." Second, Franz concluded that the ascertainment of creativity was itself a matter of "social determination and selection"; "Schopenhauer's work," Göll explained, "was as good as unsellable in his lifetime," and "Nietzsche remained mostly misunderstood by his contemporaries." With this sociology of knowledge, Franz had completely torn apart his youthful arguments about supermen and comets. It was not the case that only genius recognized genius, but quite the opposite: posterity appreciated genius in the same way as it bestowed a title of distinction.[39] Society created and cradled the genius.

At first glance Franz seemed to have wiped away the prophetic and innovative potential of the genius by making it a function of social estimation. Genius was not the fiery eruption of the volcano, but the potentially deceptive *Aschenregen* of legend. But Franz took one more step, arguing that it was precisely the recognition of the social constitution of knowledge and creativity that made it possible to perceive and therefore potentially overcome their arbitrary or nonnecessary limits. Knowledge about the containment of knowledge served as the premise for new knowledge. This self-consciousness about the problem of knowledge was difficult to achieve, Franz conceded, but its attainment in varying degrees was what distinguished human beings from all other forms of life. The mark of genius was thus the ability of individuals to use knowledge about the self. Thus by proceeding with an analysis that denied genius, Franz ended up retrieving it.

Truth and Lies

Let us go back to the aquarium. In the interaction with nature, organisms developed ever more complex adaptive systems that refined the senses and developed increasingly effective functions of aggression and camouflage. The evolution of living organisms over millions of years illustrated that life was not a fixed or closed system. For Göll, these were clear biological facts. However, human beings represented a new stage of evolution because they were "the first and only beings that thought and acted independently," self-consciously, "not instinctually." With the "perceptual apparatus" of the "highly developed brain," they could reflect on the state of nature. In highly revealing diary entries written in December 1934, Franz recognized that with the "primitive illusions of prehistoric humans," who conceived the violence of nature as the activity of "supernatural beings," humans had accomplished "the first attempt to clarify their relation to and location in nature." Religion was the first step in self-consciousness. The existence of "good and evil demons" who acted on the world was a life-enhancing "illusion" that not only offered a description of nature but also reformulated the basis for interacting in nature. "If humans are born into the world of reality," Franz maintained, "they are the only living creatures to possess the ability, thanks to their capacity to conjure up illusions, to lift themselves up over reality and to mingle with the intellectual currents of the cosmos and to give their perceptual organ, the brain, the impulse for further refinements." The production of illusions, say, about the existence and power of gods, constituted the specific adaptive mechanism of human beings. "This thread of refinement will be continually spun out further," he continued; "scientific research" in the modern era was the most refined means to gain "clarity and knowledge" and made the impulse "to always go further and deeper" its organizing principle.[40] The explanatory function of "illusions" about demons, what Nietzsche had referred to as fictions and lies in *Beyond Good and Evil* and especially in his posthumously published essay "On Truth and Lie in an Extra-moral Sense," written in 1873, served as the premise for new knowledge that might destroy the demons that had served as its inspiration.[41] Unlike animals, which existed completely in the security and self-evidency of their environment, "man wants to know how, why, and to what purpose he is here." Therefore, humans no longer lived with the unselfconscious security of ignorance.[42] They had the drive, as well as the capacity, continually to produce illusions (or notions or ideas) about the world in their reflections about and engagements with the state of nature. All forms of knowledge were, in crucial respects, illusions, just as all illusions constituted better or worse forms of knowledge.

"The first act of humans," Göll wrote in 1955 about self-reflection, "which was at once the greatest and most consequential in all humankind, is expressed in the idea of the 'expulsion from paradise.' Humans developed out of animals. As a result, new, unknown tasks completely preoccupied the 'first' humans, giving them intellectual nourishment and spurring their intellectual activity. Humans had to adapt and orient themselves anew; instincts had only secondary importance. [Now] the intellectual-spiritual struggle for recognition, progress, knowledge, truth, for God could begin."[43] Expulsion was the precondition for the self-conscious activity of worlding the earth.

According to Göll, falsehood was the primary basis for humans to find themselves at home in conditions of homelessness. However, "The disposition to illusions in each human being is constituted very differently," he explained.[44] Given the violence of nature, most people preferred to make themselves at home in the myths they had fabricated. They therefore refrained from revising them and soon forgot their false nature. (This is why Nietzsche observes that most people "tell the truth"; they resist becoming conscious of the falsifying process of cultural production.)[45] Without knowing it, Göll adopted Nietzsche's assertion that the moment of invention in which myths and gods had been created had been forgotten by all but the most distinguished individuals. The free act of reflection was ultimately consumed by the abiding desire for certainty, "to tell the truth." In Göll's view, as in Nietzsche's, human beings generally hankered after "safety, security." In the present day, an "age of technology, machines, atoms, the theory of relativity, synthetics," "the 'ordinary consumer,' for whose needs civilized life is tailored, feels at home in this world." Only "the thinker who feels dragged out into no-man's-land, only the man in contemplation, lapses into existential fear," Franz maintained; "That is how I see the situation of contemporary humanity."[46] Göll might have added that he saw himself, in the 1950s the watchman on the late shift at Carl Holz's lumberyard, close to "no-man's-land." In other words, most people ended up living in cocoons of their own making, while only a few endured the pain of unraveling them; Göll certainly believed that he was among the latter, even though, as the next chapter will suggest, many of his political ideas about Germany and its enemies in the world wars were uncritical and self-serving.

Göll's father, Franz von Göll (1864–1915).

Göll, ten years old, with his mother, Anna von Göll, née Liskow (1874–1954).

Göll and friends from the Coal Distribution Office (early 1920s);
Else Landwehr is kneeling.

School picture; Göll is seated at lower left (ca. 1911).

Göll at sixteen, when he
started the diary.

Picture postcard ideal of Klara (1916).

Daß sich also der Winterknäuel auflöst,
den sie bildeten, um sich gegenseitig
zu erwärmen. Nun dringt die Kälte ein,
die Bienen erstarren, und oft geht auch
solche Weise ein ganzes Volk zu grunde."
(Seite 16). . .
(Aus: <u>Leben und Weben in Wald und Feld,</u>
<u>von Christian Brüning).</u>

. . . Hier sind ihre (Eichhörnchen) Fußspuren,"
ruft Eduard.   „Haben
Die aber ungleich   H.   große Füße.
Die Vorderpfoten sind   viel größer
als die Hinterpfoten."   „Du meinst
wohl umgekehrt,"   V.   verbessert
der Vater. „Nein,   Papa, sie
selbst! Hier im   weisen
Spuren sind sie   deutlich
abgedrückt. Die Vorderfüße sind viel größer."
„Höre zu, Eduard! Das Eichhörnchen hat an
jeder Vorderpfote vier und an jedem

Papier 13 Kg.

Göll retraced animal tracks from a children's book into his notebooks
(February 1918).

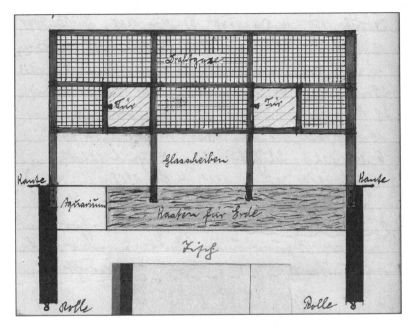

Göll sketched his aquarium (October 1939).

Einnahmen		Ausgaben	
Oktober		**Oktober**	
Tag	In Tausenden von Mark	In Tausenden von Mark	
29.	66 789 695	Übertrag	57 712 800	Übertrag
30.	10 000 000	Eisenbahnfahrt	5 000 000	Besondere Stiftung im Verband (d. A.)
"			3 500 000	Flugblätter u. Tageszeitung
31.	45 000 000	"	33 530 000	Steuerabzug
"			5 120 000	Angestelltenversicherung

| Sa. | 121 789 695 | | 104 862 800 | |

In Tausenden von Mark:

Einnahmen:	121.5.50.000	121.789.695
Ausgaben:	104 862 800	−104 862 800
Bezahlt:	16 687 200	16 926 895 Geldbestand

1923

Einnahmen		Ausgaben	
November		**November**	
Tag	In Tausenden von Mark	In Tausenden von Mark	
1.	16 926 895 Geldbestand	Steuerabzug	40 060 000	Steuerabzug
"	120 000 000 Firmen Bedarf	Öl usw.	39 000 000	Öl usw.
"			14 000 000	1 Paar Handwerkerknöpfe
"			2 000 000	Volksküche: für …
"			2 000 000	Fahrt auf der …
"			9 500 000	3 Flaschen Tinte
3.	30 000 000	"	54 680 000	Krankenkassenbeitrag
5.	90 000 000	"	40 060 000	Steuerabzug
6.	120 000 000	"	40 060 000	Steuerabzug
"			17 500 000	Flugblätter u. Tageszeitung

| Sa. | 376 926 895 | | 263 860 000 | |

Page from the account books during the inflation
(October and November 1923).

Göll the dandy (July 1920).

Göll, front left, with workers from the post office (1925 or 1926).

Göll on his balcony at
Rossbachstrasse 1
(late 1920s).

"My girlfriend" Hildegard Meissner, in the woods around Berlin (June 1930).

Franz's thirty-second birthday with Hildegard Meissner, Eva Wulkow,
and his mother.

Eva Wulkow vamping
(October 1931).

Göll on vacation (1931).

Springer workers on Tempelhof meadow for Nazi May Day 1934.

Göll on a Strength through Joy hiking trip, Bayerischer Wald (August 1935).

With a fake moustache, Göll vamps Hitler, while a friend vamps Göring. Strength through Joy trip to Rothenburg ob der Tauber (May 1939).

A haggard Franz Göll after the war (March 1946).

Göll as night watchman (late 1940s).

Brigitte Otterstein, another "love" interest at Springer (late 1940s).

Göll in his apartment in the Rote Insel (July 1950).

Göll with friends, New Year's Eve 1962.

The fiftieth anniversary of Franz's 1913 confirmation;
there are sixteen women but only five men.

The adaptive nature of illusions made it possible for people to gain knowledge and to make a home, but also to live without complete knowledge about themselves. This was the general condition of existence. "How is that even supposed to happen?!" Göll asked about Socrates' injunction to "know yourself" in 1955. "I mean, whoever wants to know himself inside and out must be able to exhaust himself, must first have the will to place himself in many different circumstances in order to know how he reacts and relates to them and to know whether he can master them. . . . Everyday people, who complain and bicker that they do not get ahead, are usually too inert, too comfortable, too lazy, too indecisive, too hesitant, in short, too negative to take the opportunity to prove themselves. Many people do not recognize where the limits of their abilities lie, that is, they do not know themselves and are surprised when push comes to shove and they are able to act. And there are others who have too much faith in themselves, again because they do not know themselves."[47] People remained trapped in categories that offered consolation but limited insight. They assumed that they possessed a recognizable self, but "the word *character* already assumes that we understand and value the idea of a strongly constructed, stable, and thus calculable state of being." Here Franz undermined the idea of the unitary self that was the foundation of the entire autobiographical project. But the insight was valuable: the vocabularies of our inquisitiveness are not alert to dispersion and contingency. The slogan "Know yourself!" simply invited deceptions in which fragmentary, contingent responses to the environment were rebuilt into false coherences.[48] To seek genuine knowledge about oneself did not end with the discovery of an essential self, but with the awareness of the partial and mutable nature of character and personality. "The truth about a person is not a formation fixed for all time," Göll explained; "It transforms itself over time and is really only apprehended as an outline." "Indeed, the man has already become a stranger to his own former childhood self."[49]

Franz made it clear that people possessed a certain amount of self-consciousness about the quality of illusions. As his examples suggested, the grown man understood that he did not recognize himself in the small child, and society celebrated new lines of thought in the figure of the genius. The less "disposed to illusions" individuals were (about the truth), the more able they were to comprehend the inadequacy of knowledge about the world and to create new, more sufficient interpretations. For Franz, Copernicus was exemplary for his courage to undermine the stability of authoritative truth statements about the nature of the universe in the search for more comprehensive explanations. "Consider and immerse yourself in the concept: our earth a swirling piece of dust in the immense ocean of the universe, and you have to admire the inner courage of a Copernicus who held a view that would release the earth from its anchorage in which it had been commonly regarded as the stable foundation of the world and would fling the planetary sphere into an unknown outer space." With this gesture, "the earth, God's work of creation, had become a plaything of still-unknown forces, robbing the soul of its security." Although "over the course of time, human beings regained the balance that had been upset because they learned to find a new internal footing in the newly flourishing sciences," the aspiration to test assumptions, to scrutinize categories, and to find better explanations remained. Franz summarized: our "disposition desires" security, but our "intelligence demands" new answers, a reworking of his two-stroke model of accommodation and resistance.[50]

"If man were totally ignorant of himself, he would have no poetry in him," wrote Alexis de Tocqueville in *Democracy in America*. He went on, "If man clearly discerned his own nature, his imagination would remain idle and would have nothing to add to the picture. But the nature of man is sufficiently disclosed for him to know something of himself, and sufficiently obscure for all the rest to be plunged in thick darkness."[51] It was in this twilight state of both ignorance and clarity that Franz Göll suspected that the nature of being human emerged.

For Göll, new knowledge rested on doubts about the sufficiency of old knowledge. It relied on acknowledging the partial and fragmentary nature of the new answers that had been advanced. *Weltfremdheit,* literally "unworldliness," was the condition of what Göll referred to as the genius, the foundation to create new descriptions of and new illusions about the world.[52] "For the philosopher, nothing is self-evident," he aphorized in 1974.[53] Acccording to Göll, knowledge proceeded by blows rather than accretion: "Our intellectual development does not move forward in the regular oscillations of the pendulum, but proceeds in spurts [*stossweis*]"; new knowledge entailed the destruction of what had previously been taken for granted, a 1950 insight that anticipated Thomas Kuhn's notion of how "scientific revolutions" overturned dominant research paradigms.[54] Not surprisingly, the genius, the fabricator of new illusions, that representative of ourselves who willingly abandoned the shelter of home, inhabited a "no-man's-land" from which the dark side of the moon could be sensed.[55] "We human beings," wrote Franz in 1934, "possess only a dubious capacity to intuit the dark connections of our universe through the ages. This capacity we express in our human language with the word 'God.' "[56] In other words, religious feeling was ultimately sustained by the suspicion that our own descriptions of the world remained inadequate. For Franz Göll, new knowledge and old gods went hand in hand.

5

Franz Göll Writes German History

One had only to go out into the streets to bump into German history, as Franz did one fall afternoon: "As we left the theater around 6 p.m., we were hit with a thunderous commotion. We heard the chants 'Down with . . .' and 'Up with . . .'" as well as "'Revolution!' 'An End to Militarism' . . . and 'Never Again War!'"[1] Thus Franz walked into the German Revolution on 9 November 1918. In the years that followed, he also wandered around demonstrations against the French occupation of the Ruhr in January 1923 and milled among the crowds who rallied in Berlin's government district to cheer Hitler's conquest of power almost exactly ten years later. Franz joined the Nazis' May Day celebrations and signed up for their Strength through Joy holiday programs later in the 1930s. As an air-raid warden for his apartment building on Rossbachstrasse, he watched how Allied bombers destroyed much of Berlin in the last terrible years of World War II. At the very end of

April 1945, Franz huddled in the basement as Russian soldiers took away and raped his neighbors. Franz Göll was an eyewitness to many dramatic events of what the historian Eberhard Jäckel has referred to as the "German century."[2] But throughout these decades of war and revolution, Franz mostly stood by as a detached observer. He prided himself on his "objective examination of history," and he wanted to expose the mechanisms of his times for future readers, but, in fact, he interpreted political history mostly as a natural historian would, seeing events as a "struggle for existence" through the glass of his aquarium and the cages at the zoo.[3] This was a highly ideological stance. For Franz, the field of politics simply extended the struggle for recognition, advantage, and power that he had observed on Berlin's schoolyards and in its workplaces. As a result, he tended to diminish the role of ideas and ideology, which for him simply camouflaged the play of interests. Moreover, he generally did not view history as a poignant national drama in which the fate of Germany played the leading role. As a result, he incisively analyzed the patriotic politics of the Third Reich as a struggle for advantage without sentimentalizing Germany's cause. But by focusing on huge assemblages of power operating on a global scale, he was less able to see the degree to which ordinary Germans desired the Nazis or the particular, incomprehensible nature of German crimes in World War II. As an observer, he avoided the morally charged vocabulary of perpetrators and victims. Instead, Franz's intellectual method was to create equivalences and homologies in order to integrate phenomena around him into a comprehensive, almost cosmic worldview rooted in natural history. Therefore, the catastrophe of the Holocaust tended to get lost in his grand theories. And as a self-styled observer who generally wrote in the third person, he evaded any question of his own responsibility for the course of German history.

The struggle for existence was inexorable, although Franz's position was that of a weak and vulnerable player. He viewed the world from the bottom of the social heap, which both colored and sharpened his political observations. His opposition to war and especially the sacrifices it demanded of the poor made him sympathetic to revolution in 1918, but he was also frightened of what followed, especially the new democratic state's aggressive interest politics. From Franz's perspective, hucksters and confidence men had so riddled the Weimar Republic in the 1920s that he initially welcomed the Nazis and their emphasis on the commonweal over individual interests when they took power in 1933. However, the unforgiving militarism of the National Socialists, who sought to totally mobilize society in order to unleash their wars of conquest, quickly shredded his support. The violence and aggression of the Nazis constitute a primary theme in the diaries. In one of the most moving scenes, Franz described his 1938 visit to the propaganda exhibition Degenerate Art, in which his encounter with modernist portraits of maimed soldiers and crippled veterans left him profoundly shocked. More than most German diarists, Franz was alert to the persecution of Jews, but the "objective" composition of his entries and their frequently cynical tone kept him from expressing genuine empathy for the victims of the war. His detached account of rapes in Rossbachstrasse at the end of World War II is also unsettling. Franz was observer and naturalist first, *Kümmerform* second. He rarely saw himself as a participant or agent in historical events, although in this regard he shared with many of his contemporaries an astonishing lack of any sense of culpability.

The Weimar Republic

Franz Göll was a child of the revolution. His endeavor to realize his ambitions after his father's death in 1915 coincided with the overthrow of the German kaiser and the establishment of the German Republic. The early entries in his diary registered the "cultural wars and revolutions" that had begun to break down the old order in the last year of the war. "The people were only evaluated numerically as designated matériel," he explained in 1919; "at home, money speculation; at the front, cannon fodder." Wounded soldiers, long lines for scarce goods, and usurious prices on the black market—these "events and experiences" of the war had led more and more of his neighbors, he explained, to resist the "oppressive yoke of militarism." The new political and social setting of revolution also energized him. He did not march with revolutionary soldiers or workers because he was neither a soldier nor a worker, and he did not join a political party or attend party meetings, although I suspect that Franz voted early on for the moderate party of the revolution, the Social Democrats, before moving to the right. Nonetheless, the revolutionary spirit of the age propelled him around Berlin, enticing him to attend Expressionist plays and "life-reform" lectures, to sample occultist gatherings, and to visit Bible study groups. The revolution fortified his sense of spiritual exploration as a fatherless adolescent. He railed against the dogmas of organized religion and its preoccupation with identifying sin and dispensing mercy. Instead, he thought, the church should guide "us to find our way to ourselves."[4] Franz also praised the frank and open discussion of human sexuality. Although Franz Göll was no revolutionist, he was an unmistakable beneficiary of the revolution. Beginning in 1919, employees at the Reich Coal Distribution Office received annual three-week vacations and regular cost-of-living adjustments to salaries.

At the same time, Franz wondered whether the "wave of freedom" threatened to overwhelm Germans, who had hurriedly cast off the old but stood "perplexed" in the face of so much that was new.[5] He saw the dissolving power of the revolution but missed its unifying potential. Like many middle-class Germans, Franz was unnerved by the militancy of mass politics and the political fragmentation of parliamentary democracy. With the establishment of the Weimar Republic in 1919, the lenient system of proportional voting ultimately led to the creation of twenty-eight separate parties that over the course of fourteen years rearranged themselves in some twenty mostly rickety coalition governments. Right-wing coup attempts in 1920 and 1923 tested the Republic's fragile stability early on, and the reliance on antidemocratic parties into which it was forced undermined it in the long run. As a result, the revolution repeatedly deflated its utopian promises; its effect, Franz thought, was not to suspend the struggle for existence in a higher union but to sharpen its terms. The people's protests in 1918 against "the fat cats," the monarchists and militarists who had misled and misruled them, dissolved, as Franz saw the situation, into an unpalatable brew of competing factions and fragmenting interests. It is certainly true that the revolution came with an explosion of interest in politics; even Berlin's prostitutes found their lobbyists. Whatever happened to basic "Christian precepts?" Franz wondered caustically; "Why do people chase after money, goods, property, honor?"[6] Just two months after the abdication of the kaiser, on New Year's Day 1919, he argued for the strong hand of a *Führer,* a leader: "Not everybody can rule," he explained.[7] Sensitive to the evidence of postrevolutionary chaos, but not necessarily to the benefits offered by democracy, and, as a result, attracted to the idea of a strong, regulating hand, Franz increasingly adopted the political concepts of the right-wing nationalist forces that would eventually destroy the Weimar Republic.

Göll bounced from one idea to another, the disappointment with one project gradually sapping his enthusiasm for the next. In November 1919 he quit the spiritualist Johanni-Bund to pay his dues to Marschél's Society for Research into Psychology and the Occult, only to quit a short time later: "It was all just cold calculation, egoism . . . trawling for new members."[8] Immediately after World War I spiritualism became something of a rage as the bereaved tried to make contact with fallen soldiers, many of whom lay unburied and unidentified on the western front; indeed, as many as one in five Germans believed that the dead might return to the land of the living. One of the best-selling books in the postwar period was Walter Flex's novel *Wanderer between Two Worlds* (1917), which was widely read in a way that kept the living alert to the call of the dead. Indeed, Germany's greatest living novelist, Thomas Mann, not only placed Joachim at séances in the closing scenes of *The Magic Mountain,* which he published in 1924, but let himself fall, as he admitted, into "the hands of occultists," attending three gatherings at the palatial residence of Albert Freiherr von Schrenck-Notzing, director of Munich University's Psychologisches Institut, in December 1922 and January 1923. (Apparently Mann observed "materialization" when a handkerchief levitated, a wastepaper basket fell over, and typewriter keys typed.)[9]

One day in 1921 Göll decided to contemplate the *Germanen* (German stock). With "the cleansing of everything foreign, degenerate, negative" that would come in their wake, he thought that the *Deutsch-Germanen* might reign as "the spiritual leaders of the globe."[10] This was his flirtation with Germany's woodland *völkisch* ideas.

On another day in 1923 Franz picked up Karl Radek's Communist pamphlet, *The Progress of the World Revolution*. Thereafter he showed little interest in Bolsheviks.

At home, still other answers: flipping through the pages of *Psyche,* the occultist magazine to which Franz subscribed, readers could consider "the coming Uranian age" and the "perfection of Aryanism," a new era of global wars and the resurrection of Germany, as well as articles such as "The Karma of the German People" and "The Butterfly as a Greeting from the Afterworld."[11] He quit reading *Psyche* in 1925; it closed up shop two years later.

"I strayed through the streets" was how Franz summed up his restless activity in the handful of years after the revolution. To some extent, this search for affiliation was personal because the fatherless Göll was looking for a "paragon, the teacher and sculptor of my life."[12] But Franz was also like thousands of other Germans who over the course of the 1920s zigzagged between the Left and the Right, between new and old worlds and afterworlds, between what would not return and what might still be, always with the hope of fulfilling the transformative ideals of revolution. For many, the bumpy ride did not end until 1933, when the Nazis seemed finally to represent the resolution of the search for wholeness; in fact, many years later, Franz ran across his old occultist mentor Marschél, who admitted to having become a National Socialist.[13] In 1933 Franz supported the Nazis as well.

There was one big idea in twentieth-century Germany that Franz did not pick up. He never believed in the Stab-in-the-Back Legend that held that political unrest on the German home front in 1918 had sapped the resolve of the German battlefront and had condemned the Reich to military defeat. In Franz's view, it was not subversives or socialists or Jews who had betrayed an innocent people; rather, the general unsettlement of war had steadily wrecked the country's "equilibrium"; the "struggle for a livelihood made [citizens] querulous, the obvious danger of loved ones out in the field made them excitably nervous, the growing black market and speculation infuriated the crowds, [and] the failures and shortcomings of the regime became glaringly evident." During the Third Reich Franz repeated himself in no uncertain terms and in noteworthy contradiction of prevailing Nazi historiography: "We capitulated in the face of the material superiority of the enemy," he explained. Indeed, 1918's revolutionaries had saved a great deal: "The runaway 'cart' was caught by the Social Democrats, who righted it as best they could."[14] Göll's functionalist reading of Germany's crisis, in this case in terms of social strain and civil stress, resisted the moralistic notions of subversion, betrayal, and purity on which the Stab-in-the-Back Legend and conventional German history relied.

In 1921 Franz attempted to clarify Germany's fragmented political situation by intervening directly. His manifesto, "A Path to Salvation," which the twenty-two-year-old offered to various (uninterested) left-leaning newspapers, was unusual because Franz, as an advocate, stepped out of his preferred role as observer on the sidelines. For a brief moment he once again heard the call of genius. Adding his revolutionary manifesto to the heap, he argued that parties and factions could not, by definition, heal the wounds of the German people. None of the political alternatives provided a genuine solution. On the extreme left, parties "believe that in waiting for the world revolution they have found a way out," but "we cannot count on prophetic events that lie in the dark womb of the future." Moreover, the socialist parties had become overly partisan and had focused their aims exclusively on workers. The nationalists on the right were no better. Their representatives "live with the conviction that the reestablishment of the old regime will deliver us from all danger. However, we do not live in the past, but in the present." Franz acknowledged the strength of more radical insurrectionists as well: "We also have adherents who believe that in anti-Semitism they have found the way to internal and external liberation." But the rush "not to recognize Germans as German" hardly served the whole; every Jew, "every German has the right to be treated and respected as a German."[15] This was a wonderfully clear statement of political inclusiveness. At this point Göll remained immune to racial thinking, making no distinction between Germans and Jews. Nonetheless, he registered the increasing currency of anti-Semitic ideas well before the Nazis had appeared on the scene. Moreover, Franz's solution anticipated basic elements of the National Socialist worldview. In his view, what Germany desperately needed was a "savior"—elsewhere Franz had mentioned a "Führer" or a "personality"—someone who was an "idealist" in character but a "realist" in political approach. Not surprisingly, the left-wing newspapers to which he offered his manifesto turned down the opportunity to publish "A Path to Salvation," but a decade later Göll believed, at least for a time, that the coming of the Nazis had proved him right after all.[16] Like many Germans of his time, Göll remained caught in the desire for what Paul Nolte identifies as a new "society beyond society," in which the interests, factions, and conflicts of contemporary social and economic life would be soothed by the caress of a newly fashioned community and the subordination and humility it enforced.[17] This vision revealed a profoundly antipolitical understanding of twentieth-century trends even when it was symptomatic of twentieth-century longings. It also helps explain how the terribly disappointed hopes of 1918 and for a break with the past prepared Nazi mobilization in 1933.

If "A Path to Salvation" was a call to action, it rested on the savior's pacification of the clamorous political programs of Germany's political parties. It indicated just how much Franz Göll valued political peace over social justice. He simply could not accept the validity of endless political struggle as a means to realize the aims of social democratic revolution. Two somewhat divergent ideas bolstered Franz's thinking. On the one hand, he increasingly came to believe, in accordance with natural laws he believed applied, that it was presumptuous for social groups to rebel against the station to which they had fallen. Drawn from his studies of nature, this was Franz's primary argument, and it marked a profound counterrevolutionary strand in his politics. On the other hand, he also saw the German people as victims of powerful, if shifting, interests. This secondary argument ebbed and flowed over the years. Sustained by his experiences with bullies on the schoolyard and careerists at work, it explained his opposition to the militarists in World War I and his sympathy for the November Revolution, and it explained as well his growing anti-Semitism and his initial support for the Nazis in 1932 and 1933. It also reappeared in his furious attack on the Nazis in the name of the terrorized German people in 1945. The two arguments could meld together when he diagnosed the dissolution of society in general into a "restless struggle for a place in the sun," as the slogan of the times put it, which was the condition of mass society.[18] Göll's masses were not an undifferentiated amalgam but a chaotic scramble for advantage, the birds in the cage at the zoo, "a soulless monstrosity."[19]

In the "biological" first argument, Göll remained an outside observer; in the "historical" or "sociological" second argument, he identified with the German people and anticipated the liberation their shackled condition demanded. As Franz's economic condition worsened after 1924, he seemed to favor arguing by means of biology, although the choice is somewhat counterintuitive. The rise of the Nazis in the early 1930s strengthened the more historical second argument and the redemptionist, nation-centered politics associated with it.

Franz could see his biological argument for the futility of working-class struggles for social uplift unfold along the streets of Berlin. In the winter of 1922 he sketched a dramatic "psychological study" in his diary: "Man and wife push a heavily loaded handcart to market. The wheels sink deep into the freshly fallen snow, and the couple has to work hard. For a moment, the wife relaxed her hold; the load came to a standstill and became stuck. The man let himself fall into a fit of rage; quiet and acquiescent, the woman endured everything." Franz supposed that this "simple woman" understood "something of the ordeals of a person who fights against circumstances in which he feels powerless" and, in frustration, finally "gives his rage free rein." He wondered, "Does not this case reflect in miniature the fate of humankind, which, stumbling from one mistake to another, groping in the darkness, searches for a way into the clearing, searches for clarity, comprehension, deliverance? Is history not simply the transcript of agonized humanity, and are revolutions not the screams and cries of distress of the people of the world?"[20] Franz heard the "cries of distress," but the composition, opening with the image of the stuck wagon and ending with the man's gesture of ineffectual anger and the woman's endurance, worked to seal the couple's fate. Three years after the November Revolution, Franz's disappointment with the ongoing turmoil in Germany reaffirmed his cyclical, natural historical view of history in which ceaseless pendulum swings left things pretty much in place. Revolution was not release or liberation but a more intense version of the terrors and errors of the weak.

"The tragedy of humanity is this," Göll summarized: "In the great battle against matter and for matter, which we call world history, people are always thrown back into the maelstrom of negative matter."[21] In other words, it made no sense to struggle against the hierarchies of nature. After all, as he wrote in 1929, "The earth compels the moon to orbit it," and "the sun, the earth." "The social stratification of a people expresses not artificial but natural selection," Göll insisted, offering an explanation of his failures that he projected onto the fate of everyone else.[22] Resistance or revolutionary action only compounded misapprehension and rage. The obedience of the woman behind the cart was more true to life than the anger of her husband. However sympathetically he rendered the winter scene, Göll's "psychological study" added up to a sweeping condemnation of human hope and the presumption on which it was founded.

In Franz Göll's more historical argument, he focused on the success-ful social climbers who were able to flourish in modern society. Eventu-ally he refined his argument to distinguish between parasites and the German people they preyed on. "There are people," he wrote in 1922, who treat the world around them as an object for their own advance-ment, "the blowhards, the shammers, the wheeler-dealers, the prigs," who were especially dangerous when they were able to hide behind a "system."[23] This list of frauds fits the topsy-turvy years of the inflation well; many Germans thought that they had been genuinely cheated at the end of World War I. A few years later Göll rewrote the list in terms more compatible with the frenetic activity of the Golden Twenties and the new American customs they introduced. Now it was "sports stars (boxers, cyclists, footballers, etc.)" as well as "unscrupulous go-getters" who knew how to get ahead.[24] In the depths of the Great Depression he switched the characters once again. "The ruthless hotshot" was no lon-ger the celebrity hailed by the mass media; he was replaced by "the con man, the spy, the Jew," darker, more camouflaged figures.[25] Leaving be-hind the classic imagery of bread and circuses, in which "sports stars" kept the masses entertained, Franz introduced a specific and sinister gallery of enemies of the people. That Franz targeted Jews as predators in 1931 after refusing to do so in his 1921 manifesto is a measure of how rapidly anti-Semitic ideas moved through German society during the republi-can period. Indeed, Franz arrived at anti-Semitism before he got to the Nazis, and it never completely released its hold on him; as late as the 1970s he continued to distinguish Germans and Jews. But targeting Jews was something fundamentally at odds with Franz's natural histories, the other register in which he worked and in which individual agents operated under the same general rules.

The voluminous diaries of Victor Klemperer, a converted Jew and a professor in Dresden, registered his distress that "the anti-Semitic case" appeared more and more frequently in the folds of everyday life, in conversations, on swastika-emblazoned flags, and in political head-lines: "It hinders me in everything and embitters me," he wrote as early as 1919. "It is a terrible misfortune" for Jews, who were blamed for everything, "the war and the revolution."[26] Suddenly Jews stood at the end of the logical train of thought about Germany's troubled political case. Franz's thinking quickly got to Jews as well. In a single 1929 diary entry Franz moved from an analysis of the sharply partisan aspect of parliamentary politics, which he had already developed in "A Path to Salvation," to an indictment of the "Jewish manner" in which the government taxed workers, and on to an attack on Jews themselves: "Why are there so many Jews sitting in the government and in the administration? Because these people have an instinct that tells them that there is something to be earned."[27] Prejudices such as these prompted Franz to pose a question in which the premise was as ugly as any answer: "What is Jewish being, and what distinguishes it from the German?" he asked in 1932. "In all cases the difference is easy to ascertain," Franz remarked as he passed along what he regarded as obvious: "What the Germans find so repugnant and dangerous about the Jews is their elaborate and immoral business conduct. In business the Jew always employs the means of camouflage, opening back doors, laying traps, and exploiting ruthlessly . . . The Jew is simply more intelligent, someone who has a more pronounced instinct to gain personal advantage."[28]

The formal properties of Franz's "historical" arguments were similar. Whether he was contrasting celebrities with the masses or Jews with Germans, he indicated the extraordinary talents that distinguished a few "chosen" people. But the implication of each pairing was radically different. The category of "the Jew," compounded from one sentence to the next into the collective singular, suggested the presence of an active danger and made the case for immediate political action; the rogue celebrity did not. This urgency was the premise of what the historian Saul Friedländer has termed "redemptive anti-Semitism," a salvation theology in which German well-being could be guaranteed only by locating and expelling "the Jew."[29] With his notion of the "pure" German, his fabrication of the street-smart, parasitical Jew as the toxic contaminant on which the idea of purity rested, and his confidence that Jews could be identified and Germans saved, Franz tried on the full-dress costume of "*völkisch* nationalism," and it seemed to fit.

The refinement of wheeler-dealers and sports celebrities into Jews indicated the extent to which Franz was not just observing different kinds of "hotshots" in the mass media but also arming himself to join the political battle against the "ruthless exploitation" of Germans by Jews and others. Along with millions of other German voters, Franz mobilized himself in the broad National Socialist drive for power, but he did so after his period of despair had ended with his job at Springer, while he resumed his vacations, and as he romped through the city with Hildegard Meissner and Eva Wulkow. He became a Nazi and an anti-Semite from a position of strength in which his natural histories perhaps seemed less pertinent.

Throughout the 1920s the political landscape of the Weimar Republic shifted dramatically as Germany's old established middle-class parties were besieged by new right-wing movements such as a paramilitary group, the Stahlhelm, and various *völkisch* groups whose politics were premised on direct, insurrectionary action. By September 1930, when their party gained 18 percent of the vote in the Reichstag elections, the National Socialists had emerged as the most powerful challenger to the status quo.[30] Franz did not comment on the Nazis until the autumn of 1932, by which time they constituted Germany's largest party, the choice of more than one in three voters, but his political diagnosis revealed his sympathies. Because the diary covered such a large span of time, it is possible to see how Franz's explanation for the extraordinary appeal of the Nazis in the early 1930s shifted.

After World War II Franz interpreted the Nazi phenomenon as a function of crisis. The Great Depression had created "a million-headed army of unemployed," and with its emergency decrees "the government gambled away any trust it possessed among the populace" and thus stood totally isolated, "like a skeleton without flesh and blood." At the same time, the latent civil war between Communists and Nazis for political territory had completely eroded the foundations of the centrist parties. Writing some of his political reflections during the last stages of World War II, Göll inserted the war between Nazi Germany and the Soviet Union back into the Weimar Republic, during which Nazis fought Communists.[31] However, at the time, the diaries did not mention the Communists at all. In fact, in an October 1932 fan letter that he wrote to President Paul von Hindenburg, Franz's diagnosis of Germany's problems takes aim at the generic "party" and "its corrupting play with the masses." There is no reference to civil war or the destruction of the "middle" parties. What is disclosed on the eve of the Nazi assumption of power is a deep yearning for a more unified political form that would provide Germany with international recognition and domestic freedom.[32] Seen from Franz's perspective in 1932, the German problem was deeper than the Communists or the Great Depression. To vote for the Nazis was not a desperate choice in emergency conditions but the expression of a long-cherished desire for national unity, for the fresh start that Franz had already championed in his 1921 manifesto.

An unexpected hopefulness breaks into the diary entries in the Depression year 1932. Franz introduced the Nazis for the first time in September 1932 as a "movement of renewal of the German people." He still thought of himself as "an outsider," but the Nazis provoked him to think about Germany's salvation in the real time of the present day. "In any case," he continued, and here, crucially, Göll stepped out of his role as observer to write in the first person, "we have certainly gained the insight in the last years that the democratic system of governance with its motto 'Everything for the Individual' is politically the wrong way"— *Irrbahn* was his neologism. Rather, Germany's recovery depended on a government applying "the motto 'Everything for the Whole,'" which he identified with the Nazis. Moreover, he admitted that "a radical confrontation" with the Jews "was to be expected," and thus the union of "the whole" and the recovery of Germany's future rested on the exclusion of the Jews. The remaking of Germany seemed to depend on the unmaking of Jews. In the end, every single German belonged to the state's "community of fate," which Franz compared to a "living organism," whose prosperity depended on the "intellectual-spiritual constitution" permeating it. In other words, the fate of the individual depended on the security of the collective. "Therefore: Germany must live, so that we do not go under," he concluded his diary entry of 20 September 1932 with the fanfare of mobilization.[33]

It is important to recognize that Franz's new politics contradicted many of his earlier social and economic analyses of the Weimar Republic. With his analysis of the Nazis, he transformed the masses into the virtuous, long-suffering German people and thereby recoded social degeneration into political possibility, and he inserted his fate into the reanimated fortunes of the German nation. Both the "mass man" and the distanced observer who beheld him had recombined into a collective national "we."[34] By 1933 Franz had accomplished for himself nothing less than the renarrativization of German history.

The Third Reich

Franz Göll's use of the first person and his "if/then" construction—"Germany must live so that we do not go under"—marked the culmination of a remarkable political journey in which Göll came to identify his fate with that of Germany. The composition held in place his sympathies for the Nazis, his antipathy for the Jews, and his conviction that Germany stood at the cusp of a new era of political renewal that he himself had outlined in his 1921 manifesto, "A Path to Salvation." Not even during the November Revolution had Franz felt so much a part of the forward movement of history. It is important to realize what hopes the Nazis mobilized among Germans, at least at some point during the twelve years of the Third Reich. However, when his identification with National Socialism broke apart in the mid-1930s, Franz once again resumed the role of outside observer. He revived his cool, detached tone and his biological analyses of world history and abandoned a large part of his anti-Semitism. Instead of regarding the Nazis as redeemers, he cast them as highly skilled, if voracious, predators. He dropped ideas about the salvation of the German fatherland or the liberation of the German people, whom he unsentimentally dissolved once again into a weak, victimized mass. After 1935 no single German political or military victory—not the Anschluss with Austria, not the return of Danzig to the Reich, not the defeat of France—moved him to realign himself with Germany's national history. And Franz Göll never described the defeat of the Third Reich in 1945 as a "German catastrophe," as millions of Germans did, because his whole analysis of the war was governed by his analysis of the great powers as interchangeable global competitors. The entire nationalist vocabulary of Germany's rights, Germany's honor, and Germany's freedom made sense to him only in the relatively short period of his political career as a Nazi supporter in the early 1930s. All this said, however, National Socialism and anti-Semitism left their mark on Franz. His revived natural history analysis of the global competition for scarce resources meshed with key National Socialist assumptions, and the memoirs indicate that Franz found parts of the Third Reich quite attractive. He also prospered professionally during the war years. In many ways Franz Göll lived the best years of his life during the Third Reich.

Franz's judgment against National Socialism can be dated quite precisely to 1935–1936. Even so, deep satisfaction with the advent of the Third Reich on 30 January 1933 still shimmered through his recollections ten years later. He remembered the "tinkling beat of the drum bands," the "soldierly pluck," and the "rejoicing of the masses." He wrote from the more neutral perspective of the third person, but Franz was actually there in the streets with the jubilant crowds. He was probably cheering the Nazis: "One found oneself pulled into the wake of this singular experience as if one had fallen into a delirium."[35] Diary entries confirmed his appraisal of the new regime as "the amalgamation of the two contrary principles of nationalism and socialism according to natural laws." National Socialism had finally healed German history. "The personal achievement and greatness of our Führer Adolf Hitler," Franz wrote Hindenburg on the occasion of the president's eighty-sixth birthday in

October 1933, provided "the basis for . . . overcoming the problems and challenges that our era had presented us with."[36] In September 1935 he agreed that National Socialism had in large part realized his 1921 appeal in "A Path to Salvation."[37] Franz continued to sample National Socialist literature, reading Hermann Göring's *Germany Reborn*, Alf Krüger's *10 Years Fighting for People and Country*, and Otto Dietrich's *With Hitler on the Road to Power* in 1934, Hitler's *Mein Kampf* in 1935, and Alfred Rosenberg's *Myth of the 20th Century* in 1937 before abandoning the fascist bookshelf altogether.[38]

Perhaps not least because of these terrible books, Göll turned increasingly critical and even derisive of National Socialism, referring in December 1935 to the regime's habit of "serving up anti-Semitic atrocities" (he meant alleged Jewish actions against Germans) as a "diversionary tactic" and, a year later, correcting Nazi accounts of the 1923 Beerhall Putsch, which had in fact amounted to "high treason."[39] Right up to the end of the war, Franz Göll never again had a positive word to say about the Nazis. If his turn away from the Nazis in the mid-1930s is consistent with his self-conception as a *Kümmerform* who despised schoolyard bullies, his initial attraction is more difficult to explain. Economic resentment is one possible reason, and he easily, if arbitrarily, fitted the Jews into his notions of the mighty few who beset the downtrodden many that he elaborated in the difficult years after 1924. The first anti-Semitic remarks come in 1929, but they may have been nurtured by previous experiences. But Franz was doing relatively well in the early 1930s when he turned to the Nazis. In fact, he was doing so well that he might have regarded the political division of Germany not as a natural state but as an unnecessary circumstance that invited efforts of political reunion and regeneration. In terms of Franz's personal political development, both the diary and the memoir are evasive rather than illuminating. And as a natural historian, he never explored the ethical or moral dimensions of political choices, his own or those of his fellow Germans. Göll's self-stylization as a victim made him an insightful observer but a poor witness.

Franz reckoned with the legacy of the Nazis the rest of his life, writing long reflections three times: over the course of the last months of World War II, from November 1944 to February 1945; again in February 1946; and one more time in his memoirs, which in November 1947 covered the beginnings of the Third Reich. The three accounts are very similar. Each is highly impressed with the sheer power of the Nazis and the fearsome dictates of total war. This stress on the Nazis' aggressive mobilization of society is often insightful and reveals the usefulness of Göll's natural history method, but it leaves out the ideas, dreams, and fears that millions of Germans shared with the Nazis. To an important extent, Göll exaggerated the total power of the Nazis and overdramatized the helpless position of ordinary Germans. He kept the two collective nouns far apart. What his analysis of the operations of power did not recognize was the degree to which the Nazis enjoyed substantial public appeal.

After the fall of the Third Reich, Göll admitted his initial support for the Nazis, although he took care to show where he had reservations. "I will not deny," he wrote in 1946, "that at the time I did not consider it impossible that Adolf Hitler might be the coming man who could prevail."[40] A year later he elaborated on the virtues he had once seen in National Socialism: "Up to that point, what I considered to be positive was the noteworthy struggle to master the situation on a grand scale, to guard what had been gained and to complete the task, to guarantee domestic peace, to promote the culture and treasures of the People, to advocate the rights of the People, and to attend to the improvement of social conditions."[41] However, he noted, "My skepticism grew steadily; I was offended by the aggressive way" in which the Nazis "used terror against groups, social classes, and their way of life."[42] Amid the cheering on 30 January 1933, Franz had seen how uniformed Sturmabteilung (SA) men had "with a thump on the back forced dawdlers and neutrals to give the Hitler greeting."[43] Göll had always been alert to the doings of schoolyard bullies, so I think that this postwar recollection of Nazi intimidation is credible.

It was the extraordinary intervention of the National Socialist regime in everyday life that disturbed Franz Göll. His 1947 recollection of the delirious celebrations of 30 January 1933 gave way, from one sentence to the next, to an account of the totalitarian reach of the new rulers: "And then came the measures, directives, orders, installations, and reforms . . . with which National Socialism, with its penchant for drastic turns of phrase, accompanied the upheaval."

Everything not to the taste of the Nazis was "prohibited, burned, interdicted, dissolved, obliterated, and then the Nazis carried, blew, drummed, and organizationally built their valuable corpus of National Socialist ideas into every cell of the people, into even the smallest and most remote corners of the country." Franz's inventories reproduced the onrush of Nazi vocabularies, militarized action verbs, and building-block acronyms denoting the new fascist designs. "From the infant in the cradle to the old-age home . . . now there were only NS (short for national socialist)"—as Göll informed future readers—"things." The rhythm of his sentences reproduced the frantic mobilization of society. "Effective immediately," he continued, "every citizen was a slave to his community and his nation, a bondsman, a serf, an automaton."[44] Franz concealed his initial enthusiasm by stressing the immediate totalitarian reach of National Socialism, which he had not registered in his 1933 diary entries. His 1947 recollections also left the majority of other Germans completely powerless, the objects of Nazi designs, not the subjects of their own actions and intentions. But by the 1940s Franz had left the scene, for as an observer who had long since dropped the pronoun "we" for "they," he was neither a supporter of the regime nor an automaton in its hands.

What authenticates Franz's 1947 analysis of National Socialism was the degree to which it followed conclusions already drawn in October 1944. From 1933 on, he argued, "The National Socialist regime aimed to commit and bind—preferably crisscross—every single person." "The individual was shaped, schooled, drilled, and trained for whatever special purposes needs dictated, his intellectual-spiritual independent existence was deadened, [and] young people were weaned from their parents' homes to be brought up for a nomadic, herdlike life." Emphasizing the degree to which the individual had been "degraded" to a "state slave," Franz drew parallels between National Socialism and Communism.[45] Both regimes sought to harness power through the mobilization of the masses; the Nazis did so on the basis of race, the Soviets on the basis of class.[46] With his 1944 study, Franz had returned to a broad natural history perspective in which he analyzed the internal dynamics and external relations of states as functional adaptations to assemble power. In this view there was no special German story. Except for a brief but crucial period in the early 1930s, Franz found the Nazi narrative, in which Germany was struggling to overturn the Versailles settlement and restore its national rights, to have no salience. Ultimately the Nazis replaced the Jews in Göll's schemata of predatory behavior, which both sustained anti-Semitic ideas that never completely disappeared and nurtured an eventually unyielding mistrust of the Nazis. In this case anti-Semitism did not inhibit anti-Nazism, and anti-Nazism did not completely undo anti-Semitism; both antipathies issued out of Franz's notions of the struggle for existence.

The aim of the Nazis as Franz Göll understood it was the establishment of a powerful military state to wage war. Indeed, as a natural historian he accepted the Nazi diagnosis of world politics as a continuous struggle for power. He also agreed that the competition for scarce resources provided the primary motivation for state actors. In these conditions Germany faced a calamity. "You can compare the German People to a family," Göll explained at the end of 1935, "which has its little garden and its small farmstead, but which can only just support the—by its head count—large family with the exertion of all its energies and only under the best circumstances. In any case scarcity prevails."[47] The state of nature knew only the "offensive will" in order to "procure raw materials" and the "defensive will" to avoid one's own destruction as someone else's quarry. This either/or applied to plants and animals, as well as to human beings.[48] Political survival depended on mobilizing the resources of society to assemble more power. "On the basis of population, social and ethnic unity, energy, and drive, every people constitutes a field of power within its borders," Göll surmised;[49] the Nazi project aimed to augment the "field of power" by producing more ideological "resolve" and more productive "energy," or, as Göll put it, by creating "raw material," "commodity goods," and "state slaves" out of the Germans themselves.[50] For example, in 1938 Göll compared the convalescent homes that the Nazis had opened for expectant and new mothers to "human breeding installations." Here, as in other Nazi institutions, "Maturing adults are professionally raised for future use and exploitation according to a coordinated and normatized schema."[51]

Göll was unusual in seeing so early and so clearly National Socialism's intention to cultivate a new race of productive (and pliable) men and women, although he put the emphasis on selection rather than extermination. (At the same time, Ernst Jünger had dreams of similar *Zuchtanstalten* that grew human beings for food, prepared at a "luxury gourmet shop" with what provided the title of his horrific vision, "Purple Endives.")[52] Göll's background in natural history undoubtedly helped him apprehend the revolutionary nature of a racial state built on allegedly scientific biological principles. Therefore, he quickly recognized the deeper purpose of National Socialism's interest in euthanasia. In November 1941, after watching *Ich klage an* (I accuse)—a riff off Emile Zola's progressive turn-of-the-century manifesto, *J'accuse*—the popular film which advocated for the right to die voluntarily, Franz expressed his nagging doubts: "It is generally known that the National Socialist state is thinking about and willing to take action against comrades who no longer contribute, on whose maintenance it no longer places value, and whom it considers merely ballast. It is completely possible that the National Socialist state will promulgate a law in which it urges the destitute, who are dependent on the alms (pensioners) of the state, to more or less 'voluntarily' commit suicide out of a sense of duty to the whole [*Volksgemeinschaft*] or eventually will, on the basis of rigorous assessment, take action on this issue."[53] In many ways he was wondering about his mother and even himself. He was also thinking for himself, and other Germans in the Third Reich surely had doubts about the Nazis' productivist dogmas as well.[54]

Franz well understood that National Socialism had a thoroughly imperiled sense of world history in which every being faced the alternative of aggression or destruction. "Friss, oder du wirst gefressen!" (Devour them, or you will be devoured!) was the way the Nazis put it at the end of the war.[55] The general conditions of scarcity upholstered this zero-sum conception of politics, but the threat of Bolshevism created a sense of urgency, which Franz interpreted as the premise for further waves of mobilization, each one enhancing the power of the regime. Göll repeatedly compared Nazism and Bolshevism, but he also saw the way they needed each other in order to militarize their own societies. It was precisely the "opposition" of National Socialism and Bolshevism that stabilized "both systems in the entirety of their outlooks, their strength, their will, their objectives and directions, their intellectual character, and their actions and intentions."[56] "Indeed, the key attribute of an authoritarian system," he argued in 1939, was "its 'constant' agitation and restlessness, the never-ending battle for or against something. Unrest secures its existence, whereas being at rest would cause it to fall apart into itself," he continued: "So battle at any price."[57] In the Third Reich, Göll remarked in this incisive analysis, "Events literally fall over each other; in all sectors, brisk activity takes over."[58] As he saw it already at the end of 1938, "constant motion" prevented "the accumulation and solidification of one's own thoughts, opinions, and perspectives."[59]

In Franz's view, the state of emergency was the key to the authority and legitimacy of both systems, because each depended on conditions of jeopardy in order to assemble power. Such conditions also brutalized society. "This mutual hatred," Göll concluded, was "nurtured, fanned, preached, and presented as justified through clever fabrications, disinformation, and atrocity legends. One no longer sees the individual, only the murderous firebrand, the criminal, the idiot, the slave of his own system, the hideous spawn of hell."[60] These lines were written in

November 1937, just as the Nazis launched a ferocious anti-Communist propaganda campaign; they foretold with astonishing prescience the frame of mind of many of Germany's soldiers when they invaded the Soviet Union in June 1941. Franz used the comparison of Bolshevism and Nazism to focus on the destructive dynamic of the Third Reich. But he was also describing Bolshevism, and by making Bolshevism so dangerous, something the National Socialists themselves propagated, Göll ultimately kept a key aspect of Nazi doctrine in place even while he mounted a comprehensive critique of it. The natural history vocabulary of the "struggle for existence," the competition for raw materials, and the state of emergency explained the behavior of sets of global actors; it was less useful in focusing on the Nazis' near monopoly on preemptive violence unless Göll had analyzed the Nazis' use of biology as ideology rather than seeing ideology as a function of biology. But for that Franz was too indebted to natural history as a way of making sense of the world around him.

Germany's annexation of Austria in March 1938 provided Göll with a textbook example of the ways in which Nazism exploited the sense of national injustice to further its political ends. If there was any moment when the Third Reich seduced even its political opponents, it was Tuesday, 15 March 1938, when Hitler addressed a cheering, delirious million-headed crowd on Vienna's Heldenplatz to celebrate the Anschluss. The screenwriter Erich Ebermayer, a determined foe of the Nazis, at least in the privacy of his diary, admitted that he wept for joy on the occasion: "*Not* to want it," he wrote, "just because it has been achieved by Hitler would be folly."[61] It was the remarkable individual who defied the jubilation that electrified Germans. Franz, however, did not even nod in the direction of national triumph; his diary entry for 13 March 1938, the day after German troops entered Austria, gave a long historical account of how Hitler had gone about undermining Austrian sovereignty. Göll's more comprehensive reckoning with Nazi methods a month later, just days after the 10 April plebiscite to formalize the Anschluss, did not even make reference to the specific historic event, which he scooped up in his larger conceptual framework. Without mentioning Austria, Göll outlined the general lesson that conquest was more easily achieved if it was accompanied by high-minded justifications of liberating "one or another ethnic group, racial minority, or religious community from its oppressors, from servitude, bondage, and humiliation."[62] In 1938 the drama of German and Austrian history, the aim of uniting all Germans, left the diarist completely cold. The conquests of empire merely spurred him to further scientific-historical commentaries.

Göll pushed his analysis in the fall of 1938, when the Nazis were able to force an international agreement to annex the Sudetenland, the German-speaking border regions of Czechoslovakia. That the Nazis had achieved this by means of an extraordinary propaganda campaign characterized by "lies, distortion, concealment, malice, deceit, underhandedness, pugnaciousness, and other base qualities" impressed him. It put the most brazen talents of the German creature on display. Propaganda was "ultimately the effect of human beings' inherent natural tendency to defend existential interests; the counterpart in the animal and plant kingdoms is the ability to outwit and entrap through enticement, camouflage, and mimicry." Indeed, "recognizing the value of political propaganda, the individual renews his connection to nature."[63] In this perspective the authoritarian state stood out as the most refined and skillful player in the global struggle for resources. Once again, Göll naturalized the objects under study. He thereby disabled a moral or ethical critique of Nazism.

It was precisely Franz's alertness to what he took to be his racial and biological debilities and to his general vulnerability in society, to his unsuitability to be an "Aryan" *Herrenmensch,* that pried open his reservations about National Socialism. Franz had frequently compared his manifesto, "A Path to Salvation," with National Socialist aims, but in 1935 he acknowledged that his 1921 effort failed to provide a racial perspective. On the one hand, in a spirit of self-criticism, he explained that the "racial question" was "not relevant back then"; on the other hand, opening a new line of thought, he disregarded it "because as a person I am too tolerant a judge"—"tolerant" was a word that rarely appeared in German vocabularies during the Third Reich. Over the course of the 1930s Göll rolled back his anti-Semitism, withdrawing from the positions he had adhered to since at least 1929. Göll's view on the Jews had rested on the premise that the Jews imperiled the well-being of the German people, but by 1935 he no longer saw the Nazis as guardians of the German nation, nor did he really concern himself with Germany as a subject in history at all. He bored into the maneuvers and tactics of the Nazi predators, who Göll believed used anti-Semitism as a diversion. But because he saw anti-Jewish policy as a mere feint by the regime, he was never able to see how seriously the Nazis took the purported Jewish threat or how jeopardized the Jews really were.

After the pogroms in November 1938, when the Nazis destroyed thousands of Jewish shops and torched synagogues across Germany, Franz remarked that "now that we have squeezed the Jews out of their specific economic living space, a vacuum has been created"; because racial Jews had been pushed out, the newly opened "gap in economic life will be filled with customized 'new Jews.'" These comments do not exactly disassemble the stereotype of Jews as exploiters, even though they suggest that the Nazis were poised to step in as the "new Jews." It is possible that Göll was being ironic, which seemed to be the case when he noted a few years later the "Jewish sophistication" with which the Nazis had misled Germans into the war.[64] Even so, the sheer violence of the pogrom became clear to the diarist only during the bombing of Berlin, when Göll himself had become vulnerable to attack. After a big bombing raid in March 1943, Franz walked the streets from Spittelmarkt to Schöneberg: "I have waded through so much glass only once before, namely, on that notorious 8 November 1938, when the hate of the 100 percent Nazis ran wild in the demolition of Jewish businesses."[65] Again and again Göll inhabited the role of victim, which made him alert to predators but not to his responsibility in judging the world from the self-righteous vantage of a victim who let himself off the hook without exploring his prejudices and actions at the crucial moment of the Nazis' rise to power,

Nonetheless, Göll's diary stands out for its sober appraisal of anti-Semitism. It was remarkable that in the middle of the summer of 1940, after Germany had defeated its historic enemy France, and when Hitler's popularity had never been higher, Göll pushed the idea of parasites right back into the face of the Nazis: "What was the line back in those years? Help kick out the Jews, and you will live a happier life because Germany will become more beautiful." Well, he noted, "The Jews have been taken care of, but there is no sign of relief." From this perspective, the Jews were no longer like the Nazis but were similar to all the Germans who had been cheated or expropriated. Franz finished his analysis with a flourish, the first of many anti-Nazi jokes that he would pass along in the last years of the Third Reich: "Before we had it good, today we have it better; but it would be better if we had it good again."[66] In 1941 Göll condemned rumors that the Jews who remained in Germany would be marked with the Star of David as a regression to the "revived Middle Ages." Because he was writing on 3 July 1941, just eleven days after the invasion of the Soviet Union and some six weeks before Hitler agreed to the star decree, Göll probably simply guessed that what was already happening to Jews in occupied Poland would come to pass in Germany. "It is an open secret," he continued, "that they are proceeding against the Jews in the most rigorous way with sterilization, removal to the eastern territories . . . expropriation by the state of private inheritances, jewelry, and other valuables." There were not many Germans in the summer of 1941 who demonstrated this kind of clarity of thought. "The National Socialists are actually masters of the expropriation of private property, the exploitation of human beings, and other machinations." The entry is reminiscent of Paul Celan's line from his poem "Death Fugue" (written in 1944), "Death is a Master from Germany." Göll concluded the diary entry at this point with the words "Germany, awake!"[67] For the first time since 1933 or 1934, he dropped his guard as observer and wrote again in the exhortative second person, but this time not to join the Nazis but to urge the Germans to see the crimes committed in their name, especially the crimes against the Jews.

By the end of the war, Göll seemed to have rejected anti-Semitism; the Jews were marked only by the "tenacious-fanatic" anti-Semitism deployed against them. "What we call trickery and deceit with regard to Jews, we describe as industry, proficiency, and entrepreneurship when it comes to Germans."[68] It would be nice to think that Franz had completely freed himself from the prejudices that had contaminated him since the late 1920s, but unfortunately this is not the case. After the war, when Göll, like many Germans, tried to explain the rise of the Nazis, he passed on old anti-Semitic lies and continued to think of Germans and Jews as separate people. He wrote in 1977: "Now that some distance has been gained from the Third Reich, we have to admit that back then Jewish influence in certain sectors such as medicine, law, banking, culture (theater, film, media, science), and politics represented a brewing danger for our way of life, whereby I certainly do not want to reevaluate or excuse the inhumane implementation of the final solution to the Jewish question." This is very careful, awkward phrasing, suggesting considerable agreement with the premises of Hitler's anti-Jewish actions. At once, Göll switched gears: "Today, when the Jews have been awarded the right to a state, I support giving Israel more security guarantees and other assistance." In the end, Germany's Jews were not Germans; they were Israelis. This identification was typical of Franz's generation, but a far cry from the injunction in his 1921 manifesto: "Every German has the right to be treated and respected as a German."[69] The Nazis lived on for a long time even in such a sensitive observer as Franz Göll.

Franz's natural history perspective on National Socialism attuned him to the totalitarian reach of the regime, in which "the concept 'soldier' has been extended to the entire people." The instruments of power turned the German into "an aggregated Raw Material Man," who Göll believed was the premise and basis for the political successes of "Adolf Hitler's authoritarian system." Göll also understood the violence that threatened dissidents and naysayers. Only a small minority of citizens had the strength to defy the claims of the collective. "Depending on context,

one refers to them as bellyachers, grumblers, fuddy-duddies, intellectuals, religious fanatics, Catholics, Jews' lackeys, traitors, etc.," he explained
in 1939.[70] These groups had been declared *vogelfrei,* beyond the law, and
threatened with "blacklists" and "concentration camps."[71] Absent from
this list, it must be noted, were the primary objects of the ferocious terror of Nazism, that is, racially unworthy groups, Jews (and not "Jews'
lackeys"), and so-called genetically defective Germans. In 1939 concentration camps filled up with "asocials," homosexuals, and Jehovah's Witnesses (Göll's "religious fanatics," perhaps), but not primarily, as Göll
wrote, with "bellyachers" or intellectuals or Catholics. Franz had a harder
time understanding the degree to which Germans quite willingly accepted
the premises of Nazi rule and Nazi racial policy. Ordinary citizens certainly did not think of themselves as either slaves or merely soldiers. They
were also patriots, consumers, and beneficiaries of the regime that had
engineered a return of "good times" for racially acceptable Germans, as
Franz's memoirs occasionally revealed.

Franz railed against the notion of the *Volksgemeinschaft,* which was
not, as he had believed in 1932, the national organization of the common interest. It was nothing less than a "new system to exploit German
workers whose deductions under the slogan 'Winter Aid' are two or
three times more than their penny-ante raises."[72] Taxes for social welfare
projects such as Winter Aid cost Göll nearly one-quarter of his gross
income. But National Socialism provided Franz with the highlight of
his year in the form of Strength through Joy trips—people's holidays
that were subsidized by tax revenues. As Franz noted, the subsidized
holidays were among the most popular programs in the Third Reich.
And although his recollections kept a discreet distance from the collec-
tivist spirit of the vacations—their borderland destinations, the commu-
nal kettle of goulash on arrival, and the singing of Nazi anthems—he
cherished the ability to travel throughout Germany, to test his physical
limits, and to enjoy comradeship; social relations and escapades took
up a greater and greater portion of his descriptions ("Willi and I" and

the "single widow") as time went on.[73] To be sure, Franz was by temperament an outsider. He took his social status as a white-collar professional seriously and dressed the part. Nonetheless, the vacationer felt treated like a "guest" and responded to the warm address of the informal "comradely 'Du.'"[74] National Socialism created new forms of social engagement in which Franz felt picked up rather than left out, as had often been the case in his life. It invited him into the *Volksgemeinschaft*, and he accepted its embrace. And what do we make of the 1939 holiday photograph of Göll (with a fake moustache) and a friend vamping like Hitler and Göring?[75] This is not an outsider's criticism of the regime's theatrics, but a lighthearted tease ventured by a generally contented insider.

There was something homespun about Göll's "Aryan" identity. He characterized the requirement to prove "Aryan" ancestry in order to receive entitlements from the state or to take a Strength through Joy holiday as "very interesting and informative" as late as 1947. It "produced a romantic note" and "yielded some surprising connections" as Franz was finally able to trace his noble lineage back to the von Gölls, von Repperts, and von Zeugens of the eighteenth century. Over the course of his research, he even located and befriended his von Zeugen cousins.[76] National Socialism thus restored to Franz parts of the noble identity he believed his family had frittered away. However, Franz's primary interest in heredity was always the fate of the individual rather than the racial group, and neither his "Aryan" identity nor his noble roots shook Franz's obsession with his mediocre genetic inheritance. His assessment remained self-incriminatory.

Thinking about family trees and biological destiny also sent Franz off into directions completely inconsistent with Nazi racial doctrines. In his view, Hitler's strength derived not from his "Aryan" status but from the fact that he was a half-breed, a *Mischling* of sorts. "It is a remarkable fact," he wrote in June 1933, when he was still enthralled with Hitler, "that the cradle of great popular leaders is located on the borderlands. Napoleon was a borderland Frenchman," that is, from Corsica; "Stalin is a borderland Russian" (Georgia); "Hitler is a borderland German" (Austria); and "Mussolini stems from a German family that emigrated to Italy," which was not true. This itemization "actually argues against the now-dominant scientific-dogmatic assertion about the allegedly exclusive positive influence of racial purity," he affirmed in a conclusion strengthened by his study of the psychologist Ernst Kretschmer.[77] Precisely because of what he considered his phlegmatic inheritance from his parents—"there was too little of a mix and thus too much homogeneity present," as he put it—Franz always prized mixtures of genes and personalities. His friendship with Brigitte Otterstein was so easy because "we make a harmoniously complementary opposition."[78]

World War II

"Hitler means war." This was the hotly debated proposition throughout the 1930s. Hitler's aggressive posturing in his speeches, his withdrawal from the League of Nations in 1933, and his unrelenting attacks on the Versailles Treaty threw the question of a new war into everyday conversations across Germany and across Europe. Memories of the previous war, the Great War that had cost the lives of 2 million German soldiers in the years 1914–1918, became topical and compelling. At the Dürkefäldens, a working-class family in Peine, the talk veered toward war one Sunday afternoon not long after Hitler came to power. Emma's new boyfriend recalled his temporary blindness after being shot in the head in the last war; "He does not want to take part in any war again," Emma's brother Karl reported; "He has had enough."[79] In her autobiographical novel Margarete Hannsmann remembered her father and uncle bickering constantly over whether Hitler intended to go to war. When Eva Sternheim-Peters's father indicted Erich Maria Remarque for besmirching "the honor of German soldiers" after he found the best-selling 1929 novel *All Quiet on the Western Front* on Uncle Anton's bookshelf—the year was probably 1935—his brother-in-law, a decorated reserve officer, spoke up in Remarque's defense: "But that's the way it was!"[80] For Georg

Hensel, later a journalist in West Germany, descriptions of "soldiers blistering with enthusiasm" for the opportunity to sacrifice themselves for kaiser and fatherland in Franz Schauwecker's novels, which figured in his Hitler Youth training courses as "on the level," were nothing more than "nationalist kitsch"; "No one talks like that . . . certainly not a soldier."[81] The young Hensel went back to Remarque's book, which, having sold over 1 million copies in 1929 alone, remained on German bookshelves. Over the 1920s and 1930s Eva Sternheim-Peters recalled, "Tannenberg, Skagerrak, Marne, Somme, Verdun, always Verdun" embedded themselves in the private vocabularies of countless Germans.[82] "Hitler means war"—conversations in the Third Reich circled endlessly around the theme.

On Saturday, 12 March 1938, Franz viewed the exhibition Degenerate Art, which had originally opened in Munich in July 1937 and was seen by more than 3 million visitors as it toured Germany. Organized by the Propaganda Ministry, the exhibition's purpose was clear enough to Franz: "To arouse the regime's abhorrence of the premises" of modern art "in the broad masses and to justify, substantiate, and strengthen the required opposition."[83] Open eleven hours a day, until nine at night, it was designed as a chamber of horrors to display the moral depravity of modern art and its deliberate distortion of pictorial realism. "The dismay you feel should indicate from what abyss German art was rescued," commented the long-since politically loyal *Berliner Morgenpost.*[84]

Göll had occasionally referred to art in his diaries, noting his preferences for "landscape and idyll," "the carefree splash of children," or "German ways in German lands."[85] Landscapes were "calming"; they were "simply pretty."[86] His decorating style was conventional: "Goethe's garden house" and Frederick the Great. But Franz, a scrupulous observer, had some feeling for modern art. In 1923 he maintained that "even the artists of the modern possess a way of seeing that goes beyond the crude sensibility of the majority. One could almost speak of atomistic perception; the brain's snapshot of the ceaseless alternation of the world. Hence the distortion, the amorphousness, the confusion of form and color."[87] Would Franz see through Nazi propaganda? What follows is the most moving entry in the diary.

Franz found himself standing in front of Otto Dix's Expressionist triptych *Der Krieg*, painted in 1929–1932 and now on display in Dresden's Gemäldegalerie. He admitted that "the sight of this picture is not pretty; it is horror-inducing, shattering." "But the repulsion you feel is not because of the representation," Franz explained, "but the subject of representation, war with its ruination and destruction of property, blood, and soul. It presents a cross section of the war, not as the general staff would see it, for whom the individual is merely matériel to be thrown into battle, but as the front soldier experiences it." In an extraordinary declaration that turned the aim of the exhibition on its head, Franz summarized: "The picture is not a bloody-minded depiction of the degenerate, war is." Franz returned to this picture when he thought about the "brutality and unrestrained destructive urge" of the war that Hitler had unleashed against the Soviet Union: "Soldiers will experience the war as it was symbolically depicted in the exhibition Degenerate Art," he predicted in June 1941.[88] Most Germans probably disagreed with him, but the one response of ordinary visitors to the exhibition we have is Franz's.

The paintings prompted Franz to consider literary representations of the war. Faced with the kitsch of nationalist novels such as *Faith in Germany* (1931) by Hans Zöberlein, forgettable but enthusiastic in its celebration of "glorious objectives" and molded heroes who "can pick off a hundred men from their secure lair and see the enemy as 'dogs' who need to be sent to their maker as fast as possible," Franz preferred Remarque (whose *All Quiet on the Western Front* he had read when it came out in 1929). What distinguished Remarque was that he "stands up for humanity and does not comport himself as a mass butcher like Zöberlein, bloodthirstily clobbering baby seals and hunting down buffalo." (The gestures to the future and past causes célèbres of animal

rights are fascinating.) Franz showed himself to be immune to the piti-
less worldview of the Nazis, for whom the redemption of Germany's
loss in World War I was central. In other words, Franz remained caught
in the nets of what the Nazis dismissed as *Humanitätsduselei,* or "sloppy
sentimentalism."

One reason that Franz was sloppy was that as a *Kümmerform* he had
a feeling for incapacity and loss, as a final turn around the Degenerate
Art exhibition confirmed. "And then one more picture," he wrote in his
diary, one more "of great sadness that really strikes a chord. A war invalid who wants to tenderly draw his wife to him with his prosthetic
arms. He awkwardly places his artificial arm outfitted with a claw hook
around his wife. From their expressions, it is obvious that this caress is
not regarded as a moment of bliss, but as a painful disappointment over
a happiness that is gone forever." Franz's feelings were not encumbered
with rude references to a "nervous Nelly" or absorbed by his own feelings of inferiority; his empathy recalled his adolescent tenderness that
had permitted him to tame birds and to feel their warm-blooded vulnerability. It directed him to condemn the violence of war, to acknowledge its horrific costs at home and on the battlefront, and to deride
Germany's "glorious objectives" in the present day of 1938.[89] As Franz
exited the House of Art that Saturday, Wehrmacht soldiers had already
crossed the border and occupied Austria. The next day he opened the
fifth notebook of his diary with denunciations of the annexation as sober and scalpel-like as Dix's painting.

The wartime diary did not follow the chronology of the Blitzkrieg,
the rapid-fire triumphs in the campaign against Poland in September
1939 and against France and the Low Countries in May and June 1940
that otherwise kept Germans riveted to their radios. Only when the
war crashed onto Germany with massive air raids on Berlin itself did
the diary register the impact of the day's or the previous day's onrushing events. Otherwise it was left to the memoirs, in which Göll recollected the war years in 1948, to establish an encompassing narrative to
hold fast the major turning points of the conflict. This is interesting

because most Germans were very attuned to Germany's military victories. In Franz's case, however, the chronology of triumph did not matter because Göll did not consider the goals of the war or Germany's declared national interests to be justified or even pertinent. "The actual cause" for the war with Poland was "irrelevant," Franz maintained a few weeks after the invasion; war with Poland had been "predetermined." Hitler had prepared the campaign for months, if not years.[90] Official propaganda claimed that the war had been forced on Germany, Franz reflected at the end of 1944, but "the lightning of this war was already visible on the day of the seizure of power, when I myself heard groups of young people marching past and singing the Engellandlied, 'Wir fahren gegen Engelland,' on the evening of 30 January 1933." (How does the old war song go? "Today we want to sing a song . . . for we go to England, England!") Danzig and the Polish Corridor were secondary issues; with the war Hitler had achieved a key political goal, which was "the chance to satisfy his hunger for power, his thirst for glory, and his ambition."[91] Thanks to the "ruthless" deployment of "modern weaponry, airpower and tanks," Poland capitulated in less than four weeks.[92]

Not even Germany's victory over its historic foe France budged Göll. This was an exceptional position to take in the summer of 1940, when one diarist after another basked in Germany's triumph. "Oh, I cannot believe our luck!" exuded the twenty-one-year-old student Lore Walb.[93] What struck Göll was the total and brutal escalation of violence. He pressed on: "The conduct of war in the Middle Ages, with its depredations, conflagrations, plundering, reprisals, appeared to us until now to be raw, brutal, barbaric," he wrote in July 1940 as Germany pursued the same sort of "economic-political enslavement." "In olden days a city was besieged, blockaded, and starved to force it to give up resistance. Today blockades are imposed on entire nations . . . And just as in the Middle Ages when tower sentinels announced the approach of an enemy attack with bugle signals, so today alarm sirens warn of enemy air attacks. The methods are the same, although technology has been improved and the scale of operations has expanded." Moreover, there was nothing substantially different about the German empire, which would "exploit other people and countries as colonies" just as the British had.[94] Göll watched from a remove, seeing both the British and the Germans through the same natural history lens. At any rate, there were few Germans that summer who shared Göll's thoroughly unsentimental perspective on events.

The Germans took the moral high ground with the invasion of the Soviet Union on 22 June 1941. It was the largest offensive mobilization in history and caught ordinary Germans as well as the Soviets by surprise because Germany had signed a nonaggression pact with the Soviet Union in August 1939. Göll simulated how the propaganda offensive suddenly reversed course: "Justice, civilization, providence, etc. are naturally on our side and stand united behind us in the *defensive* fight against the World Enemy, the All-Destructive, Bolshevism, against World Jewry and World Plutocracy." But "in reality," Göll objected, "Hitler's purpose is to proceed with his plans for conquest under the cover of destroying World Jewry."[95] Already with the Anschluss with Austria, Göll distinguished between the righteous language of justification, a mixture of indignation and jeopardy that was necessary in order to arouse public opinion, and the imperial aims that sought to conquer "new territory." In a democratic age the fabrication of the one was required to pursue the other. What Göll missed, however, was the fact that the destruction of "World Jewry" was not propaganda for another end but the end of Nazi policy itself.

Göll was astonished by how easily National Socialism could shuttle Germans from one position to another. After years of anti-Bolshevik propaganda, they had accepted without a beat *(hinnehmen)* the 1939 pact of friendship with a regime that the Nazi playbook had previously identified as "World Enemy Nr. 1." Less than two years later "the Russians are once again murderers, sadists, criminals, idiots, Jews, the dregs of humanity, the inhabitants of the nether world, etc., and Stalin is the beast in human form, the bloodsucking butcher, the hangman." Joseph Goebbels remarked with extraordinary frankness in his diaries that with the war against the Soviet Union he would have to put "the anti-Bolshevik waltz" back on the phonograph.[96] Hurrying from one position to another and back again, Nazi propaganda did not cater to the sentiment of public opinion but shamelessly steered it. Göll was appalled more by the witless consumption of the masses than by the cynical production of the manipulators. Only after the war would he restore to the German public a degree of moral sensibility when he recalled in his memoirs the "profound dismay" induced when the radio announced the invasion of the Soviet Union. However, his diary entries give the opposite impression.[97] Nonetheless, Göll held out some hope that Germans would attain moral clarity: he concluded his 25 June 1941 diary entry with the words "Germany, awake!" It was the first such appeal since his pro-Nazi affirmation "Germany must live" in September 1932.[98]

Göll repeated the appeal "Germany, awake!" a week later, in the entry of 3 July 1941, in which he discussed regime plans to mark, expropriate, and deport Jews; in the entry of 4 November 1941 condemning euthanasia; and finally in the entry of 4 February 1942, in which he compared Nazism with Bolshevism. Thereafter while his critical analyses of the Nazis continued, his personal appeals did not. One reason for dropping his exhortations might lie in Göll's growing despair over the ability of the German people even to see what was going on. If they could not see, the appeals simply wasted hope. "Through the instruments of terror combined with the slogan of the *Volksgemeinschaft*, [Hitler] has erected a system to dominate the masses," Göll commented in July 1943. "The masses are restrained and therefore no longer dangerous. National Socialism considers the biggest danger to be the crumbling of the masses into individual lives"; precisely the opposite had been the case during the Kaiserreich when the masses expressed the "chaos of modern life." "Whoever opts out of the masses separates himself," Göll continued, and "is regarded as a parasite [*Volksschädling*] and falls into the hands of the Inquisition. The masses are everything, the individual nothing, without moral or legal rights. And the party organizations eagerly attend to the masses (herd) to keep them under constant surveillance and in rhythmic motion."[99] "Mass," "herd," "ant colony"—these were the images Franz chose to emphasize the dullness and passivity of Germans whom the mighty Nazis could easily control with, as Franz put it in a calculated blow to the Nazis, "Jewish" refinement.[100] There was no need to combat Bolshevism because there was no difference between the Nazis and the Soviets. Both aimed at "the complete dissolution of the individual personality into a raw material being" so that all that remained of the people were "machines and animals," "'dead' and living inventory."[101]

Occasionally Göll switched images and allowed ordinary Germans just a little bit of agency: "Only the dumbest of cattle select their own butcher."[102] But on the whole Göll kept the Germans lethargic. His commentaries did not consider the acclamatory aspects of Nazism or the degree to which Germans actively supported the regime and might have felt at home in the Third Reich. On the occasion of the Anschluss, he never saw the millions of people on Vienna's Heldenplatz. During the war he did not study the legitimacy that the idea of the *Volksgemeinschaft* enjoyed. After Stalingrad he was not alert to how Germans rallied to the flag, how they feared something worse in the event of defeat. Because Göll's analysis withheld political subjectivity from ordinary Germans, he could not consider them fundamentally complicit in the actions of the Third Reich. His Germans were passive. This theorization from the realm of natural history was internally consistent, but it ignored the crucial differences that Germany's prosecution of total war produced; Germans did not share the same fate as the Europeans they occupied, the Poles they enslaved, or the Jews they murdered. The patterns of life and death in the Third Reich disappeared when Göll interpreted each along the continuum of a ruthless war for advantage and power that accelerated the general process of massification.

If Franz's diary emphasized the way in which German society had been reduced to an "ant colony," Franz's memoirs shed more light on the ways in which the war animated his life. Indeed, Franz was never more involved in public affairs than during the war, in which he served as an air-raid warden for his apartment building on Rossbachstrasse and advanced to department head at Springer Publishers. Like many Germans during World War II, Franz proved to be a resourceful manager of the new wartime problems encountered in daily life. National Socialism itself aimed at creating a cohort of self-reliant and reliable leaders who could participate in the renovation of national life. Young people found themselves quickly promoted up the administrative ladders of the Hitler Youth and the Reich Labor Service, and thus hundreds of thousands of men and women held leadership posts in the Third Reich. Two million Germans volunteered to collect Winter Relief funds every year. The People's Welfare Service, the National Socialist Women's Service, and the Air Defense League enrolled many millions more. All this was evidence for Franz's contention that National Socialism constantly kept people in motion and under control. But national service was also meaningful, even exciting, and pulled Germans into a larger terrain of activity and responsibility. The memoirs reveal how Franz participated as well.

In 1933 Franz joined the Air Defense League. Just how voluntary his participation was is not clear. On the one hand, his memoirs recalled that "he too" joined, a construction that suggests that he did so willingly, to climb on the bandwagon. On the other hand, they described Göll as being "obligated to collaborate actively as an air-raid warden." We do know that in 1933 Franz went so far as to write an essay, "Air Defense Is Urgent!" which he included in his notebooks and in which he explained the premises of civilian self-defense. He accepted the Nazi view that modern war jeopardized the home front and demanded moral and technical rearmament so that the collapse of 1918 would never occur again. Franz's participation was probably meaningful but not quite voluntary.[103] People always felt "forcibly volunteered" in the Third Reich, but the accent should fall on the implications of both words; consent as well as compliance structured everyday life in Nazi Germany.

Alongside tens of thousands of other German volunteers, Franz enrolled in air-defense courses, which were "designed to impart the necessary expert knowledge about weaponry. We were enlightened about the dangers of air war and preventive measures; we took part in exercises to fight fires, to handle defense equipment, to care for the wounded and gas attack victims, to use gas masks." Participants also learned about "building-code ordinances for air-raid shelters, antishrapnel trenches." Because Nazi mobilization expected individuals both to serve the collective and to exercise responsibility as they oversaw their patch of the *Volksgemeinschaft,* Franz advanced to the post of air-raid warden for his apartment building. He found the experience difficult but also fulfilling: "I was really out on a limb with all these obligations," which required Franz to mobilize his fellow tenants; "I often felt very pressured and mentally drained." But it was up to him "to take the initiative . . . to requisition, to arrange, to organize, to construct."

When war came in 1939 and the first bombs fell on Berlin, Franz was not impressed with the state of readiness he had been charged to oversee on Rossbachstrasse. What he did as warden was to improvise. Franz explained: "For example, we learned in the air-raid courses to use sand to seal the chambers of the cellar against shrapnel. No sooner had we carried this out than we realized that it was absurd because an airtight seal created the danger of suffocation, and water-soaked sand also damaged tools and our health. The constant and often-aimless reconstruction, tearing down, [and] rebuilding cost a great deal of resources, demanded a great deal of work, and provoked quite a bit of frustration and anger." It was often difficult to introduce new procedures among confused and even frightened tenants, but in doing so, Franz joined the ranks of what one historian has called Germany's "world champions in managing disaster." These were the "junior officers, middle management, foremen, or women who maintained the infrastructure of bureaucracy and every-day life in bombed-out cities."[104] As the bombing threats grew more serious, Franz's efforts to rise to the challenges the new dangers posed increased: "The location of the shelters was marked on the walls with arrows and excavation instructions so that in case of a direct hit rescue teams could begin their operations in the right place. Emergency exits were constructed, the purchase of gas masks was made obligatory, sand was piled in front of the walls of buildings with shelters, [and] valuable household goods were brought into the cellar."[105] Franz promoted himself to manage the crisis.

In May 1940, after the invasion of France, Franz assumed an additional post of responsibility at Springer, replacing the head of the Mail and Equipment Department, who had been drafted. This promotion relieved Franz of the requirement to train as an auxiliary policeman. Because many reserve policemen served in Poland and even participated in the roundup and murder of Jews, one wonders where Franz might have been placed and how he would have made choices had he served.[106] However, Franz was lucky: the new post at Springer functioned as the equivalent of war service. "Although this position demanded even quite physical challenges from those who had assumed it and well-intentioned colleagues urged me not to take it and prophesied that I would not last three months, I did accept it—and I did not regret it." His initial fears about organizing a department and supervising its staff were quickly put to rest. "I myself was surprised with what confidence and ease I set off into the new horizons. I felt very satisfied when my daily round of duties had been completed." Never again would Franz assume so much responsibility. It was probably the most exciting period of his life.[107] With an income of 250 marks per month in 1940, Franz was earning more than half again as much as he had at the beginning of the Third Reich.[108] It was in these positions of authority, as warden and head, that Franz began to write his memoirs (3 January 1941) to summarize world history and to see a measure of coherence, order, and direction in his life.

Given his contempt for the German masses who had allowed themselves to be seduced by Hitler, it is remarkable that Göll never reflected on how his autobiography might have helped explain the actions of ordinary citizens. Göll had supported the Nazis and had lauded "the personal achievement and greatness of our Führer Adolf Hitler" in 1933.[109] He participated in Nazi organizations such as Strength through Joy and the Air Defense League, accepting at least in part the egalitarian address of the *Volksgemeinschaft* and the geopolitical premises of Nazi rearmament. A final example from the memoirs reveals the difficulties Göll experienced making political choices in the Third Reich, a complexity his analyses did not extend to other Germans. In the last year of the war, Franz wrestled with the "far-reaching" decision whether to heed the calls to volunteer for service in the Volkssturm, the citizen army of young teenagers and old men called on to defend the beleaguered Reich in the fall of 1944. He even went to his mother for counsel. In the end he joined lest he be conscripted, explaining in 1948 "that by reporting voluntarily [in 1944] I retained a certain room to maneuver and control." Given the anti-Nazi tone to the diary entries in 1944 and 1945, Göll probably felt the need to explain himself to future readers, but he did so without exploring the wider implications of his free choice or his emotional response to the appeal to "save the fatherland." In this case his distance and his fabrication of the masses, his choreography of their seduction, and his diagnosis of their trancelike state all deterred rather than enabled Göll's insight into the political motivations of his fellow Germans.[110]

After 1943 the terrible realities of the war smashed into the diary more and more forcefully. Franz's handwriting became more hurried and sloppy as he described how the surrender of the German Sixth Army at Stalingrad at the end of January 1943 made it clearer that Germany might be defeated. His script is a material indication of a kind of breathlessness that Göll shared with many other Germans who found themselves paralyzed and shocked or who vomited and even killed themselves after Germany's great defeat at Stalingrad.[111] Lengthy diary entries also recorded the full impact of Allied bombing raids on Berlin in the last two years of the war. But the war took on such terrible shape in the diaries only after 1943, when it had already killed millions of people outside Germany. By the time of Stalingrad, the German occupation of Europe had lasted almost three years, and the majority of Jews whom the Nazis would murder had already been killed. What the diarist detailed after 1943 was the destruction of Germany, a counteroffensive that followed Germany's war of aggression since 1939.

A huge raid hit Berlin just two weeks after Joseph Goebbels declared "total war" in his famous 18 February 1943 Sportpalast speech to the party faithful. Goebbels sought to calibrate the war effort to the hard circumstances that had emerged after Stalingrad. The premise of total war was the possibility of defeat, which Goebbels described in a way that projected exactly what the Germans had already done to Jewish, Polish, and Soviet civilians onto the Germans themselves: "the liquidation of our educated and political elite," "forced labor battalions in the Siberian tundra," and "Jewish liquidation commandos." This fate could be avoided only by sheer force of will and the complete mobilization of society. Because Germans wanted to avoid defeat, they needed to adjust to a more "spartan way of life." With populist rhetoric, Goebbels attacked privileged elites and unresponsive bureaucrats in the name of the "people's community."[112] The air raids that followed Goebbels's declaration seemed to express the terrible equation of total war, in which, as Göll quoted Hitler, there would not be losers or winners, only "annihilated and survivors."[113]

Göll recounted, "In the night of the first to the second of the month [March 1943] the enemy attacked the capital in a powerful air raid, causing heavy and extensive damage. Berlin has now experienced its first really serious air raid. In cellars one listened in fright to the sirens and the crash of concussion bombs. Within an hour the racket was over." The time of *Kellerfeste* that had been celebrated in the shelters in the first years of the war was over. The next day Franz inspected the "heavy devastation in all its horror"; in "Schöneberg, Friedenau, Steglitz, Wilmersdorf and, to some extent, in Charlottenburg, Hansaviertel, and the inner city"—everywhere "one sees collapsed buildings, structures completely burned out by phosphorus canisters, the smoke-blackened outer walls standing as eerie ruins, the top stories destroyed by firebombs, roofs exposed and tenement walls ripped open by the blast so that here and there you glimpse inside the wrecked apartments." Glass littering the streets reminded Franz of the Night of Broken Glass, the Nazi pogrom against German Jews in November 1938.[114]

Three weeks after the end of the war, Franz wrote a composite account of the frightening prelude to a bombing run on the city. He recorded the soundscape of an impending attack:[115]

> What a state of nervous excitement ensued when the radio announced: "Achtung! Achtung! We have an air-defense report to give. A medium-sized bomber force is flying east and southeast over the Hanover-Braunschweig sector. An additional force with fighter-plane protection is flying into the realm in Schleswig-Holstein. Report time: 9:26." We had heard these reports so often already, but a cold shudder ran down your back and a psychological nervousness had a paralyzing effect on people. Those who were particularly over-excitable rushed with suitcases, totes, packages, and pocketbooks into the public bunkers. Everyone followed further local reports in dreadful suspense. It was not long before the loudspeaker declared, as usual: "Achtung! Achtung! The tip of the reported bomber force out of Hanover-Braunschweig sector is over Magdeburg on a continued eastward course. The force that flew into Schleswig-Holstein is now over Mecklenburg on a southeast course. A public air raid warning is in effect for the capital." All around you could hear the terrifying siren screech of the public air-raid alarm: a constant howl repeated three times. Once the air-raid danger had been determined, the Berlin radio station broadcast its special danger signal, "Kuckuck." People asked anxiously: "Will they come, or will they change course to reach another target?" In most cases it was not long before the signal "bomber alarm," a two-minute-long ghastly howl that you felt in your bones. The clarity of the situation had a slackening effect. Everyone relived all his or her experiences with this situation; appearing outwardly calm but inwardly beset by terrible forebodings, each person sought out what appeared to be a secure corner of shelter . . . It was queer to see the people colorfully thrown

together, sitting pressed closely together on the wooden casing of the conductor rail, like chickens on a sleeping perch. Some dozed, others chatted. But it was a tragic plight, when all thousands here and elsewhere quietly hoped for a happy outcome to the raid for themselves and every time so-and-so-many victims had to lose their lives. Whoever was lucky enough to be able to hear the all-clear signal left the shelter with a sigh of happy relief until the next alarm conjured up the same fears and worries.

Again and again Allied bombers broke through fraying defenses of German antiaircraft fire. "For nearly half an hour in the cellar we heard the crashing and rocking of the detonating bombs," wrote Franz after a major attack in November 1943. "Often a dust-filled wave of air pressure swept through the rooms, shaking, rattling, clanging at the barricaded walls. Everyone hunched over anxiously." To express the utter helplessness of civilians, Franz piled active, threatening verbs on each other. The next day he walked through the streets of Berlin: "Buildings still ablaze in bright flames, between plots of wreckage, piles of debris, houses in ruin. On the streets, an unusual commotion prevails; people laden with suitcases and bundles drag about their rescued belongings. Pieces of furniture and household goods have been set aside at reasonably safe locations on the street where a variety of haggard, frightened, beaten-down, and distraught-looking people have hunkered down."[116] Springer Publishers was hit in November 1943, in February 1944, and again in February 1945. The apartment building down the street at Rossbachstrasse 4 was destroyed in February 1944 (the lot remains empty to this day). Franz also described the brutalization of everyday life. City authorities moved elderly men and women living alone into old-age homes or temporary barracks in order to free up apartments for bombed-out families; Germans got used to going to bed in their clothes and packing gas masks to work; and the once-busy streets of Berlin set scenes of misery for passersby (Franz himself went to work at Springer every day until April 1945): "With a sense of gravity, because in the dark gray that has descended onto the landscape, it catches the eye, a streetcar, all but its silhouette faded out, slides out over the makeshift bridge. A timid glance scans the burned-out buildings, the stores of junk, and the bridge over the dirty-dank water of the Landwehrkanal to return to the gloom-enveloped path between the ruins."[117]

Franz observed the terrible scenes with the expertise of an air-raid warden and natural historian, but he also immediately understood the political dynamic by which the Nazis attempted to rally Berliners after the bombers withdrew. "With bombastic words" the leadership referred to the hours waiting in cellars as " 'heroically resisting attack,' sputtered on about 'Love of Homeland, Unerring Faith in Victory, about retaliation thousandfold, and about the reconstruction of the destroyed cities, which would be more beautiful and exquisite than before.'" In other words, Franz continued, "The more bombed-out, the stronger the drive and the incentive to achieve victory, because only victory promises the restitution of what has been lost."[118]

Franz Göll also observed with all the power of the poet. The bitter poem "Christmas Bombing" dates from 1943. It splices Nazi slogans into holy songs to haunting effect. I think that it is the best poem he wrote:

"O how joyfully, O how blessedly
Comes the glory of Christmastime,"
Sang once the children's choir,
It is all just like a fairy tale.

"Hard times, hard hearts,"
Demands the rallying cry of war,
"Do not let terror lead you into defeat,
All help to secure the victory!"—
"Tomorrow, children, just wait,
Tomorrow you will rejoice."

"And Peace on Earth and
Good will toward men,"
The joyous message ended so.

"Air raid!" sounds today's round;
Terror bombers thunder through the sky;
Not even the dead rest in their grave.
Bombs crash, buildings burn,
Sleep-roused people run astray
Screaming, stumbling through the night—
"From heaven above, to earth I come."

"O how joyfully, O how blessedly
Comes the glory of Christmastime,"
Once the promise of all glory
What faith, love, hope could deliver—
Today, millions flee,
fighting, dying for the victory,
In this German people's war of fate.
"O come, little children, come one and all,
To Bethlehem's stable, in Bethlehem's stall."

In fact, the bombing strengthened rather than broke the morale of civilians who rose to manage the challenges of everyday life. But as the war entered its fifth year, with Berlin a garrison city under the increasingly severe attacks of Allied bombers, Franz continued to put the blame on the Nazis. All the amenities of the *Volksgemeinschaft,* Franz argued, were promoted in the name of social progress but were administered precisely because they served the racial war. Danzig and the Polish Corridor had nothing to do with the real prize: "Land in the East" and the Ukraine. Ruins in the city reflected the false promises of the Nazis. "Ten years of National Socialism have sufficed to bring to the very edge of the abyss the Reich, which the immortalized President von Hindenburg saw himself forced, as the legacy of a heedful heart, to put into the hands of a person who, as the trustee of providence, presumed to build anew the Third Reich for a thousand years." Like many other sobered-up Germans, Göll came to realize just how accurate Hitler's election slogan from the year 1933 had been: "Give me ten years' time"—Hitler had originally said "four years' time"—"and you will not recognize Germany anymore," a remark so well understood at the time of the air war that it got people who repeated it in trouble with the secret police. Instead of "6 million unemployed," Germans had "15 million victims." (Göll never counted non-German victims.) Göll ended his diary entry for 6 January 1945 with embittered irony: "Führer, We Thank You!"[119] Göll was not arguing with the Allies, whom other Germans blamed for "terror bombing" and "terror attacks," but with the Nazis. The diaries never mention Churchill or Roosevelt; they refer repeatedly to Hitler, Goebbels, and Göring.

In the last year of the war, Göll began to pepper his diary with spot-on jokes he had picked up, which suggests that furtive conversations about the rigors of war were taking place in the workplace, in tenement stairwells, and on the way to market, although it also suggests a thickening atmosphere of fear. Transcribed, the jokes did indeed provide valuable tidbits to a "cultural history of the war" to which Göll saw himself contributing.[120]

A witty omnibus conductor calls out the last stop: "End of the line, the bus is being evacuated according to plan!" Thereupon he was arrested.[121]

Only once in a while do you hear the customary greeting "Heil Hitler" . . . "Hail Hitler" is jokingly transformed into "Heal Hitler."[122]

A sign at an old-age home: "Closed—We've Been Called Up."[123]

Soviet Russia has shown us its very humane conduct of war:
(1) It gave us a three-year tour of Russia,
(2) it lent us the Ukraine, and
(3) it now sends us back home into the Reich.[124]

Under Kaiser Wilhelm and Kaiser Franz,
We had goose for Christmas;
Under Social Democrats,
We still had roast,

Under Hitler and Göring,
There is not even herring.[125]

Hitler was supposed to have been asked whether the old German greeting should not be reintroduced. And he replied, "As long as I govern, there is no more 'good day.' "[126]

These wartime jokes are pretty good; they have a bit of bite. So one more: "Adolf Hitler thinks for us; Joseph Goebbels speaks for us; Hermann Göring pigs out for us; Robert Ley boozes for us; dying, though, we have to do for ourselves."[127]

Franz did wonder if the beginning of the end was at hand with the failed assassination attempt against Hitler on 20 July 1944. He quoted lines from Friedrich Schiller's poem "The Hostage," also known as "The Pledge" (1797), when he transcribed his response a week later:

"What would you do with that dagger,
Speak!"
Demands the despot, his visage bleak.
"I would free the state from the tyrant!"
"For that, on the cross be repentant."

Göll scoffed at Goebbels's remark that strangers had embraced each other on the street upon learning that "the Führer"—Göll had come simply to refer to Hitler derisively, and unusually as "A. H."—had survived. As it was, most Germans condemned the assassination as a stab in the back. But the problem, as Franz saw it, was that the masses could only with difficulty be roused from their lethargy or their trancelike state—Göll deployed somewhat contradictory images here.[128] When Germans did finally awake, it was at the final moment of defeat, when it was "unfortunately too late."[129]

Göll had reckoned with Germany's defeat since early 1944, but the actual end did not come for a long, long time, not until May 1945. Many Germans had suspected that after the defeat in Stalingrad and the overthrow of Mussolini, the summer of 1943 would force an end to the

war (but not necessarily the Third Reich). Göll's political analysis persistently emphasized the logic of self-destruction: the 6 million unemployed who had turned into 15 million dead (the actual figure for Germany
was probably closer to 10 or 11 million civilian and military casualties).
The fact that what Göll took to be the untenable structure of the Third
Reich did not topple under its own improbable weight forced him into
ever more extreme explanations that stressed the overwhelming might of
the Nazis and the total passivity of the German people, whom he referred
to as prisoners or slaves or coolies gang-pressed in their own land. His
commentaries produced the effect of utter powerlessness, which corresponded to Göll's theoretical and psychological inclinations. In March
1945 Göll resumed the memoirs he had broken off for six months; the end
of World War II comes in the middle of his colorful descriptions of Weimar Berlin, which perhaps represented an effort to reinvent retrospec-
tively an animated people characterized by the verve and mobility they
no longer exhibited in the present.

The feeling of powerlessness was manifest in Göll's detailed, though
cold and detached, description of the last days of the war when Göll
and his fellow tenants huddled in a basement on Rossbachstrasse in
Schöneberg's fabled Rote Insel. This is the contemporaneous transcript
of the natural historian, the air-raid warden, the "observer" on the
sidelines:[130]

> Over the course of the 27th of April, we learned our fate . . . The
> door to the cellar was ripped open, the first Russians stood before
> us. An officer and three men, soldiers in impeccable accoutrement
> with leather belts and machine pistols, but human beings nonethe-
> less. The officer, with an oval face, laughed jovially; the others had
> round heads with facial characteristics, short necks, and squat bod-
> ies that betrayed their Asiatic origins. Their smattering of German
> was eventually understandable. They asked if there were soldiers or
> weapons among us, waving their pistols about, threatening: "If sol-
> diers or weapons, then bang, bang!" Then the demand: "Watches,

watches, schnapps." We gave them our pocketbooks and wrist-watches; anyone who hesitated was treated more roughly. Thereupon the officer came around, gave us cigarettes and enlightened us: "Russians do nothing to Germans. Hitler shit, Stalin good. Russians not exterminate Germans. Russians friends. No Siberia. No murder women and children like Germans in Russia." We applauded each point and felt relieved. The officer left, and a busy coming and going of Russian soldiers of all types, from more humane European to mongoloid-animalistic, followed . . . Toward evening the Russians came back, shone a scrutinizing light into the faces of the women, and then came the order: "Come, or bang, bang!" The selected women had to go. This sudden turn of events left us depressed . . . After a while, very dispirited, the women returned and silently took back their places.

In some measure, Göll expected the women to go just as they "silently took back their places."

For many women in Berlin, the horror of the war had just begun; as many as one in three women were raped in the weeks after the Red Army occupied the city.[131] But Göll softened the blow, perhaps because he had expected worse for himself: "That is the way it was, here and elsewhere, sometimes worse and more terrible, elsewhere more civil and civilized, as is the case in war and according to the fancies of fate. Later we heard tell of terrible situations and hard fateful blows, but also of sympathy and understanding for our situation and chivalrous behavior on the part of the enemy." Göll's entry was dated 3 May 1945.[132]

Göll's diary indicated how exhausted he and his mother had become during the final bombardment of Berlin. The end of the war meant above all an end to air raids and artillery fire: "The war is over, and also the horror of the bombing terror and its nerve-racking siren howl during air raids, the quick flight into cellar, bunker, S-Bahn shaft, and the looming phantom of chemical warfare." Germany's defeat meant that Göll could get some sleep.[133]

It was a few days before Franz reflected on Hitler's "accomplish-ment," which was the "pile of ruins" he had predicted long ago: "(See diary entry 25. June 1941)." At this point, however, Göll seemed uncer-tain about what exactly he had foreseen and what register to use in or-der to make sense of it all. He tried out a moralistic vocabulary, in which Hitler was a creature out of nature altogether: "This criminal, this pretender, this Satan."[134] In Göll's widely shared view, the number of Nazis became smaller and smaller. If the Nazis were "sadistic mon-sters," then the German people were no more than "poor wretches," bewildered but basically innocent.[135] But in his 14 May 1945 entry Göll stepped back to blame Germans. "Did we not always scream for a man of action?" Göll reflected, using the self-incriminating first person: "Since 1933 deed followed deed [*Tat*] and misdeed followed misdeed [*Untat*] until our present situation as the ultimate *Endresultat*," a clever play on the word *Tat*. This line of thought left out Göll's appeal for a "savior" in his 1921 manifesto and in his 1932 letter to Hindenburg. In whatever key, however, Göll's analyses were completely self-absorbed. The catastrophe was the one the Germans brought on themselves, not the ones they had meted out to others.[136]

Göll's disregard for the torments, humiliation, and suffering of Na-zism's victims was typical for Germans of his day. His opaque, self-absorbed sense of sight recalled the "glass wall of an aquarium" through which Primo Levi believed his German superior at Auschwitz, the chem-ist Pannwitz, looked at the starving prisoner: it separated "two beings who live in different worlds."[137] Franz had looked through these same panes, sometimes with empathy for, but also often with indifference to, other lives.

Indeed, Franz began to blame the Allies, and especially the Russians, for their brutality, a theme he had first taken up toward the end of the war. "With a few words," Göll wanted to discuss the "opposing side" after a long February 1944 diary entry in which he had condemned the Nazis. They too used "many inhumane instruments of war:"[138] "parti-sans, snipers, riflewomen, commissars ready to execute, all besmirching 'the cultural values of the white race.' "[139] Göll consistently drew parallels between the two sides, but, writing as Germany began to lose the war, he started quite uncritically to blame the Soviets for ratcheting up the violence. When Germany's defeat became clear in January 1945, Göll refined his colonial references. He imagined the terrible fate of Germans under Allied control, implicitly accepting the Nazi argument that Germans were fighting against imperial domination even while he explicitly rejected the freedoms the Third Reich allegedly protected because "every German is already a coolie . . . in his own fatherland."[140] Colonial imagery provided the register for Franz to consider his condition that of a helpless victim who evaded responsibility for the disaster he helped produce.

Although Göll was quite clear that the Germans had started the war, the closer the Allies got to Berlin, the more their counteroffensive seemed to rival the aggression of Hitler. He eventually returned to his analyses of the struggle for survival. In this way Göll's biological argument allowed him persistently to evade a historical analysis. The two world wars, Franz reflected in July 1945, had been fought to drive out the competition. In his view, the defeat of Japan in Asia and of Germany in Europe allowed a more advantageous redistribution of scarce resources among the victors. The division of Europe into Soviet and American spheres was the logical consequence of the Allied victory. World economic recovery, he surmised, depended on the elimination of selected "civilized peoples" such as the Germans, whose fate increasingly resembled that of colonized natives. In the future "they will magnanimously allow us just as much economic and cultural autonomy as has been customarily granted to 'primitive indigenous people.'" Franz's postwar commentaries rested on a series of spatial homologies drawn from the realm of natural history, not on a chronological analysis of cause and effect. Everything came down to economic competition in conditions of permanent scarcity that made both domestic and international conflict inevitable and redistributive schemes such as social welfare or socialism unworkable.[141] "World history" was "robber history,"

he stated, quoting his favorite author, S. Philipp, in October 1939 after
the invasion of Poland, and Franz continued to think so in 1945 after
the defeat of Germany.[142] In other words, Franz's inability to distinguish among powerful agents and to untangle the context of cause and
effect completely dulled the critical commentaries he had developed
before the end of the war. His natural histories veiled as much as they
illuminated.

As a result, Franz, like many of his fellow citizens, was not inclined to dwell on the specifically German nature of crimes in World
War II. "Although we became culpable," he wrote somewhat defen-
sively in his memoirs as he reflected on the January 1933 seizure of
power in November 1947, "we also paid heavily, and now we should
draw a line under this completed account. We should not think of
ourselves as better than other people, but we are also certainly not
worse. We are guilty of having done too little; let the others take care
not to be guilty of doing too much. And when we are accused of being 'war criminals,' then we have every right to respond, 'Peace sabo-
teurs!' "[143] In the end, Franz Göll dismissed the case for German guilt.
According to him, no one was basically different from anyone else, a
self-righteous, self-exculpatory judgment in which Göll was unfortunately not alone.

The foundation of Franz's equivalencies between the warring parties
was the reduction of the individual to a commodity in the conditions
of modernity. What had happened in Germany between 1933 and 1945
was a symptom of larger, global processes of degradation. Even the
Americans snatched up German experts, while the Soviets deployed
labor battalions to dig mines or build canals. The Nazis had attempted
to refine the process of objectification even further:[144]

> That people who because of their racial affiliation or anti-Nazi atti-
> tudes were expelled from the *Volksgemeinschaft* were literally used
> and cannibalized as raw material for industry exceeds the normal

conception of what is human. After all, one just burned these unfortunate victims to ash in smelting furnaces to make fertilizer or boiled them in cauldrons to make soap. Undoubtedly statistics and tables gauged the productivity, quality, and cost-effectiveness of the result . . . All that was missing was to establish a corporation with common stock, dividend disbursements, and business advertising to use human beings for industrial purposes.

"Who or what will arrest this human degeneracy?" he asked. "When will humankind catch its fall and convert once again to Christian humanity?"

As a natural historian, Göll thought in predominantly material terms that permitted him to comprehend very early the centrality of racial selection in the Third Reich but left him quite blind to the specific role that Jews and Germans played in the Nazi view of history. Göll came close to adopting the position of the philosopher Martin Heidegger, who in a 1949 lecture asserted that the motorization of the agricultural food industry was in essence "the same thing as the manufacturing of corpses in the gas chambers and the death camps, the same thing as the blockade and starvation of the countryside, the same thing as the production of hydrogen bombs."[145] The difference is that Göll used a language of shock and incomprehensibility and indicated some distinctions in scale and kind, whereas Heidegger insisted, over and over again, on making everything look the same. "The war is over, nothing has changed, nothing new, on the contrary," Heidegger had written on the day the war ended.[146] Göll was misguided, perhaps, but scientific and curious. Heidegger was obfuscatory and embittered.

Franz's natural history subsumed the specificities of history in an overarching symptomatology. Göll's alertness to struggle and adaptation in life made him susceptible to National Socialism early on because he accepted the legitimacy of the state's aim to mobilize resources for national advantage and the collective good. It led him to discount specifically German crimes in a larger series of equivalencies among all political entities. But his self-appraisal as a weakling who had been unable to master life or take the offensive was ultimately more decisive in forming his view of National Socialism as relentlessly exploitative and destructive. He saw life as in an aquarium, but from the bottom up.

6

Resolution without Redemption

In 1945, at the end of World War II, Franz Göll was back where he started. He lived with his mother on Rossbachstrasse in poverty, undernourished, without prospects, and forced to divert his savings into calories. The struggle to survive in the difficult postwar years eroded whatever sense of mastery Franz had achieved in the early 1940s. The good times at Springer had come to an end. As he concluded his memoirs in the summer of 1948, he surveyed his life in the same melancholy register as the diarist had in the 1920s and 1930s. Almost fifty years were without shape or aim, a series of episodes, waves that knocked him back down to the position of rubble clearer and night watchman. Like many Germans, Franz saw both the long end to the war and its aftermath as an extended period of calamity and destitution. He experienced the years 1943–1948 without much sense that recovery in a more stable, affluent postwar epoch would be possible. And like most Germans of his generation, he felt humiliated by Germany's defeat in World War II, even though he had not identified closely with the Third Reich. Only gradually did Franz perceive improvement for himself, for Berlin, and for Germany.

The more upbeat diary entries in the 1960s and 1970s recorded Franz's reconciliation with the course of his life and that of German history. In what ended up being the final diary entry, written on the last day of 1983, Göll fashioned colorful end papers to his life, recognizing that he had achieved "a *Lebenssymphonie*"—"in some measure"—a "life symphony" that he realized was now coming to an end.[1] But Franz remained guarded, eschewing any sort of redemptive conclusion in history or in his autobiography. His legacy was not wisdom or happiness but the transcripts of his continuous endeavor to figure out what was going on and why events happened in the way they did: his diaries and his notebooks on the self, nature, science, politics, and the Nazis. His last piece of business was to historicize Jesus Christ and to argue against the sweeping motions of judgment and salvation carried out in his name.

Humiliation

The end of the war did not bring much relief. Forty-six years old, Franz Göll did not experience 1945 as the liberation of Germany from the Nazis. To be sure, right after Germany's unconditional surrender, he recognized that Germans were free of Adolf Hitler, "this criminal, this pretender, this Satan" who had so disastrously led citizens into utter defeat and ruin. On behalf of himself and his mother, "I can only thank divine destiny that helped us survive this difficult time unharmed. We have kept our lives and our apartment."[2] But the brutalization of everyday life did not come to an end. In January 1945, four months before the end of the war, there was no gas for cooking, and electricity was out for hours at a time. Long lines of people gathered in front of stores to purchase dwindling supplies with discounted ration cards. Every step testified to the degradation of life: "Just a journey in one of the overfilled streetcars is proof enough how shattered, demoralized, and embittered people have become. Getting picked up is difficult, and when after a long wait you have pushed and shoved yourself to finally squeeze into the tram car and have fought for a 'place,' you stand there in the crowded corridor like 'sardines in a can.'" He concluded, "A genuine orgy of the human, all-too-human." Franz astutely observed that "in the name of the *Volksgemeinschaft,* everyone assumes the right to demand from others what he himself would not do." The much-vaunted Nazi community was understood as license to complain, to elbow some people aside, and to turn a cold shoulder to others. Everywhere *Kippensammler* zealously trawled smoking compartments to pick up cigarette butts and sort out the ashes in order to press them into a "coveted 'sweet nugget'" of tobacco. Kept like "pets" for years by their master, "a thick-skulled fanatic," Germans were now vagabonds, bombed out, disoriented, and desperate to save themselves by any means necessary.[3]

Six months later, after Germany's defeat and extensive occupation by the Soviets, not much had changed: "Potatoes and bread are in short supply." "In order to put a little meat into the pot on Sundays," Franz complained in July 1945, "housewives have to stand in line at the butchers already Friday morning at 6 a.m. Moscow time," that is, 4 a.m. for Berliners. Full of self-pity, Franz went on to lament that the Allies "have gone so far as to deploy women standing in line to shovel debris somewhere. And this they presumptuously, proudly call a progressive, democratic system guaranteeing 'freedom, work, and bread.'"[4] The general misery squeezed "humanity, empathy, and compassion out of people. Everyone sees in another an adversary, a rival, another mouth to feed, a bothersome, annoying hanger-on and runner-up." In other words, sharp elbows and cold shoulders were now licensed by humiliation and privation, which weakened individuals "spiritually as well as physically."[5]

Indeed, Germany's humiliation had become a public spectacle when the American occupation force arrived in Berlin in July 1945. "You can see on a daily basis how German men greedily stoop to pick up the cigarette butts thrown out by the Americans, who often amuse themselves in this way." Moreover, it was not long before "German women hooked themselves to American soldiers and strolled through the streets completely at ease . . . the German soldier it took five years to conquer, the German woman not even as many days."[6] This gendering of collaboration was pernicious but widespread in the 1940s. Popular myths held that French women had yielded to the seductions of German soldiers during the war; a few years later it was German women who supposedly yielded to the victorious Americans. The female figure both exposed and expressed national weakness.

Berlin itself was wrecked. Franz walked around in May 1945 and sketched the sorry scenes three years later: "Everywhere shocking pictures of barbaric devastation. Whole blocks of buildings consisted of nothing but ruins and mountains of debris. Here and there on streets and squares, provisionally dug graves, occasionally decorated with a simple cross with lettering, a few flowers, an infantry helmet, and, for the Russian dead, stars and little red flags, all surrounded by overturned cars and military vehicles; tossed-out uniforms, corpses, half covered in dust, the pervasive stench of blood; smoke, phosphorus, mildew, decay, everything sinking into dirt, filth, slime. This was the road to the desert, where once had stood the capital, full of life, flourishing, forward looking." The ruins were thick with flies, then with spiders.[7] Not only did Franz inventory humiliation in long lists, but also humiliation itself came in the form of an inventory of wreckage and loss.

Franz quit Springer in July 1945, outraged that as a senior employee he was assigned to do cleanup work for the Russians; instead, he ended up doing cleanup work for the city. It was like being back at the post office, except that Franz was now twenty years older. He performed heavy manual labor among the ruins of apartment blocks on Kolonnenstrasse in his neighborhood, then on Olberstrasse near the Jungfernheide S-Bahn station, and finally in Neu-Westend. In the best Berlin tradition the city organized a steamer trip for workers in June 1946. From Beelitzhof to Glindow, the cleanup crews enjoyed a break with "two barrels of beer," "a tasty stew of kohlrabi and potatoes," and "an accompanying ship-board band."[8] Even so Franz resented the physical labor and poor wages and especially the calibration of rations according to the grade of work. Because money had become worthless, he estimated, "manpower" was measured according to "horsepower and caloric intake," a new denomination that characterized the "materialism" that had "run amok" since the war. Göll wrote about the statist "biotech" regimen: "In an hour, a worker produces so many pieces, in eight hours that many more pieces . . . Engaged in strenuous activity, a worker needs so-and-so many calories a day to remain productive; working less hard, only so many calories. In this way, supplied foodstuffs are distributed to animals and people." He could just as well have been writing about Siberian penal colonies in one of Varlam Shalamov's *Kolyma Tales,* in which Soviet prisoners realized that "the mysterious charts of proteins, fats, vitamins, and calories intended for the convicts' table did not take a person's weight into consideration," with the result that "a scrawny intellectual lasted longer than some country giant."[9] Göll continued his analysis: "The eggs that hens lay, the tapped milk production of cows, the output of sheep, the meat consumption of pets, the productive efficiency of human beings, the energy expended in completing particular tasks, the wastage of material and power, psychological factors in work productivity—everything is assessed, monitored, controlled, and registered with technically sensitive and sophisticated equipment."[10] As Göll saw it, the end of the war was not a difficult time that would pass, but the intensification of the ongoing objectification of humans by larger and increasingly oppressive and mutually supporting technological and authoritarian structures. Theorizing in this way, Göll did not accentuate the end of the war or the opportunity of peace but stressed instead the destruction of human forms by gigantic processes that did not distinguish between victors and vanquished. His theory depended on the evacuation of history.

The "cynical way" in which calories were counted left Franz and his mother hungry. Franz had to dig into savings for several months in 1946 in order to purchase bread or cigarettes, a "hard currency" that could immediately be converted into bread. In a business transaction straight out of the short stories of Heinrich Böll, whose postwar characters always ended up a nickel short, Franz wrote up his accounts for April 1947:[11]

> Sold bathrobe = 1500 g bread + 80 [cigarettes]
> Sold women's stockings = 1500 g bread + 50
> Sold dress shirt = 1500 g bread + 30
> Sold dress shirt = 1500 g bread + 30

Too few calories and too little coal during the bitterly cold winter of 1946–47 weakened the physical bodies of Berliners; between December 1946 and February 1947 over 1,000 people died of malnutrition, and 250 froze to death.[12] On Rossbachstrasse, Franz's mother had several frozen toes amputated in March 1947, and she remained in the hospital for weeks. Even when she was released "once improved," Anna stayed in bed for a long time and never walked properly again; in October 1948 she fell and broke her leg, a "black day" that eventually forced Franz to move her to a rest home in 1952. Franz himself had to seek medical attention several times in 1947 for "general physical deterioration, nervous breakdown, boils," all the result of "insufficient nourishment."[13] The war and immediate postwar years left deep physical and psychological scars. Although Franz's were relatively minor, the haggard 1946 portraits of him and his mother revealed the imprint of hard times. What was entirely missing in the diaries and memoirs, however, was reflection about the fate of other Europeans either before or after 1945.

In April 1947 Franz landed a job as a night watchman on Schöneberg's Sachsendamm, not far from home. It came with the advantage of a coveted "ration card II," which entitled him to more calories and extra coal but was a far cry from his senior position at Springer. What it did do was leave him time to go to the library and read.

Always moving from the specific to the general in his endeavor to find larger patterns, Franz interpreted his misery not as the result of postwar scarcity after a ruinous war started by the Nazis but in grand geopolitical terms in which state actors continued their wartime struggle for advantage. This time the Germans were being expropriated as they had once expropriated others: "It is all strictly business and is handled and conducted accordingly. Apparently [the Allies] are dealing with us as if they were buying up the competition and closing and liquidating the enterprise." In his helplessness Franz identified once more with Germany, retying many of the bonds he had loosened during the war and rehearsing Nazi positions he had rejected years earlier. In his view, both the Russians and the Americans were determined to take what they could from the defeated nation. "It is only the sake of outward appearance that gives them the moral responsibility to provisionally provide for us," he commented in his completely self-absorbed manner, but "they hope for and even propose our eventual extinction as a nation."[14] Schiller may have said that "the old is crumbling . . . And from the ruins blooms a fairer life" (from *William Tell*), but, as Franz noted ruefully, although "the old has crumbled around us, in fact often completely," there was little evidence of new life. "The black market, criminal activity, and moral squalor"—Franz could see all this; otherwise, "People and nation" led "a life without future, a knocked-into-unconsciousness, miserable zombie existence." Franz continued his lament: "Germany has become a plaything in the hands of economic-political forces, strategies, and special interests; everyone works to gain his own sphere of influence." Germans were as powerless after the war as they had been under Hitler during the war: On the one hand, "raw materials, food supplies, and finished products are extracted from Germany," the aim of the Russians, in particular, "and on the other hand, we are supplied basic necessities on account at exorbitant prices," the specialty of the Americans. In the end, "We are in arrears with no means to pay." Franz drew this sorry balance on New Year's Day 1948.[15]

Economic fortunes eventually improved, and Franz's commentary became less drastic, but the basic themes of his analysis of postwar Germany remained in place. The two new superpowers, the Soviet Union and the United States, had divided the spoils of Germany and had established their own expansive imperial regimes in Europe. Franz referred to a new "'cold' war" in March 1948; George Orwell had begun to use the term in 1945 to denote a "peace that is not a peace," and the columnist Walter Lippmann popularized it in a 1947 book, *The Cold War*.[16] "The end result of the Second World War," Franz explained the situation as he quite perceptively saw it, was "the crystallization of two political superpowers, the USA and the Soviet Union. All other countries are forward areas, the glacis surrounding these two fortresses. Before the decisive engagement between these two bulwarks is played out, each party attempts to gain as much forward area for security as possible . . . Europe no longer has a role to play; it has played itself out and has lost its economic-political independence as a result of blindness, internal disorders, and quarrels. The actual survivors of the Second World War are the USA and the Soviet Union; the other nations are mere satellites without volition or purpose, simply chess pieces of world politics."[17] "The question of national self-determination," and certainly the question of German reunification, Göll asserted, "is as good as eliminated from world politics; there is only the choice: East or West." Europe would be either Asian or American, for Franz a poor choice that confirmed the "decline of the West" that Oswald Spengler had foreseen a generation earlier.[18]

Hitler, too, had anticipated the threat to the sovereignty of Europe, Franz recalled, and although his goal of a "middle bloc" had been misunderstood by some and misused by Hitler's own ambitions, he had been right to try "to maintain Europe in its historical form and culture."[19] This was an extreme, truculent hypothesis in which resentment over the historic fate of Germany shattered all understanding of the fundamentally criminal nature of the foreign policies of the Third Reich or of the liberal structures that the presence of the United States fortified in Western Europe. It also contradicted Franz's disavowal of Hitler's foreign policies before 1945. After the war Franz began to take his German being more seriously, as his entire commentary from the first postwar years right through the Reagan presidency demonstrated. In March 1948, as in October 1932, Franz identified his impoverishment with the destruction of Germany, but this time, after World War II, he could not imagine and never ventured to formulate ideas about the redemption offered by Hitler the first time around. He did not subscribe to literature imagining the "perfection of Aryanism" or the "karma of the German people," as he had after 1918, and he struck the idea of a *Götterdämmerung* or a phoenix rising from the ashes from his cultural index. The disaster was complete—for Franz, adrift again at the end of his forties; for his fellow workers, whom a thoroughly rationalized marketplace judged by their muscle power and caloric intake; for Germany, whose debasement not even Schiller could console; and for Europe as a whole, overrun and overtaken. There was "no exit" and "no future."

Although Franz had invested little of his political self in the enterprise of National Socialism, he resisted facing the fact that Germany was basically to blame for its fate. He responded indignantly to the new international order that Germany's aggression had called forth. Indeed, his angry indictments of the Allies put him closer to the Nazis than he had ever been in the Third Reich. In his humiliation, in which he identified his impoverished self with the wrecked, humiliated body of the German nation, he subscribed to what Michael Bodemann has labeled "late Nazism."[20] He spoke in his diary as a shamed loser without feeling a sense of vindication that would have been more consistent with his unsparing commentaries on the Nazis during the war. Göll hated the Nazis, but something about the Third Reich and its promise of a greater Germany had struck a deeper chord, a resonance he shared with many other Germans who were suddenly without orientation when the norms and values of the Nazi era broke apart. Contemporaries flailed about in the ruins of Germany, often holding on to this or that piece of the Nazi wreckage.

One part of Nazism that Franz Göll refurbished was racism, for he spoke out against his avowedly shameful treatment in part as a white man. During World War II he had condemned the "instruments of war" used by the "other side" as a "scandal" to the "cultural values of the white race."[21] After the war he continued to associate the Soviet Union with its Asian or "Mongoloid" racial features (already standard Nazi propaganda). "Asia" now threatened Europe by advancing as far west as Berlin and the Elbe River and showed itself to be "nonwhite" by stoking anti-imperial struggles against the European metropolises around the world. Imperiling the political superiority of the "white race," the Communists overturned what Göll took to be history's judgment on the moral and cultural superiority of Europeans. Göll could well imagine the distress people suffered around the world, but until the end of the war he never imagined that misfortune could befall the "white race." "When will the white man properly recognize his cramped, dishonorable situation," he mused in 1947, when the European empires were still largely intact, "and find the strength to confidently tread the path to genuine humanity?"[22] The strange crossing of "white race" and "genuine humanity" attested to both the shame and the humiliation he felt. He and his mother suffered as Germans, but Franz also blamed the Americans as much as the Soviets for putting "whites" in the subordinate position of the colonized.

The presence of American troops in Europe also brought Franz Göll face to face with a situation in which "whites and blacks live cheek by jowl." He worried about the American model (incomplete though it was) in which "legally binding civil rights" would force whites "to be treated by a black doctor, to be held responsible by a black judge, or to sit amid blacks in movies or on public transportation. In such conditions tolerance really reaches its limits."[23] In this case the post-1945 discussion around the world about human rights, decolonization, and the color bar, rather than power politics, jeopardized Göll's self-satisfaction as a white man. Göll did not embellish racist themes; for him, the Cold War was much more dangerous. Nonetheless, the diary continued to refer to planetary struggles between whites and blacks or between Europeans and Asians.[24] Franz's whiteness clothed his nakedness. The voyages he had made to

Asia and Africa in his wide-ranging reading program, his scientific curiosity, his exploration of nature—none of these kept him from fortifying racial hierarchies precisely at a moment when his and Germany's place in the world had become insecure. In this regard Franz was not a man of the world, despite the transcontinental reach of his imagination.

But when Franz thought about the universe during the space race in the 1950s and 1960s, he responded quite benevolently to the extraterrestrial beings that he believed might well exist. He did not consider aliens, as he did many of his fellow human beings, threats to the species. "If we ever could hear from the inhabitants of other stars," he suggested in an interesting analysis, "this eventuality would have a cataclysmic effect on the Christian church, its theology, and its message"; as the "son of God" and "redeemer of humankind," Jesus Christ "has relevance and meaning only on this earth."[25] "Even if we could understand one another's language," he concluded on a fastidious note, "I cannot imagine that one could convince these hitherto hypothetical beings . . . of the truthfulness of divine grace in the face of their conceptions of faith."[26] It was in the ultimate space of space that Franz worked out the earthbound nature and this-worldly origin of revealed religion.

Private Satisfaction, Material Prosperity, and the Cold War

At the end of 1976, seventy-seven-year-old Franz Göll sketched the world he saw from his perch in the Rote Insel. "I live a satisfying, quiet, and trouble-free life in my neighborhood Schöneberg (zip code 1000 Berlin 62), have diverse and good shopping outlets, relaxing parks, and cultural amenities. Children can enjoy playgrounds with climbing structures and other amusements." In many ways Göll described the idyll of postwar West Germany (his West Berlin included), which had recovered from the war to enjoy substantial material prosperity and even serenity. This was an "Economic Miracle" that Franz, along with most other Germans, could not have anticipated in the first years after World War II. At least in the West, generations who had grown up in the first half of the twentieth century, punctuated by the catastrophes of war, revolution, and economic misery, came to enjoy unprecedented civic and economic security that was valued all the more because it was unexpected. Older Germans especially prized order and homogeneity in order to preserve the comforts of peace. They were quick to point out blemishes in the picture, as Göll did: "Somewhat strange behavior can be observed among the guest workers who for several years have been brought here, mostly Turks, Yugoslavs, but also Greeks, Italians, Spaniards, etc., who have taken over the lower-paid work that German workers will no longer accept." Not since the war had there been so many foreigners in Berlin, and Franz felt as uncomfortable now amid the *Gastarbeiter* in Schöneberg as he had during the war when he had watched the so-called *Ostarbeiter* on Alexanderplatz. But he moved on, and did not dwell on foreigners. More disruptive were Germany's young people with their "sloppy clothes" and "often-unkempt manes of long hair." Franz could not stand their "arrogant" and "snotty" attitude, not least because it did not defer to the cherished order that he believed had been achieved since the war.

Beyond Franz's safe, if not completely harmonious, neighborhood, West Berlin "bordered on East Berlin and the German Democratic Republic along what the infamous wall created as a flat expanse of territory." Behind the German-German border dividing East and West, the enclave of West Berlin symbolized the ongoing tensions of the Cold War, in which the two superpowers, each armed with thousands of nuclear weapons, faced each other in an uneasy peace that each believed the other was stealthily working to undermine. But whatever difficulties a West Berliner might encounter when entering or leaving the city, Franz knew that "in the West anyone can determine by himself his own lifestyle at his discretion at liberty and without coercion."[27] As in the late 1940s, the Soviet Union and the United States of America dominated the political fortunes of Europe, but since then the West had become prosperous in the "glorious thirty years" that followed currency reform in 1948. Geopolitical dangers persisted, particularly in the late 1950s and early 1960s and again in the early 1980s, but did not disqualify the feeling of economic security at home. In the Federal Republic of Germany full employment, consumer goods, and a social welfare state overcame the bitter scarcities that had dominated daily life in the late 1940s. As Franz put it, life in the neighborhood was relatively "trouble free." Franz's postwar politics revolved around the principle of keeping matters just so, "trouble free," which justified skepticism about immigrants, fortified disdain for hippies, and animated his support for East–West détente.

After Franz took a position as night watchman at the lumberyard of Carl Holz and Company in April 1947, he regained modest financial stability. The work was tedious; Franz traded off with another guard the two nighttime shifts, one from four to midnight, the other from midnight to seven. But Franz found friends and enjoyed respect. Fellow tenants in the Rossbachstrasse apartment building augmented his social circle. In the evening neighbors would visit Göll, bringing a phonograph and records, or accompany Franz to the movies. Franz, "Frau Bo," and "Hans W" celebrated at a neighborhood bar with *Bockbier*, schnapps, and "Mosel wine" in March 1951. After twenty years Franz also renewed contact with his Amboss cousins; a legal claim over Grandfather Hermann's inheritance had long estranged Franz's mother from her sister's family in Kladow. Franz even attended the funeral of his pushy, disagreeable uncle, Carl Amboss, who died in 1963 at the age of ninety-three.

Franz's Economic Miracle arrived when he unexpectedly received an invitation to return to Springer Publishers as head of his old department in 1959, an offer he accepted because of the financial rewards and pension it promised. But he outlined the disadvantages. Springer meant stress as well as an early morning start at 7:30 am. Franz missed his old friends at the lumberyard and the surrounding garden allotments and the long stretches of free time that allowed him to check out books from the Amerika Gedenkbibliothek at Hallesches Tor and pursue his studies.[28] As it was, Franz made new friends at Springer, resumed the holiday trips that had come to an end with World War II, and added steadily to his wealth; he died in 1984 with over 100,000 marks in the bank. Like most West Germans, by 1979 he had acquired a color television ("Brand: Philips") and a private phone line (with the number 7817276).[29] Franz retired at the end of 1964 at the age of sixty-five, but he maintained contact with friends and colleagues at Springer, especially Rudolf Müller, who shared his intellectual habits and interest in postcards. The two companions often went to the movies, *Doctor Zhivago* in 1971, for example, or *Julia* in 1978; they spent Christmas and New Year's together; and they explored the countryside around Berlin, as Franz had with his mother in the 1920s: Gatow, Tegel, Kladow, the Grunewald. The gang at Springer sent "Papa Göll" cigars for his birthday and reassembled during annual Christmastime reunions that took place at the Palace Hotel in Berlin's Europa Center, the epitome of West Berlin's new modern American look.[30] Göll looked back with satisfaction at the friendships he had made and the "Life Symphony" he had arranged.

By his own testimony, he never regretted not marrying.[31] Like his fellow diarist Fernando Pessoa, Franz averred that he never loved anybody: "No one was ever so close to me that I could say in all honesty that I loved that person."[32] There was always something prickly about Franz's sense of sovereignty, as was the case with many diarists who lived on the islands of their own writing. In the event, "a slight toward me" caused Franz to end his friendship with Rudolf Müller in 1978; he ended his renewed contacts with his Amboss cousins in discord around the same time.[33] Quick to take offense and withdraw into his shell, Franz had become very much like his mother. Franz lived alone until the end of his life, stubborn but generally at peace with himself and content to have been able to offer the world his "Life Symphony," the notes and reflections he had kept for seventy years.

However, Franz Göll was increasingly uncomfortable with the public disorder of a diverse, youthful democratic society. "The order of our

state takes the form of a democracy," explained Franz somewhat hesi-
tantly in a formulation in which democracy justified itself by providing order. "This means," he continued more confidently, that "every
citizen has the right to enjoy as much personal freedom as possible."
Unfortunately a large number of citizens did not adhere to "personal
limits within these accorded freedoms." In other words, democratic
practice required the ceaseless reassertion of order and discipline so as
not to disrupt the repose of others.[34]

Like Goethe during the time of the French Revolution, Göll preferred order over freedom. This was the case in the 1970s as much as it
had been in the 1920s. The foreign-born guest workers "are not exactly a
disruptive element," Franz conceded, "but they are conspicuous on account of the mentality that differentiates us from them. We find their
speech, with its loud and hard cadence, accompanied by arm-waving
gestures, disagreeable to our ears. Especially the women dress in colorful clothes and distinctive head scarves. You can recognize them immediately by their profile and external appearance." This was a mild judgment, but Franz turned ferocious at one point, comparing the "foreign
infiltration" of "guest workers" in the 1970s to the presence of Jews in
the 1930s: "A large number of these guest workers, mostly from eastern
countries, intend to stay here and become citizens. For the most part,
they come from fresh and sthenic ethnic groups whose birth rate far
exceeds ours."[35] As a result, he predicted, in twenty or thirty years Germans would feel overwhelmed and invaded; as it was, foreign "guest"
workers made up 10 percent of the German workforce in 1973, up from
1 percent in 1960. Göll's assignment of jumbles of people to "us" and
"them," family and strangers, was also a remnant of Nazism. Ideas about
racial or ethnic exclusivity apparently had cut deep because they reproduced themselves effortlessly after the war. Franz's idea of Germany had
become much more rigid and exclusive in the sixty years since he had
written his 1921 manifesto. Franz understood the horrors of the Holocaust;[36] his racism stemmed not from ignorance of Germany's twentieth-
century history but from his nearly automatic association of normality

and prosperity with order and sameness, an old formula from the Third Reich that still seemed to make sense in the Federal Republic.

Franz was even more disturbed by the culture of youth in the 1970s. In the so-called juvenile delinquents or *Halbstarken* in the late 1950s and then the "hippies" a half generation later, Franz recognized the children of the bourgeoisie, not proletarianized or impoverished subgroups. They came from Schöneberg, not somewhere else. During the Third Reich the "snide-irreverent manner" of young people who had grown up in the Third Reich had irritated him.[37] But the problem of youthful rebelliousness had deeper causes, Franz surmised, and here his analysis improved on his resentments and anxieties. In an age of technical progress, in which "robots" and "automated factories and offices" displaced human beings and the media displayed the "meteoric rise" of young stars in film and sport, it was not surprising, Göll contended in an entry from 1956, that "attention-starved adolescents gather in parks and side streets in the evening to make mischief" as a way to overcome feelings of inferiority. A lingering sense of unmet expectations accompanied the modernization that had destroyed the former "authoritative frame of reference" in which "station" and "milieu" had once provided codes of behavior. A culture that celebrated the "'hot' jazz music" and "the sharp, nervous rhythms" of "popular dances" and produced "superficial films (Wild West, gangster, crime—with riotous scenes)" and other "obscene scandals" had lost "an assured sense of limits."[38] Göll had received more than his early experience had led him to expect, and he was both grateful and highly protective. As a result, he could not sympathize with the sense of disappointment held by younger Germans.

Franz understood the important role of youth in questioning premises and renewing society as he contemplated rowdies in the 1970s. "When you reach a certain age, you do not want to relearn . . . you want to continue on the well-trodden, familiar path," Franz explained. For its part, youth had an instinct for loosening up "institutions, facilities, perspectives, and customary practices" that "over the course of time had threatened to become dogmatic and rigid." Even so, Franz was put off by the arrogance with which '68ers opposed the entire system. The city districts that young people inhabited had become squalid: "They are partial to occupying the front hall of Bahnhof Zoo, gathering to block pedestrian traffic, talking, arguing in loud voices." Around the corner "they crowd the steps to the new Kaiser-Wilhelm-Memorial Church in their shabby getups and rude behavior, carrying on like rowdies, leaving behind batteries of empty bottles, and otherwise spreading garbage around." This behavior was ungracious, given the city's "effort to give Berlin a friendly, embellished appearance by planting greenways, tree-lined boulevards, and floral arrangements."[39] Interestingly, Franz was bothered by public disorder and socially inappropriate behavior, not by the contagions of sex, drugs, or rock and roll, which, except for the single reference to "jazz" in the 1950s, the postwar diarist did not discuss.

The left-wing terrorists of the Red Army Faction who in February 1975 kidnapped the chairman of Berlin's Christian Democratic Party, Peter Lorenz, were also an affront to the political order. In Göll's view, radicals needed to be dealt with harshly, both in the courts, to which he recommended the reinstitution of the death penalty, and in public opinion, which tended to treat the "anarchists" as "gangster heroes."[40] Franz Göll could not comprehend the well-brought-up children of Germany's postwar prosperity despite his study of the rebellion against the commodification of modern society: "It is as if a virus had infected their brains, blocking normal thought."[41] Perhaps it was noteworthy that the old man tried to understand the revolutionaries of the 1970s at all.

In basic ways, however, Franz was on the side of the rebels as a result of his untiring opposition both to the nuclear brinkmanship of the two superpowers and to the unrealistic political demand at home that Germany should be reunified in the pre-Anschluss borders of 1937—that is, without Austria, but with the Prussian East. In his view, the rigors of the Cold War and the dogmatism of German nationalists left West Germany without a creative political role to play in the world. It was in the name of a more independent Germany that Göll moved to the left in the 1950s and 1960s to become an unabashed supporter of the Social Democratic chancellor Willy Brandt. The resentments of the late 1940s, when Göll felt that he was living in a newly conquered colony on a par with "natives" in the non-European world, gave way to more levelheaded Social Democratic politics in the 1960s and 1970s in favor of détente and mutual accommodation; he opposed arming the new Bundeswehr with nuclear weapons or stationing short-range nuclear missiles in Germany, and he supported Brandt's Ostpolitik as an attempt to find a third way between the two superpowers. Göll mistrusted the Americans because he believed they proposed to defend the United States on the banks of the Rhine River. "There is not much I can do with the new American president Reagan," he averred toward the end of his life.[42] Franz Göll was not free of resentments, but he also was not so burdened by them as not to undertake the remarkable journey back into the Social Democratic camp. Göll began his political life somewhere around the moderate socialists, moved decisively toward Hitler in the early 1930s before backing away, and ended up near Willy Brandt, a supporter of compromise, toleration, and openness.

What most imperiled the tranquility of Franz Göll's life in Schöneberg was not the appearance of guest workers or the rebelliousness of young people but the proliferation of nuclear weapons. The diaries in the 1950s and 1960s home in on this issue even as they leave unmentioned dramatic episodes in Berlin's Cold War history: the blockade and airlift in 1948, the workers' revolt in East Berlin in 1953, the erection of the Berlin Wall in 1961, John F. Kennedy's visit to the city and his famous "Ich bin ein Berliner" speech at Schöneberg's city hall in 1962, and the student riots in 1967. Nuclear bombs preoccupied the former air-raid warden.

More nuclear weapons were concentrated in Germany than anywhere else in the world, all of them controlled by foreigners, and a low-grade but palpable anxiety about whether it was possible to survive the confrontation between the two superpowers strained German public life right up to the reunification of Germany in 1990.[43] The characteristic postwar word *Angst* well describes the residual feeling of unsettlement; indeed, "The capital letter gives one the feeling one has been placed in a black box from which there is no easy escape," adds Cees Nooteboom, the Dutch writer.[44] In long, well-observed diary entries Franz brooded over the looming threat of nuclear war in Europe and Germany's powerlessness to alleviate the dangers it faced. He opposed stationing short-range nuclear weapons on German soil not only because they made Germany a target but also because they severely limited Germany's options in the event of a confrontation between the superpowers. Göll believed that the rapid integration of the Federal Republic into the military structures of the North Atlantic Treaty Organization (NATO) that the postwar chancellor, Konrad Adenauer, pursued in the 1950s in order to advance the long-term goal of national reunification was counterproductive because it tied Germany completely to the strategy of the United States while hardening the position of the Soviet Union. In Göll's view, Adenauer mortgaged Germany's future by trying relentlessly to regain its former unity. Franz understood the chancellor's position that "the Federal Republic cannot achieve success if it engages the Soviets and makes demands in isolation and without means of force. For this, it needs to be strongly backed up by partners in the alliance." But he found the Social Democratic position more persuasive. Global tension would remain heightened, German reunification would be postponed, and the provisional status of West Berlin would be made more tentative as long as NATO did not accommodate the security concerns of the Soviet Union. Moreover, Franz noted, the United States did not really care about German reunification. Every step that Adenauer took in step with the Americans made it more unlikely that West Germany would be able to pursue its own interests.[45] Although Göll underestimated Adenauer's willingness to accept the division of Germany, he stressed the need for détente in the context of the Cold War.

The flash points of the Cold War, Germany's decision to accept rearmament and join NATO in 1955, the ongoing discussion of the Rapacki Plan that envisioned a nuclear-free zone in central Europe, the placement of nuclear weapons on West German soil in 1958, and the sharpening conflict over West Berlin in 1960 and 1961, prompted Göll to undertake rigorous analyses of what he considered to be the flawed premises of the military strategy of the West. He was particularly unnerved by the crash of an American bomber armed with nuclear weapons that newspapers had reported in January 1958 (it is not clear what incident he is referring to, but there were several mishaps in 1957). There was no immediate danger because the bombs had not been set to go off; they were designed so that the nuclear capsule was inserted only immediately before deployment. But these precautions hardly reassured Franz, who realized that "for quite some time now in the USA, planes with atomic bombs on board are continuously in the air, ready when notified of an attack to move into action immediately." In other words, he continued incredulously, "We are already so close to a Third World War as to be prepared for its outbreak 'by the hour' and to have taken the necessary precautions." What frightened Franz about the superpowers was their shared suspicion that nuclear warfare was imminent, which drove the United States to deploy nuclear weapons on hair-trigger alert and to station short- and mid-range rocket launchers in the Federal Republic.[46] It was like living permanently in 1938 and 1939, between the Sudetenland crisis and the invasion of Poland. Like most left-leaning West Germans, however, Göll did not analyze Soviet actions in any detail, nor did he quite understand that the postwar recovery of Germany he cherished was not simply threatened by the Cold War but in fact depended in large part on the conflict between the superpowers and on the United States' economic as well as military commitment to Europe that followed.

Although Franz noted that "authoritative voices argue that Europe would long ago have become sovietized had it not been for the deterrence exercised by the NATO power block in alliance with the USA," he was skeptical. One thing was certain: "If we allow the construction of launching platforms (for long-range missiles and atomic bomb stockpiles) on German soil, in time of war, such action will be reciprocated with launches by the other side." "To be sure, a zone that is not secured *can* be attacked without risk," he added, "but a zone that is secured *will* be attacked with *certainty*." Franz concluded his 1958 analysis, "Our alliance with the West provides us with a certain security guarantee," but one that "can easily have the opposite effect if we feel compelled or are compelled to go along with the West in support of a certain policy in which the risk of danger is greater than the gain in security." He called for Germany to adopt a strategy "suited to our own interests."[47]

Moreover, Franz disputed the logic of mutually assured destruction. Hair-trigger timing, permanent sorties in the air, and ever-larger nuclear stockpiles, all justified in the name of an imminent threat, "will bait the button-pushers." Deterrence depended on an unchanging balance of forces that was illusory in an age of extraordinary technological development. Because "each side will attempt to gain a head start, however small," not only would the arms race accelerate, but also the likelihood "that one side finds itself compelled at what it considers an advantageous moment to take preemptive action" would increase. Göll carefully plumbed the psychology of the nuclear age, which he believed favored preemptive action. The Cold War leaned toward a hot war rather than a cold peace. Besides, as he noted, in the 1930s observers had agreed that Europeans would not stand by and let their cities be bombed into wastelands, but deterrence had failed. (Actually there was no such agreement; on the contrary, the consensus held that cities were quite vulnerable to obliteration by long-range bombers.) Given these conditions, "It is completely mistaken," indeed, "frivolous," "cynical," and even "barbaric," "to use words like courage and cowardice in connection with the atomic threat. We can only really speak of murder and suicide, of . . . responsibility and collective guilt."[48] Like many other Europeans, Göll imagined the mass deaths that would result if a nuclear bomb were dropped on a city. He recalled the terror of being bombed in World War II; his anger and anxieties were real, and his positions anticipated the general demilitarization of European foreign policy attitudes after 1945.[49] But he also stood out for offering a precise and levelheaded analysis. He judged as a former air-raid warden and as a German quite aware of being caught in the middle, not as a natural historian observing an ongoing struggle for existence. In any case he maintained the perspective of the underdog.

For the rest of his life, Göll opposed tying West German policy exclusively to American security stakes and stationing short- and mid-range missiles on West German soil. He admitted that nothing guaranteed Germany's security, but he argued that rearmament threatened it, creating conditions in which Germans faced each other with weapons of mass destruction. The paradox of the Western European experience of the Cold War was that while nuclear weapons imported the fears associated with the military catastrophes of 1914–1945 into the post-1945 years, the period up to the 1970s otherwise came to be marked by unprecedented material prosperity, *les Trentes Glorieuses*. This created a situation where the possibility of the end of life collided uneasily with the premise of the good life, which Europeans desperately wanted to preserve, and this collision sharpened their frustrations with nuclear armament.

West Germany's justification for following America's nuclear lead was in large part the assumption that compliance would facilitate reunification. Franz considered the goal a pipe dream because West German politicians never offered a definite plan about how to achieve it or to reconcile and pay for property claims; it was not even clear that Germans on either side of the border desired reunification, which was therefore a poor guide to strategic and defense policy. It was better simply to recognize the German Democratic Republic, Franz counseled as early as 1957.[50] Even though this was a lonely position to take, he argued that most West Germans had come to implicitly recognize the other Germany simply in the way they talked about their eastern neighbor: "We used to refer to the eastern zone or the Soviet zone, but years later, at first quite timidly and only occasionally, we said the 'so-called DDR [Deutsche Demokratische Republik],' then more clearly, the 'DDR' in quotation marks, and now, lately, we say DDR and refer accurately to two states on German soil."[51] Franz was remarkably unsentimental about reunification, perhaps because he was anxious to maintain the status quo, which, after many turbulent decades in which catastrophe seemed to be around the corner, finally offered him economic security and peace.

Franz's perspective on the German Democratic Republic turned increasingly positive as well. A witness to the new state's declaration of sovereignty in October 1949, Franz had nothing but contempt for the ceremonies. "I felt that I had been transported back into the days of the 'Third Reich,'" he reported. "Then, as now, it began harmlessly with a torchlight procession and marching columns (then it was brownshirts, today the decision was made in favor of blue), with the fetching melodies of the battle songs and serrated marchers, with flags and standards, speaking choirs, spontaneous cheers and oaths, with pledges, with pinched-earnest, dogged battle-ready expressions, and with the resounding, spiritedly enthusiastic broadcast of the proceedings over loudspeakers and radios. Only the slogans had been switched."[52] A visit to East Berlin neighborhoods eight years later revealed the tawdry backstage of the patriotic proscenium: "Although there are many pedestrians on the main streets, there is very little motorized traffic. You only see a few automobiles of an older make alongside the horse-drawn carts. Everything looks a little worn out. With their weathered paint jobs, carriages smeared with dirt, and drawn blinds, the streetcars and omnibuses—also older models—are a wretched sight . . . It is obvious that public life is tailored and geared toward the 'producers' [*Werktätigen*] . . . There is lots of talk . . . about 'retail culture' [*Verkaufskultur*]—another buzzword in the East— but the state-run shops . . . do not make an especially tidy impression. The shopwindow displays reveal scarce and meager goods, a big mockup, lots of propaganda, and what you can catch a glimpse of through the often-drawn blinds is disheveled and unattractive."[53] Already in 1957, two years before his well-paying return to Springer, Franz reported on the East from the perspective of the relative material well-being he enjoyed as a consumer in the West. In any case the Berlin Wall, erected in August 1961, put an end to his journeys to the East.

However, a visit in April 1972, after German-German negotiations opened some traffic across the Berlin Wall, impressed Franz. There was something both orderly and congenial about East Germany that the more Americanized, rough-edged West Germany lacked. "Invited by a friend, I went for a visit abroad to the East yesterday," he reported. "After lunch we took a walk around Alexanderplatz. Although I recognized certain streets," the new configuration of the square, which had recently been completely revamped in socialist international style, was "foreign to me. I was very impressed with the size of the space reserved for pedestrians, with the surrounding apartment buildings, and the height and size of the newly built television tower with its rotating restaurant and fabulous views. Laid out in modern design, fountains, flower beds, and benches adorn the square." Moreover, "In contrast to our Bahnhof Zoo, the train stations have not been occupied by annoying *Packzeug,* and the streets are generally very clean." Indeed, as Göll commented elsewhere, "If you take a careful look, over there German culture and tradition are usually better maintained than over here, with our heavy American influence."[54] What he saw in East Germany was exactly what he had come to hold most dear in Schöneberg: safety and security after two world wars and after the economic calamities he and his mother had suffered in 1915, upon his father's death; in 1924, when he lost his job at the Coal Distribution Office; and again in 1945, with the end of the war. Hence the West German's appreciation of East Germany's repose.[55] Göll had anticipated what would become a familiar dichotomy at the time of German reunification in 1990: "An East German life that had preserved much of its German integrity and a superficial fast life in West Germany in which much of history and tradition had been forgotten."[56] In Göll's view, expressed already in the 1970s, it was West Germany's modernity and its alliance to the United States that endangered the security the "West" supposedly guaranteed.

Détente appeared to be one way to procure a margin of security from the brinkmanship of nuclear confrontation. Détente also seemed a way to protect the benefits of the economic miracle from the vicissitudes of world history. And Willy Brandt represented détente. First in 1966 as foreign minister and then from 1969 to 1974 as West German chancellor, Willy Brandt was the right man for Göll because he pursued a policy that recognized existing realities, making possible visits between citizens of the two states, diminishing German-German tensions, and laying the groundwork for the policies of both states eventually to regain a degree of independence vis-à-vis the superpowers.[57] Similarly, Franz greeted Brandt's recognition of the Oder-Neisse line as the permanent border between Germany and Poland. He did not believe that anyone really wanted to go back to Germany's old eastern territories that now lay in Poland and the Soviet Union; the unforgiving "Old Homeland Associations" which opposed any territorial concessions and served at the same time as "catchments for foreign Nazis, revanchists, and similarly dark figures," were as harmful to Germany's interests in the 1960s as the pro-Soviet Victims of Fascism had been in the late 1940s.[58] Writing in December 1970, Franz focused on the importance of reconciliation to overcome the conflicts and resentments of the past. "German politics has now taken exactly the direction that I have supported for years in my political commentaries."[59] Willy Brandt had been able to sort out and "develop" German history, although he had done so without providing Germany a grand design or a conclusive resolution. In Brandt, Franz recognized the modest scale of future German politics; there would be no powerful statesmen on the order of Bismarck; the unified Reich under which Franz had grown up and to which so many memories were tied had broken up into two German states, while Prussia, "the nucleus of this former empire, has been obliterated."[60] Franz found the ending of German history to be bittersweet, but he preferred the security of the present to the grandeur of the past.

"I myself have become acquainted with several systems of order," Franz mused at the end of 1970. This was a historical perspective he shared with most Germans of his generation, all of whom could speak of having lived in four different Germanys. From his perspective, "There was no overarching dynamic to German history, simply a ceaseless rhythm of assertion and resistance," the insight of the natural historian. The "monarchy with its class state" fell apart with Germany's defeat in World War I. The "socialist" Weimar Republic that followed "found little resonance among the broad masses"; war, revolution, and inflation kept Germans unreconciled, paving the way for Hitler's Third Reich. "There has hardly been a sovereign who understood, exploited, and abused his position of power better than Adolf Hitler"—an interestingly mixed judgment. But "with the huge drama of the Second World War, this form of government and its creators found their well-known and infamous end." For all its dissatisfactions, the Federal Republic of Germany was the best of the four systems because of the comforts and security it offered: "Today we simply live in a society of affluence with sufficient income, generous vacations, modern comfort, and reasonably priced trips abroad."[61] The Germany of 1970 was appropriately sized to Franz Göll's modest sense of proportion. It no longer invited the schoolyard bullies, careerist strivers, or political dreamers who had bothered him in the first half of his life.

Franz died in 1984. He did not have the chance to reevaluate the long course of twentieth-century history from the perspective of the end of the Cold War and the reunification of Germany. Had he lived on, my guess is that in his diary entry for October 3, 1990, the official day of reunification, Göll would have recognized the liberation of millions of Germans from dictatorship and from the threat of nuclear annihilation and perhaps would have recalled the east German lands where he had spent his first holidays in the 1920s, but he also would have noted the financial cost of reconstruction and the brittleness of "the feeling of belonging together" that he had anticipated thirty years earlier (as he might have put it at the end of the entry, "Compare with the diary entries from 18.11.57, 18.11.59").[62] In 1992 an elderly Franz Göll might have noted one more development: that year the United States grounded its permanent air-based strategic bomber fleet for the first time since the 1950s. North American air bases such as Chanute in Rantoul, Illinois, in my own neighborhood, shut down.

Bones and Ash

In the last years of the diary Franz put aside his reflections on German history and politics to take up Christianity and the figure of Jesus Christ. When I first examined the diary, I assumed that Franz had found religion at the end of his life, perhaps moved by the Jehovah's Witnesses who had come to his apartment door in the late 1940s and with whose missionaries the solitary bachelor stayed in friendly contact. For example, he accompanied Jehovah's Witnesses to church services in April 1977, the first such reference in the diary.[63] But Franz remained a religious doubter all his life. A self-described "skeptic" and "pantheist," Franz contended that he believed in God, although his God was not a "superman" sitting on a "throne" but an idea, a principle of superordinate, though as yet uncomprehended, harmony, an idea that was a fundamental precept of monism.[64] Franz believed that life in all its forms was interdependent; it was a universal principal that each strand reflected and owed something to a larger, not clearly comprehensible whole. This interdependence was visible as well in the illusions that human creatures assembled and the truths they sought. Franz certainly did not believe in a Christian God because he could not imagine that God distinguished between world religions that were, in any case, to his mind quite similar and because the possibility of life beyond earth strained "the truthfulness of divine grace."[65]

Given his theory of knowledge, in which the world that humans experienced was the world they pictured and described, it is not surprising that Franz regarded gods as human inventions, marvelous fabrications. "Man created his gods in his own image," he concluded after reading Karl Löwith's *God, Man, and the World in Metaphysics from Descartes to Nietzsche* (a book he described as "difficult material"), "and his pious devotion built them into independent and rule-bearing entities, whose dominion he subsequently recognized and to whom he subordinated himself in humility." The gods were the first attempt of human beings to interpret and reflect on the world around them. Religion provided a sense of security and orientation and offered the needy self the promise of an eternal afterlife amid a lifetime of destruction and disappointment. Over time, however, people opened up new avenues of understanding, imagining the world in more lawlike terms that facilitated the consolidation of the gods into a monotheistic "main God," with whom they secured a more personal, less arbitrary relationship, but whom they also banished from the earth to the heavens.[66] As long as God was "the embodiment of the incomprehensible," Göll explained, he "lived" among people and "could be recognized in nature's violence and in mysterious signs and miracles." "But as people began to discern and interpret their surroundings," the incomprehensible was "anthropomorphized" into a single humanlike being whose "wrath" turned into "benevolence, grace, charity, and love."[67]

There were always doubters and skeptics, Franz insisted; these individuals were the daring few who produced new knowledge. Strong men such as Copernicus proved able to bear the burden of exploring "no-man's-land." Franz counted himself among these Nietzschean strong: "Where most other people impose a secure framework around their religious beliefs, one in which they can feel snug and wait faithfully and confidently for eternal life, in contrast, I search for the wide, free ocean in order to take audacious intellectual journeys with unbounded far-sightedness to new shores, to new understandings of being."[68] As the realm of knowledge expanded and the necessity of belief receded, more and more people rejected religious faith and grounded their daily lives in notions of scientific and technical mastery and in the idea of progress. As a result, faith in religion withered. Franz spoke as a typical secular European of the second half of the twentieth century. "What does Jesus Christ still mean to us today?" Franz followed up his conclusions with a question in 1976. "Christianity has used itself up, its power is drained,

its theology has no conviction. It cannot lead us any further to the creator and is being superseded by technology, which opens up new ways of
understanding the universe and brings us closer to creation."[69] For Göll,
science and faith stood against each other as opposites, but this formulation was certainly not the only way to interpret modern times because
faith has not receded uniformly, and science appears nearly as dangerous as it does emancipatory. Franz remained a classic nineteenth-century
secularist, unmoved and untouched by the existential dilemmas posed
by the years after World War II.

Indeed, Franz Göll thought that the twentieth century confirmed
just how disastrously the Christian God had failed. All his life he had
been appalled at the church's teaching that "heaven is more pleased with
the one sinner who repents than with ninety-nine righteous who do not
need to do so. That might be a satisfying consolation for the sinner, but
a humiliating putdown for the righteous." Did preachers and teachers
really believe everything they said? Franz wondered. The schoolteacher's
version of God he objected to was at once too arbitrary in his distinctions, too intolerant of the quietly righteous, and too willing to receive
the wicked. On the one hand, the God of the Old Testament demanded
obedience, but not self-discipline or self-mastery; Catholics had even
invented the living devil as a "means to train and discipline," ventured
Franz.[70] On the other hand, the notion of the "elect," to be chosen by
God, put the emphasis on selection, encouraging a conception of the
world in which great battles had to be fought for the souls of human
creatures, which incited relentless intolerance and unending violence. In
modern times, Franz argued, Christianity's "God of war and revenge"
was put into the service of political and military struggles, for which
Franz chose the fitting example of Germany's popular singsong appeal
during World War I, "May God Punish England."[71] In his view, the sacrifice of Jesus did not redeem his followers, who instead endured "much
sorrow, pain, destruction, persecution, and injustice."[72] With the German
translation of Norman Cohn's 1957 book *The Pursuit of the Millennium*
in hand and its account of messianic and millenarian violence over the

centuries in mind, Göll wondered whether the "promise of salvation" and "protection" that God promised his creatures had not become a "curse." Nazism stood out as the greatest rebuke to the conviction that Christianity had saved people. "Well, people overcame polytheism, and they will now have to overcome this anthropomorphized single God," Göll concluded.[73]

Göll wrote the historic failure of Christianity back into the life of the historical Jesus. Like many contemporaries in modern Europe, Göll repeatedly returned to biblical accounts of the birth of Jesus and of the Passion and his death. Nineteenth-century readers also had actively pursued the modern search for the historical Jesus that made best sellers of Ernst Renan's *The Life of Jesus* (1863) and Albert Schweitzer's *The Quest of the Historical Jesus* (1906). Martin Scorsese's film *The Last Temptation of Christ* (1988) and Mel Gibson's film *The Passion of Christ* (2004) indicate the continuing appeal to this day of the search for connection to the actual life of Jesus. In his first reading cycle in 1913–1916, Göll took up Otto Schmiedel's study, *Main Problems in Research into the Life of Jesus* (1902), and he returned to the theme more energetically after World War II. As Bible researcher, Franz was an autodidact; he read widely and picked up compelling details and apparent contradictions, but he skirted the main texts (such as Schweitzer) and never distinguished among the four Gospels, which were written at different times and thus revealed the transformation of Jewish messianism into Christian faith in the three generations after the death of Christ. Göll read literally but not systematically. What did he come up with in his quest?

Göll disputed the divinity of Jesus because only man, not God, would have been tempted during forty days in the desert. Moreover, he considered Jesus an individual of high social rank whose enterprise as a wandering preacher offering the kingdom of heaven to his fellow Jews revealed a fundamental political ambition, which Göll the natural historian could easily make sense of. Göll guessed that Jesus of Nazareth was probably a "royal scion" of one sort or the other, a notable whose birth threatened King Herod—as the Gospels report—and who, as a result of some sort of "palace intrigue," had to be placed with "foster parents," Joseph and Maria (this was Göll's conjecture).[74] In his view, the virgin mother was really the foster mother, neither biologically nor ontologically related to Jesus. Sufficiently well born and well dressed both to command authority to drive the money changers from the temple, who would not have heeded commoners such as Jesus's disciples, and to make it worthwhile for Roman soldiers to bid for his clothes after his crucifixion, Jesus possessed earthly powers to hold in thrall the followers he attracted from among the credulous masses. Jesus was a celebrity like the media stars Göll had identified in the 1920s. Göll is probably following false leads here because most scholars emphasize Jesus's strongly religious conception of his role as "God's last messenger before the establishment of the kingdom," a kingdom that was God's, not Israel's.[75] Göll was also not alert to the powerful messianic message of Jesus, who expected God to deliver the kingdom in the very near future. Nor, as a natural historian, was he sensitive to the Christ of faith. For many Christians, belief and profound religious experience governed the interpretations of the historical circumstances of Jesus's life; scientifically deciphering the Gospels did not change the way they viewed the biblical narrative as a matter of faith and tradition.[76] With the idea of Jesus's wealth, Göll did not want to license material prosperity, as some megachurches in America have; he simply intended to puncture the picture of Jesus's unalloyed, humble, pristine virtue.

Göll considered (not inaccurately) Jesus's disciples to have been mostly poor and naïve, except for Judas, whom Göll considered a kind of "manager" for Jesus.[77] It is hard to believe that Göll was not deliberately sharpening his words in this 1956 diary entry, but he took up a fruitful line of inquiry employed by other scholars who use a vocabulary of branding and franchising to explain the spread of Christianity in the ancient Roman world.[78] In Göll's view, it was Judas in whom Jesus confided once his return to Jerusalem failed to make the desired impression. Göll offered the hypothesis that Jesus and Judas planned Jesus's sacrifice in order to jump-start the salvation movement, whose gospel Judas would spread after Jesus's death. And it was probably Judas, Göll continued, who emptied Jesus's grave in order to demonstrate that the dead man was the resurrected son of God: "Then everything rolled as planned."[79] Completely misunderstood by history, Judas had no incentive to betray Jesus (in the Old Testament thirty pieces of silver denotes a paltry sum), but helped plan the drama whereby Jesus would be arrested, would be crucified, and would be seen as having risen from the dead in order to have one more chance to spread the good news. It was no surprise that as a rebel and visionary, Jesus drew the ire of Roman and Jewish authorities. But Göll believed that his crucifixion was a deliberate self-sacrifice carried out in order to save a failing movement of religious renewal. Göll is not alone in thinking of Judas as a midwife to the birth of Christianity. Even Scorsese's film and Nikos Kazantzakis's novel on which it is based suggest the "willed" nature of Judas's betrayal. But it is important to note that Göll's rehabilitation of Judas ran completely in the face of dominant Christian tradition that rendered Judas as red haired, dark skinned, bloated, unscrupulous, and, inevitably, Jewish.[80]

Göll went on: just as Jesus failed to save Jews before he died, Christianity failed to redeem believers after his crucifixion, not only in the years immediately after Jesus's death when his followers waited in vain for his return and for the imminent kingdom on earth, but also in historical time when twenty centuries of religious warfare, a period, in José Saramago's words, of "iron and blood, of fire and ashes," and of "sorrow and tears," revealed that Christians had not become better people.[81]

At first glance, Göll's life of Jesus paralleled his account of himself: noble birth, misplaced family, early talents, and a sense of extraordinary mission coupled with an admission of basic failure. There is something to this because Franz was fascinated with the figure of Jesus. "In particular periods of my life, my thoughts have repeatedly returned quite spontaneously to the person of Jesus," he acknowledged in 1966. "Again and again, my attitude to life, my intellectual journey, as well as my inner feeling for justice, strike comparisons with the Prodigal Son."[82] But Göll felt called to greatness only at the very beginning of his life, and he did not feel so much misunderstood as out of place. The more applicable parallel is between the excruciatingly exact work of self-scrutiny that Göll undertook in the diary and the sober historical method that Göll applied to the life of Jesus in long, recurring entries. To comment on Jesus in the diaries was to take up once again "the effort to appreciate and understand Jesus as a person and to extract him from the thickets of self-interested disguise."[83] Göll remorselessly scrutinized all the conceptions by which people oriented themselves, whether through an imposed sense of coherent self, belief in the gods and their mercy, or consoling categories of knowledge. Göll was like Jesus only in the sense that he spared neither himself nor the son of God critical analysis. He did not seek solace, not even at the end of his life, but looked on new shores to which Nietzsche had urged his new men. Göll did not expect to go to heaven or to live another life; he would live on only in autobiographical reflections and scientific notebooks in which he wrote up his life story, the history of Germany, and the genealogy of the gods.

Working the theme of new knowledge, Franz Göll also returned repeatedly to the image of Adam and Eve expelled from the garden of paradise. This expulsion was the beginning of human life, for "Adam and Eve's fall from grace, which in the imagination of humankind has such devastating consequences, is for me a symbol of the process of development. This is when the actual human being was born, a freethinker who has grown out of the sphere of instinct. But he had to become himself at home in a still-unfamiliar world . . . As a result, all the drivel about original sin can be dropped." Expulsion began a lonely and difficult journey for men and women, a journey in which there was no destination and no return; Göll prized for its intellectual opportunity precisely what Genesis offered human beings as fateful ballast: "A fugitive and a vagabond shalt thou be in the earth" (4:12). Vagabondage required from people the task that they make their own way and find their own markers and points of orientation. This was how Göll interpreted his life after his father's death. There was no redemption for the expelled, only mutation and development and perhaps self-knowledge. "After the expulsion from paradise it quite rightly is said: 'In the sweat of thy face shalt thou eat bread' [Genesis 3:19] . . . and with this threat, humans became the creative designers on earth, because they were forced to rely on themselves."[84] At the end of life, there was just a "few bones" or a "pile of ash," nothing that could be reawakened or resurrected, a view most Berliners held in common with Franz.[85]

Franz always noted precisely the locations of the graves of his relatives—his little sister's, by which he had written an early poem; his father's ("II. Luisenstädt. Friedhof [Abt. 12, Reihe 5, Grab 17]"), which he visited thirty years after the elder Göll's death; his grandfather's; even those of the Ambosses ("Luisenfriedhof III . . . on the Fürstenbrunnerweg [Abt. B1, Reihe 18]").[86] Visited and tended, the graves stood for the endurance of memory, which was all that remained of life after death, until eventually no one was left to remember the dead, at which time the "period of repose" would be terminated, the gravestones broken up, the names "effaced," and the resting places "leveled." Only German soldiers who had fallen in battle got to lie in their graves forever, and none of the Gölls had been soldiers.[87] Today there are no more von Gölls in Germany, nor are there any Ambosses in Kladow or any Waskos (Klara) or Wulkows (Eva) in Berlin. The graves that Franz von Göll once tended in the Luisenstadt cemeteries in Westend have disappeared, removed long ago by regular "reburial work."[88] Across the street from the cemetery, the well-named Wirtshaus zum kühlen Grunde, the Tavern at the Cold Cellar on Fürstenbrunner Strasse, run by "Tante Paula" in a Göll-like stretch of time from 1907 to 1974, has also shut its door.[89]

Afterlife

Göll died alone sometime between 1 and 4 June 1984; he was eighty-five years old. In his will, dated 1 January 1977 and opened on 12 June 1984, Göll instructed that his writings be left to the Berlin State Library and his huge collection of postcards to Berlin's state senator for education and art. Both collections were deposited in the Berlin State Archives in August 1984. That is where Marie-Odile Berne, a French graduate student, first found the diaries ten years later and made them the subject of her excellent but unpublished 1995 master's thesis for the University of Paris in Nanterre, "A Berlin sous le National-Socialisme: Vie et réflexions de Franz von Göll à travers ses journaux intimes et autre notes."[90] That is also where I found them almost ten years later, in June 2003, while I was researching another book.

Aside from his personnel file at Julius Springer Verlag on Heidelberger Platz, there is nothing except the diaries to memorialize the life of Franz Göll. During his lifetime Franz tried but failed to publish his manifesto and his poems, which he steadfastly defended despite publishers' rejections. They were not "contrived rhyming but the expression of the most intimate experience." Even so, as long as he lived, Franz's work found no public echo. "I have always had terrible luck with my contemporaries," he acknowledged in 1935. As a result, "I went my designated way, alone and lonesome." "I have not written down these lines to make an accusation or reproach," he hurried to add, "but to state the facts so that no contemporary can later claim to have been my patron, sponsor, friend, adviser, discoverer."[91] But after death Göll did find "discoverers," first Marie-Odile Berne and then me. It is not a conceit but a fact to say that Franz Göll will be known to the world as a result of this book. Moreover, the posthumous discovery of his work and representation of his life are precisely what Göll ardently wished for. Not only did he leave his diary to the public library system where he had spent so many hours since 1913, but he also inserted reading aids for future readers in his entries and crafted his prose as answers to implicit questions that might be posed long after his death. What does it mean for me to be his medium?

Of course, I am not channeling Franz Göll, but I am the means by which he has found some sort of voice. First of all, with this book, I am glad that I helped rescue Franz Göll from obscurity, something I had already tried to do for Lucie Berlin, a nine-year-old Berlin girl who was brutally murdered by her neighbor's pimp on 9 June 1904.[92] I have also overlapped with Franz Göll's life; I remember reading about the world's first heart transplant in *Life* in 1968, an event Göll mentioned in his diaries; I remember seeing the movie *Julia* in 1978, which Franz and his friend Rudolf Müller also saw; I opposed Ronald Reagan's plan to station midrange nuclear missiles in West Germany in 1982, and Franz did so as well. And I happened to be in Berlin researching my doctoral dissertation on Weimar politics when Franz Göll died there in early June 1984, although I never knew about Rossbachstrasse or the Rote Insel until I began writing this book twenty-five years later. More than that, I find Göll to be a genuinely interesting man whose explorations of the foundations of knowledge I consider incisive. Maybe he was not the first person to think of different kinds of being in terms of the caterpillar that has no knowledge of what it will become or of the butterfly that has no idea where it came from, but to me such images about the frontiers of knowledge are striking. I am also impressed with Franz Göll's analysis of Cold War nuclear policies. And I find his entire effort to critically analyze himself extraordinary and both breathtakingly honest and revealingly pigheaded. For a historian, Göll's diaries indicate quite independent thought about the racial designs of the Nazis and the strategic calculus of nuclear war, but they also reveal how the self-dramatization of the victim obscured the role of the protagonist in the rise and consolidation of the Third Reich. As a weakling, Franz Göll was especially alert to the constraints and violence of society, but he was also misleading about his active role in advancing anti-Semitism and authoritarian rule, which he effaced with one portrait after another depicting himself as a mere extra, a sidelined observer. Franz shared this work of concealment with a great many of his German contemporaries, who, in the years after World War II, regarded themselves as passive victims of extraordinary, almost supernatural forces rather than as active subjects in history and politics.

In many ways my method of analyzing the diary project follows Franz Göll's. He was aware of different kinds of selves and narratives and drew attention to the constructed nature of knowledge about the world. Göll's self-consciousness about how people retrieve knowledge would blunt his excessive surprise if he, Franz Göll, now more than twenty-five years after his death, would ever be able to read this book. Biographers dissect their subjects, but Franz Göll also dissected himself, sometimes mercilessly. It is precisely Göll's effort to view himself from different angles, in the diary entries that turn over the same material again and again and in the distinct genres of reportage, recollection, and crafted memoirs, that makes his life illuminating. It is an effort that is representative of those twentieth-century practices that think about the self, about knowledge, and about the individual's relations with the world. But the effort also makes vivid how strange or idiosyncratic Franz Göll, 1899–1984, from Berlin-Schönberg, was. Here I also do not think that Göll would have disagreed with me because he was aware of his obsessions and preoccupations, even to the point of denouncing them in his diary.

However, Franz Göll would undoubtedly have been angry about my willful act of changing his name from Franz von Göll to Franz Göll. I did so because modern readers would otherwise assign him to a social and cultural category to which he does not belong and in which his voice and insights would have been dulled. In my view, Franz Göll amplifies rather than diminishes Franz von Göll. Nonetheless, Franz considered himself to be unequivocally Franz von Göll. The title gave him some cultural capital, but it also made poignant—certainly to Franz himself—the declined fortunes of his family, the persistent hard luck he confronted, and the imagined itinerary of poet, zoologist, and genius he never completed.

Overall, I think that Franz von Göll would have been pleased that his account of the century, which is also an account of his making an account, found an interested author, an American even, and perhaps a worthy book. I have tried to recover his self-authorization to say things about the world, the authorization he claimed to see and to interpret and to make a rendering that is at the origin of the diary in 1916. I think that he would have recognized himself in this story: his general part as observer; his intermittent role as political partisan in 1921 and again in

1932; his overall sense of modesty and his arguments on its behalf; the schoolboy's attempt to duck imposters and bullies, but also to fit into his big winter coat; the lonely individualist, frightened by mass men and standard work routines; the early but lapsed Nazi; the sober, wide-ranging natural historian and aquarium fan who never quite got over the gloomy tragedies of Germany's modern history; the white man who tamed a sparrow; the inexperienced, self-absorbed, but horny lover shuttling between vamp and princess; the graphomaniac and Copernicus-like explorer; the prickly loner—in other words, an opinionated, telling commissioner of twentieth-century life. The century demanded a struggle for existence, on which Franz von Göll reported from a lower-middle-class milieu in which he inhabited a modest apartment for almost a century, across two world wars. But Franz the diarist also dramatized this struggle for existence; he read shelves of books about biological competition and social life; he psychologized, biologized, and Darwinized; he interpreted and plotted—all this in order to make a case for himself through an analysis of milieu, heredity, and his experience and reflection, to make vivid the part that he played in twentieth-century life and the part twentieth-century life was to have played in his development, which was deeply affected by the shock of war in 1914, the fantastic opportunity of revolution in 1918, the worries of complete failure in economic misery in the years that followed, the false promise of national redemption in 1933, and the unexpected second chance for (West) Germany's people after 1945. This dramatization of victimhood also exposed Franz von Göll's fear of freedom and flight from responsibility, and in this regard he was an active protagonist in Germany's twentieth-century trials and crimes.

    It is not surprising that the diary project made insecurity in its many forms—economic, political, moral, epistemological—a master narrative of the twentieth century, and, in turn, Franz von Göll's representation of insecurity or homelessness (or exile) formed the premise for writing the diary and constituted the platform for his insights into general and specific causes: nature, heredity, milieu, circumstance, history, and the nature of being a human, more or less in that order. Thinking about his case, Franz gave von Göll the opportunity to announce his words, his views, his tentative conclusions, his incomplete self, and his homelessness, which he believed was the modern condition. As *Kümmerform,* he set the exemplary scenes again and again: the occasion when his mother could not find her dead husband's insurance papers in a disheveled hamper; when his fellow students believed Franz to be so unsuited to professional life that they teased him about ordering his coffin early—"Blacksmith"? "Tailor"? "Kaufen Sie sich einen Sarg"—when Franz believed that to actually become a blacksmith, a tailor, or a clerk was to inhabit what Ishmael knew to be "coffin warehouses," as Herman Melville's character described workplaces in the opening pages of *Moby Dick* (1851); also when Franz watched the poor couple get their cart stuck in deep snow; when he observed the crippled veteran extend his prosthetic arm to embrace his wife tenderly, awfully, in Dix's painting; when he thought about his mother's cold war on account of her amputated toes.[93] Franz surely exemplifies the psychopathologies of everyday life; his diary over seventy years confirms much of the evidence in the famous Grant Study at Harvard University that tracked 268 men over the course of seventy years beginning in the late 1930s.[94] But he also registered the instability and violence of social and political life in the twentieth century, combining psychological and sociological insight to expose the injured self, which endured but remained vulnerable in moral, economic, and political as well as interpersonal contexts and which deployed that vulnerability to obscure its own faulty judgments. If the Grant Study stressed coping skills developed over American lifetimes, Franz's diary project attended to wider injuries of twentieth-century men and especially the (self-inflicted) injuries of German men in a terrible zone in which hope mingled with disappointment, mobilization with war, and suffering with self-righteousness. What does the deer caught in automobile headlights come to realize? Franz von Göll might well have told you.

Notes

Index

Notes

1. The Case of Franz Göll, Graphomaniac

1. Entry for 20 May, 1941, "6. Buch," Nachlass Franz von Göll, Landesarchiv Berlin, E Rep. 200-43, Acc. 3221, Nr. 6. I will henceforth abbreviate the Landesarchiv Berlin as LAB and refer to the 23 volumes of the diaries, which are also the first 23 volumes of Göll's papers as Göll does, simply as "1. Buch," "2. Buch," and so on. Göll's diary titles thus correspond to the archive provenance so that "1. Buch" is located in LAB E Rep. 200-43, Acc. 3221, Nr. 1. With the eighth volume, Göll switches his designation to "Tagebuch Nr. 8," a format he maintains to the end with the twenty-third volume. All other materials in the Göll papers—the poems, the reading diaries, the account books, the scientific notebooks—will be designated with a full archival provenance as well as Göll's title. My explanation for using the name "Franz Göll" instead of "Franz von Göll" is provided in the beginning of chapter 1 and the history of the Landesarchiv's acquisition of Göll's papers is told at the end of chapter 6.

2. Entry for 17 Aug. 1948, "Tagebuch Nr. 12."

3. Charles Darwin, *The Origin of Species* (New York, 1996), p. 394.

4. See Paul Nolte, *Die Ordnung der deutschen Gesellschaft: Selbstentwurf und Selbstbeschreibung im 20. Jahrhundert* (Munich, 2000).

5. See Helmut Lethen, *Cool Conduct: The Culture of Distance in Weimar Germany* (Berkeley, CA, 2001).

6. According to Martin Heidegger, "The world picture does not change from an earlier medieval one into a modern one, but rather the fact that the world becomes a picture at all is what distinguishes the essence of the modern age." See *The Question Concerning Technology and Other Essays* (New York, 1977), p. 130. On the artist, see Matthew Tanner, "Chemistry in Schlegel's *Athenaeum* Fragments," *Forum for Modern Language Studies* 31:2 (1995), p. 145.

7. H. G. Wells, quoted in Joseph F. Kett, *The Pursuit of Knowledge under Difficulties: From Self-Improvement to Adult Education in America, 1750–1990* (Stanford, 1994), p. 346.

8. Jeremy D. Popkin, "Philippe Lejeune, Explorer of the Diary," in Philippe Lejeune, *On Diary,* ed. Jeremy D. Popkin and Julie Rak (Manoa, 2009), p. 2.

9. On the confirmation reunion, see the 1963 photograph in Nachlass Franz von Göll, LAB E Rep. 200-43, Acc. 3221, Nr. 93.

10. Gustav René Hocke, *Das europäische Tagebuch* (Wiesbaden, 1963), p. 26.

11. Victor Klemperer, *I Will Bear Witness, 1933–1941: A Diary of the Nazi Years* (New York, 1998); Klemperer, *I Will Bear Witness, 1942–1945: A Diary of the Nazi Years* (New York, 1998).

12. Paul John Eakin, foreword to *On Autobiography,* by Philippe Lejeune (Minneapolis, 1989), p. xv.

13. Mark McGurl, *The Program Era: Postwar Fiction and the Rise of Creative Writing* (Cambridge, 2009), p. 12.

14. Quoted in Jerrold Seigel, *Idea of the Self: Thought and Experience in Western Europe since the Seventeenth Century* (New York, 2006), p. 291.

15. Ibid.

16. Fernando Pessoa, *The Book of Disquiet: A Selection,* trans. Iain Watson (London, 1991), p. 6.

17. Ibid., p. 9.

18. Entry for 21 Sept. 1943, "7. Buch."

19. Entry for 26 Aug. 1943, "7. Buch."

20. "Ahnung und Gegenwart," 19 Jan. 1916 in "Gedichtsammlung. 3 Buch: Vom 24. November 1915 bis 12. Juni 1916," LAB E Rep. 200–43, Acc. 3221, nr. 26.

21. "Ahnung und Gegenwart," 19 Jan. 1916; "An Klara," 2 Aug. 1915; and "Rätsel (Klara)," 3 Nov. 1915, all in "Gedichtsammlung, 3 Buch: Vom 24. November 1915 bis 12. Juni 1916," ibid.

22. Entries for 1 Jan. 1916, "1. Buch"; 15 Oct. 1943, "7. Buch"; and 31 Jan. 1916, "1. Buch."

23. Entry for 14 May 1916, "1. Buch."

24. Joseph Roth, *Flight without End* (New York, 2003), p. 63.

25. Entries for 2 June 1916, "1. Buch"; and 21 Mar. 1917 and 3 Feb. 1918, "2. Buch."

26. Entries for 25 Jan. and 22 Feb. 1916, "1. Buch"; and 20 and 21 Oct. 1916, "2. Buch."

27. See entries for 22 and 29 Oct. 1916, 5 and 11 Nov. 1916, and 21 and 25 Mar. 1917, "2. Buch."

28. Theodor W. Adorno, "In Memory of Eichendorff," in *Notes to Literature,* vol. 1, ed. Rolf Tiedemann, trans. Sherry Weber Nicholsen (New York, 1991), p. 62.

29. Entry for 15 Oct. 1943, "7. Buch."

30. Entry for 27 Aug. 1928, "3. Buch."

31. Entry for 4 July 1943, "7. Buch." On his mother, see entry for 18 Dec. 1942, "7. Buch."

32. "Berlins Volksbibliotheken," *Vorwärts,* 16 Nov. 1928, Morgenausgabe.

33. "Die Stadt- und Volksbibliotheken in Berlin," *Der Tag,* 12 Nov. 1924.

34. S. Philipp, *Über uns Menschen* (Leipzig, 1908), p. 72. See also Heinrich Michelis, "Ernst Haeckel und die deutsche Jugend," in *Was wir Ernst Haeckel verdanken: Ein Buch der Verehrung und Dankbarkeit,* ed. Heinrich Schmidt, 2 vols. (Leipzig, 1914), vol. 1, p. 267.

35. Alfred Kelly, *The Descent of Darwin: The Popularization of Darwinism in Germany, 1860–1914* (Chapel Hill, NC, 1981), pp. 7, 37.

36. Antoon Berentsen, *"Vom Urnebel zum Zukunftsstaat": Zur Problem der Naturwissenschaften in der deutschen Literatur (1880–1910)* (Berlin, 1986), p. 178.

37. Friedrich Nietzsche, "On Old and New Tablets," in *Thus Spoke Zarathustra,* trans. Walter Kaufmann (New York, 1966); entry for 4 July 1943, "7. Buch."

38. Entries for 28 July 1943, "7. Buch"; and 16 Jan. 1949, "Tagebuch Nr. 12."

39. Entry for 14 Oct. 1916, "2. Buch"; "Lektüre Tagebuch 1913–1922; 1. Buch," LAB E Rep. 200-43, Acc. 3221, Nr. 31.

40. Entry for 21 Sept. 1943, "7. Buch."

41. Entry for 16 Feb. 1916, "1. Buch."

42. Entry for 1 Apr. 1916, "1. Buch."

43. Entry for 16 Aug. 1942, "7. Buch."

44. Entries for 20 Feb. 1916, "1. Buch"; 15 Oct. 1916, "2. Buch"; and 31 Dec. 1954, "Tagebuch Nr. 15."

45. See entry for 16 Feb. 1949, "Tagebuch Nr. 12."

46. See entry for 22 Jan. 1948 in "Allgemeines Notizentagebuch, 1. Januar. 1948−14. Juli 1948, 14. Buch," LAB E Rep. 200−43, Acc. 3221, nr. 14.

47. Entry for 9 Aug. 1950, ibid.

48. Entry for 20 Jan. 1950, "Tagebuch Nr. 15."

49. Entries for 18 Aug. 1920, "3. Buch"; and 16 Jan. 1974, "Tagebuch Nr. 21." See also entry for 28 July 1943, "7. Buch," in which Göll describes knowledge as an "open book."

50. Entry for 28 Jan. 1949, "Tagebuch Nr. 12."

51. Entry for 4 Nov. 1917, quoting Meyer's *Der Untergang der Erde und die kosmische Katastrophen* (Berlin, 1902), p. 87, "Wissenschaftliches Notizen-Tagebuch, 3. IX. 1916−16. XII. 1917, 1. Buch," LAB E Rep. 200-43, Acc. 3221, Nr. 40.

52. Elizabeth Boa, "The Trial of Curiosity in *Der Zauberberg*," *Oxford German Studies* 38 (2009), p. 184.

53. Entries for 28 Sept. 1919 and 18 Apr. 1920, "3. Buch"; and 24 Jan. 1933, "4. Buch."

54. Karl Sajo, *Krieg und Frieden im Ameisenstaat* (Stuttgart, 1908), pp. 103−104.

55. Entry for 4 Feb. 1942, "6. Buch."

56. See the references to the zoo in the entries for 23 Sept. 1938 and 16 Feb. 1939, "5. Buch"; and 18 Nov. 1943, "Tagebuch Nr. 8." See also Philipp, *Über uns Menschen* (Leipzig, 1908), p. 104.

57. Seigel, *Idea of the Self,* p. 109.

58. Entries for 22 July and 26 Sept. 1916, "1. Buch."

59. Entry for 30 Mar. 1920, "3. Buch."

60. Entry for 15 Feb. 1920, "3. Buch."

61. Entry for 5 June 1935, "4. Buch."

62. Entry for 16 Mar. 1949, "Tagebuch Nr. 13."

63. S. Philipp, *Über uns Menschen* (Leipzig, 1908), p. 15, cited in entry for 31 May 1940, "Wissenschaftliche Notizen, 1. I. 1940−12. II. 1942, 10. Buch," LAB E Rep. 200-43, Acc. 3221, Nr. 45.

64. Carlo Ginzburg, *The Cheese and the Worms: The Cosmos of a Sixteenth-Century Miller* (Baltimore, 1980), p. xxiv.

65. See Mark D. Steinberg, *Proletarian Imagination: Self, Modernity, and the Sacred in Russia, 1910–1925* (Ithaca, NY, 2002).

66. Entry for 27 Sept. 1921 in Arthur Inman, *The Inman Diary: A Public and Private Confession*, ed. Daniel Aaron, 2 vols. (Cambridge, 1985), p. 192.

67. Daniel Paul Schreber, *Memoirs of My Nervous Illness* (New York, 2000 [1903]); Sigmund Freud, *The Schreber Case* (London, 2002 [1911]); and Eric L. Santner, *My Own Private Germany: Daniel Paul Schreber's Secret History of Modernity* (Princeton, 1996).

68. Friedrich Kittler, *Discourse Networks, 1800/1900* (Stanford, 1990), pp. 295–298.

69. Heinrich Lhotzky in *Leben: Ein Blatt für denkende Menschen* 4 (1908), cited in entry for 28 Oct. 1916, "Wissenschaftliches Notizen-Tagebuch, 3. IX. 1916–16. XII. 1917, I. Buch," LAB E Rep. 200-43, Acc. 3221, Nr. 40.

70. Entry for 3 Feb. 1918, "2. Buch."

71. Entry for 20 Feb. 1923, "3. Buch." See also Ulrich Beck, *Risk Society: Towards a New Modernity* (Newbury Park, CA, 1992); and Anthony Giddens, *Modernity and Self-Identity: Self and Society in the Late Modern Age* (Stanford, 1991).

72. Roy F. Baumeister, *Identity: Cultural Change and the Struggle for Self* (New York, 1986), p. 82.

73. "Medizinischem Wörterbuch," "Allgemeines Notizentagebuch, 10. II. 1923–2. X. 1933, 7. Buch," LAB E Rep. 200-43, Acc. 3221, Nr. 49. See also Michael Hau, *The Cult of Health and Beauty in Germany: A Social History, 1890–1930* (Chicago, 2003), p. 3; and generally, Mark S. Micale, ed., *The Mind of Modernism: Medicine, Psychology, and the Cultural Arts in Europe and America, 1880–1940* (Stanford, 2004).

74. Ernst Kretschmer, *Der sensitive Beziehungswahn* (Berlin, 1927), p. 41, cited in entry for 8 Aug. 1927, "Allgemeines Notizentagebuch, 10. II. 1923–2. X. 1933, 7. Buch," LAB E Rep. 200-43, Acc. 3221, Nr. 49; Oswald Bumke, *Lehrbuch der Geisteskrankheiten* (Berlin, 1936), p. 147, cited in entry for 8 Sept. 1939, "Allgemeines Notizentagebuch, 22. VII. 1934–4. X. 1939, 8. Buch," LAB E Rep. 200-43, Acc. 3221, Nr. 50.

75. Kretschmer, *Der Sensitive Beziehungswohn*, quoted in Martin Priwitzer, *Ernst Kretschmer und das Wahnproblem* (Stuttgart, 2007), p. 183.

76. See Ernst Kretschmer, *Körperbau und Charakter* (Berlin, 1926), p. 151, cited in entry for 20 Nov. 1933 (the 1933 entry comes between 1927 and 1928, a

dating I cannot explain); and Kretschmer, *Geniale Menschen* (Berlin, 1929), pp. 46, 62, cited in entries for 15 and 17 Jan. 1930, all in "Allgemeines Notizentagebuch, 10. II. 1923–2. X. 1933, 7. Buch," LAB E Rep. 200-43, Acc. 3221, Nr. 49.

77. Karl Birnbaum, *Psycho-pathologische Dokumente* (Berlin, 1920), p. 143, excerpted in entry for 8 Dec. 1941, "Wissenschaftliche Notizen, 1. I. 1940–12. II. 1942, 10. Buch," LAB E Rep. 200-43, Acc. 3221, Nr. 45. See also the reference to Wilhelm Waiblinger, *Der kranke Hölderlin* (Leipzig, 1913), which Göll read in 1941, in "Literatur—Tagebuch" [1923–1943], LAB E Rep. 200-43, Acc. 3221, Nr. 32.

78. Entry for 21 Oct. 1956, "Tagebuch Nr. 16."

79. Entry for 10 Jan. 1941, "6. Buch."

80. Entry for 20 Feb. 1981, "Tagebuch Nr. 23."

81. See, for example, entry for 31 Dec. 1969, "Tagebuch Nr. 20."

82. Entries for 7 May 1945, "Tagebuch Nr. 9"; and 11 Sept. 1943, "7. Buch."

83. Entry for 23 Feb. 1954, "Tagebuch Nr. 15."

84. Entry for 21 May 1947, "Tagebuch Nr. 10."

2. Franz Göll's Multiple Selves

1. John Eakin, *How Our Lives Became Stories: Making Selves* (Ithaca, NY, 1999); Eakin, *Fictions in Autobiography: Studies in the Art of Self-Invention* (Princeton, 1985).

2. Entry for 14 May 1916, "1. Buch."

3. Entries for 7 Feb. 1916, "1. Buch"; 3 Feb. 1918, "2. Buch"; and 14 May 1916, "1. Buch."

4. Entries for 16 Feb. 1916, "1. Buch"; 21 and 26 Nov. and 7 Dec. 1916, "2. Buch"; and 5 Oct. 1916, "1. Buch."

5. Entry for 26 Sept. 1916, "1. Buch."

6. Entry for 24 Mar. 1922, "3. Buch."

7. Entry for 18 May 1953, LAB E Rep. 200-43, Acc. 3221, Nr. 14.

8. Entry for 24 Oct. 1916, "2. Buch."

9. Entries for 30 June 1938, 16 Feb. 1939, and 21 May 1938, "5. Buch."

10. Entries for 23 Jan. and 20 Feb. 1923, "3. Buch."

11. Entry for 16 Feb. 1949, "Tagebuch Nr. 12."

12. Entry for 8 June 1919, "3. Buch."

13. "Reisetätigket als Vertreter der Firma J. Hansen Schokoladen-Grosshandlung Bln-Schöneberg, Feurigstrasse 39, vom 21 Februar 1924 bis 19 März 1924," LAB E Rep. 200-43, Acc. 3221, Nr. 85.

14. Entries for 24 Feb., 10 May, and 6 Jan. 1938, "3. Buch."

15. Entries for 31 Dec. 1924 and 9 Jan. 1925, "3. Buch."

16. Entries for 23 Dec. 1933, "4. Buch"; and 17 Mar. 1932, "3. Buch." On incomes, see Max Victor, "Verbürgerlichung des Proletariats and Proletarisierung des Mittelstandes: Eine Analyse der Einkommensentwicklung nach dem Kriege," *Die Arbeit* 8 (1931), p. 30.

17. Entry for 30 June 1938, "5. Buch."

18. Entry for 15 Nov. 1936, "4. Buch."

19. Entry for 12 July 1951, "Tagebuch Nr. 14."

20. Entry for 12 July 1951, "Tagebuch Nr. 14."

21. Entries for 21 May 1938, "5. Buch"; 16 Feb. 1949, "Tagebuch Nr. 12"; and 18 Mar. 1952, "Tagebuch Nr. 14."

22. Entry for 1 Jan. 1958, "Tagebuch Nr. 17."

23. Entries for 26 and 10 July 1949, "Tagebuch 13."

24. See, for example, Arthur Kronfeld, *Lehrbuch der Charakterkunde* (Berlin, 1932), p. 358, cited in entry for 11 June 1936, "Allgemeines Notizentagebuch, 22. VII. 1934–4. X. 1939, 8. Buch," LAB E Rep. 200-43, Acc. 3221, Nr. 50.

25. Frank Barron, quoted in George E. Vaillant, *Adaptation to Life* (New York, 1977), pp. 3, 5.

26. Entry for 10 July 1949, "Tagebuch 13."

27. Entry for 16 Feb. 1958, "Tagebuch Nr. 17."

28. Entry for 11 Apr. 1925, "3. Buch."

29. Entries for 5 Sept. 1916, "1. Buch"; and 31 Oct. 1916, "2. Buch."

30. Entry for 30 July 1933, "4. Buch."

31. Entry for 28 July 1934, "4. Buch." See also "Literatur-Tagebuch" [1923–1943] and entry for 23 Mar. 1921, "Wirtschaftsbuch 1. Januar 1920–31. Desember 1921, 2. Buch," LAB E Rep. 200-43, Acc. 3221, Nrs. 32 and 76.

32. Entry for 11 Nov. 1934, "4. Buch."

33. Entry for 5 June 1935, "4. Buch."

34. Entry for 21 May 1957, "Tagebuch Nr. 16."

35. Entry for 2 Dec. 1945, "Tagebuch Nr. 9."

36. Entries for 15 Nov. 1936 and 31 Oct. 1937, "4. Buch."

37. Entry for 18 July 1932, "3. Buch."

38. Entries for 16 Jan. 1929 and 31 Dec. 1932, "3. Buch."

39. Entry for 31 Dec. 1932, "3. Buch."

40. See, for example, entry for 19 Aug. 1924, "3. Buch."

41. See readings for 1956 and 1957 in "Lektüre Tagebuch 1944–1980," LAB E Rep. 200-43, Acc. 3221, Nr. 33.

42. Entry for 20 May 1951, "Tagebuch Nr. 14."

43. Entry for 17 June 1956, "Tagebuch Nr. 15."

44. See, for example, entry for 6 May 1912 in Franz Kafka, *The Diaries of Franz Kafka, 1910–1913*, ed. Max Brod (New York, 1948), pp. 260–261; and entry for 16 Aug. 1939 in Ernst Jünger, *Gärten und Strassen* (Berlin, 1942), p. 47.

45. Entry for 25 Jan. 1957, "Tagebuch Nr. 16."

46. Entry for 4 Mar. 1957, "Tagebuch Nr. 16." On other "Springer dreams," see entries for 2 Feb. 1966, "Tagebuch Nr. 19"; and 20 Sept. 1978, "Tagebuch Nr. 23."

47. Entry for 20 July 1948, "Tagebuch Nr. 12."

48. Entry for 9 Apr. 1945, "Tagebuch Nr. 9."

49. Entries for 29 June 1920 and 26 Nov. 1921, "Wirtschaftsbuch 1. Januar 1920–31. Dezember 1921, 2. Buch," LAB E Rep. 200-43, Acc. 3221, Nr. 77.

50. Entry for 5 May 1925, "3. Buch."

51. Entry for 18 Sept. 1920, "Wirtschaftsbuch 1. Januar 1920–31. Dezember 1921, 2. Buch," LAB E Rep. 200-43, Acc. 3221, Nr. 77.

52. Entry for 30 Apr. 1921, "Wirtschaftsbuch 1. Januar 1920–31. Dezember 1921, 2. Buch," LAB E Rep. 200-43, Acc. 3221, Nr. 77.

53. Entry for 10 May 1943, "7. Buch."

54. On "boa-bie," see entry for 18 July 1920, "Wirtschaftsbuch 1. Januar 1920–31. Dezember 1921, 2. Buch," LAB E Rep. 200-43, Acc. 3221, Nr. 77.

55. Victor Klemperer, *Leben sammeln, nicht fragen wozu und warum: Tagebücher 1918–1924* (Berlin, 1996).

56. Richard J. Evans, *The Third Reich in Power, 1933–1939* (New York, 2005), p. 472.

57. See the entries for 10, 13, 14, 15, 16, and 21 July 1920, "Wirtschaftsbuch 1. Januar 1920–31. Dezember 1921, 2. Buch," LAB E Rep. 200-43, Acc. 3221, Nr. 77.

58. See entries for 27 and 28 Feb., 31 May, and 1 June 1923, "Wirtschaftsbuch Januar 1922–Dezember 1923, 3. Buch," LAB E Rep. 200-43, Acc. 3221, Nr. 78.

59. See entries for 30 Oct. and 2, 3, and 4 Nov. 1925, "Wirtschaftsbuch Nr. 5, Januar 1925 bis Mai 1927," LAB E Rep. 200-43, Acc. 3221, Nr. 80.

60. Entry for 3 Jan. 1941, "6. Buch."

61. Entries for 1 May 1948, "Tagebuch Nr. 11"; and 31 Dec. 1983, "Tagebuch Nr. 23."

62. Philippe Lejeune, "Composing a Diary," in Philippe Lejeune, On Diary, ed. Jeremy D. Popkin and Julie Rak (Manoa, 2009), p. 168.

63. Entries for 7 Apr. and 7 June 1939 in Victor Klemperer, I Will Bear Witness, 1933–1941: A Diary of the Nazi Years (New York, 1998), pp. 297, 301. See also Klemperer, Curriculum vitae: Erinnerungen, 1881–1918 (Berlin, 1996), 2 vols.; and Stefan Zweig, The World of Yesterday (Lincoln, NE, 1964).

64. Entry for 3 Jan. 1941, "6. Buch."

65. Entry for 10 Jan. 1941, "6. Buch."

66. Entry for 6 Sept. 1942, "7. Buch."

67. Entry for 3 Oct. 1942, "7. Buch."

68. Entry for 6 Jan. 1941, "6. Buch."

69. Entry for 8 Apr. 1942, "6. Buch."

70. Entries for 20 Apr. 1941 and 16 Feb. 1941, "6. Buch." On Staudacher, see Einsamer Weg (Berlin, 1938), p. 43.

71. Entries for 28 July 1943, "7. Buch"; and 29 Dec. 1943, "Tagebuch Nr. 8."

72. Entry for 6 July 1942, "7. Buch."

73. Entry for 16 Feb. 1942, "6. Buch."

74. Entry for 18 Nov. 1943, "Tagebuch Nr. 8."

75. Entry for 30 Oct. 1946, "Tagebuch Nr. 10."

76. Entry for 17 June 1948, "Tagebuch Nr. 11."

77. Entry for 20 Apr. 1941, "6. Buch." On new historical consciousness, see Peter Fritzsche, Stranded in the Present: Modern Time and the Melancholy of History (Cambridge, 2004).

78. Entry for 10 Aug. 1942, "7. Buch."

79. Entry for 2 Nov. 1943, "Tagebuch Nr. 8."

80. Entries for 3 and 4 Oct. 1946, "Tagebuch Nr. 10."

81. Entry for 21 Sept. 1943, "7. Buch."

82. Entry for 11 Sept. 1944, "Tagebuch Nr. 8." On the flaneur in the suburban landscape, see T. J. Clark, The Painting of Modern Life: Paris in the Art of Manet and His Followers (Princeton, 1986), pp. 25–26, as well as Peter Fritzsche, Reading Berlin 1900 (Cambridge, 1994).

83. Entries for 5 Oct. 1943, "7. Buch"; and 6 Mar. 1948, "Tagebuch Nr. 11."

84. Friedrich Nietzsche, "On the Uses and Disadvantages of History for Life," in Untimely Meditations, trans., R. J. Hollingdale (Cambridge, UK, 1997).

85. Entry for 6 July 1942, "7. Buch."

86. Entry for 30 Mar. 1945, "Tagebuch Nr. 8."

87. Entries for 25 Mar. and 5 Apr. 1945, "Tagebuch Nr. 8"; and 9 Apr. 1945, "Tagebuch Nr. 9."

88. Hans Fallada, *Little Man, What Now?* (Chicago, 1983 [1932]).

89. Entry for 20 Sept. 1932, "3. Buch."

90. Entry for 9 Jan. 1948, "Tagebuch Nr. 11."

91. Entry for 21 May 1947, "Tagebuch Nr. 10."

92. Entries for 6 and 17 July 1947, "Tagebuch Nr. 10."

93. Entry for 31 Dec. 1947, "Tagebuch Nr. 10."

94. Entry for 12 Apr. 1948, "Tagebuch Nr. 11."

95. Entry for 18 Apr. 1948, "Tagebuch Nr. 11."

96. See also Fred Miller Robinson, *The Man in the Bowler Hat: His History and Iconography* (Chapel Hill, NC, 1993).

3. Physical Intimacies

1. Entries for 6 Jan. 1941, "6. Buch"; and 23 Oct. 1945, "Tagebuch Nr. 9."

2. Entry for 21 July 1942, "7. Buch."

3. Entry for 21 July 1942, "7. Buch."

4. Mark Micale, *Hysterical Men: The Hidden History of Male Nervous Illness* (Cambridge, 2008), pp. 138–139.

5. Entries for 2 Dec. 1945, "Tagebuch Nr. 9"; and 23 Sept. 1949, "Tagebuch Nr. 13."

6. Entry for 23 Oct. 1945, "Tagebuch Nr. 9."

7. Entry for 18 Aug. 1947, "Tagebuch Nr. 10."

8. Entries for 23, 25, and 26 Oct. 1945, "Tagebuch Nr. 9."

9. Entries for 13 Feb. and 7 Nov. 1955, "Tagebuch Nr. 15."

10. Entry for 25 Jan. 1916, "1. Buch."

11. "Rätsel," dated 3 Nov. 1915, "Gedichtsammlung, 3 Buch: Vom 24. November 1915 bis 12. Juni 1916," LAB E Rep. 200-43, Acc. 3221, Nr. 26.

12. "Liebesahnung," dated 1 Jan. 1916, "Gedichtsammlung, 3 Buch: Vom 24. November 1915 bis 12. Juni 1916," LAB E Rep. 200-43, Acc. 3221, Nr. 26.

13. "Seliger Traum," dated 27 Apr. 1916, "Gedichtsammlung, 4 Buch: Vom 22. August 1915 bis 23. Januar 1919," LAB E Rep. 200-43, Acc. 3221, Nr. 27.

14. "Herzenszwiespalt," dated 25 Mar. 1916, "Gedichtsammlung, 3 Buch: Vom 24. November 1915 bis 12. Juni 1916," LAB E Rep. 200-43, Acc. 3221, Nr. 26.

15. Entry for 14 May 1916, "1. Buch."

16. Entry for 30 Oct. 1916, "2. Buch"; Otto Weininger, *Geschlecht und Charakter: Eine prinzipielle Untersuchung* (Vienna, 1903), p. 298, excerpted in entry for 18 Sept. 1916, "Wissenschaftliches Notizen-Tagebuch, 3. IX. 1916–16. XII. 1917, 1. Buch," LAB E Rep. 200-43, Acc. 3221, Nr. 40. See also, Weininger, *Geschlecht und Charakter,* p. 12.

17. Entry for 20 Apr. 1934, "4. Buch." See also entries for 19 Feb. and 18 Apr. 1935, "4. Buch."

18. Entry for 8 Nov. 1916, "2. Buch."

19. Entry for 20 Nov. 1923, "3. Buch."

20. Entry for 18 Apr. 1935, "4. Buch."

21. Entry for 5 Oct. 1943, "7. Buch."

22. Entries for 27 Sept. and 22 Oct. 1920, "Wirtschaftsbuch 1. Januar 1920–31. Dezember 1921, 2. Buch," LAB E Rep. 200-43, Acc. 3221, Nr. 77.

23. "Lektüre Tagebuch 1913–1922; 1. Buch" and "Literatur—Tagebuch" [1923–1943], LAB E Rep. 200-43, Acc. 3221, Nrs. 31 and 32.

24. Entry for 20 Dec. 1919, "3. Buch."

25. Undated entry for 1952, as well as entries for 29 May 1922 and 30 Oct. 1923, in Arthur Inman, *The Inman Diary: A Public and Private Confession,* ed. Daniel Aaron (Cambridge, 1985), pp. 100, 210, 220.

26. Entry for 5 Feb. 1920, "3. Buch."

27. Entry for 28 Aug. 1953, "Tagebuch Nr. 14."

28. Entry for 10 Nov. 1939, "5. Buch."

29. Entry for 9 Aug. 1925, "3. Buch."

30. Entry for 28 Feb. 1946, "Tagebuch Nr. 9." See also entry for 4 Sept. 1946, "Tagebuch Nr. 9."

31. Entry for 2 Dec. 1947, "Tagebuch Nr. 10."

32. Entry for 28 Aug. 1953, "Tagebuch Nr. 14."

33. "Eine Stellungnahme," in "Gedichtsammlung, 5 Buch: 1. I. 1920–April 1947," LAB E Rep. 200-43, Nr. 29. As will become apparent later in this chapter, Eva Wulkow was more important than Hildegard Meissner, but Hildegard rhymes better than Eva.

34. Entry for 4 Mar. 1944, "Tagebuch Nr. 8."

35. Entry for 11 Aug. 1944, "Tagebuch Nr. 8."

36. "Freudesaugen," dated 25 Dec. 1918, "Gedichtsammlung, 4 Buch: Vom 22. August 1915 bis 23. Januar 1919," LAB E Rep. 200-43, Acc. 3221, Nr. 27.

37. "Abschiedsgedanken," dated 23 Jan. 1919, "Gedichtsammlung, 4 Buch: Vom 22. August 1915 bis 23. Januar 1919," LAB E Rep. 200-43, Acc. 3221, Nr. 27.

38. Entry for 22 Dec. 1918, "2. Buch."

39. Entries for 11 Aug. 1944, "Tagebuch Nr. 8"; and 20 Nov. 1923, "3. Buch."

40. Entries for 6 and 7 Nov. 1923, "Wirtschaftsbuch Januar 1922–Dezember 1923, 3. Buch," LAB E Rep. 200-43, Acc. 3221, Nr. 78.

41. Entry for 1 June 1924, "3. Buch."

42. Entry for 4 Oct. 1946, "Tagebuch Nr. 10."

43. Letter to "Mein Liebes Gretchen!" dated 11 Nov. 1924 and "Liebessehen," dated July 1925, both inserted into the diary.

44. Entry for 21 Sept. 1947, "Tagebuch Nr. 10."

45. Entry for 19 Aug. 1948, "Tagebuch Nr. 12."

46. Entry for 30 June 1947, "Tagebuch Nr. 10"; "An Hilde," dated 14 June 1930, "Gedichtsammlung, 5 Buch: 1. I. 1920–April 1947," LAB E Rep. 200-43, Acc. 3221, Nr. 29.

47. LAB E Rep. 200-43, Acc. 3221, Nr. 87.

48. Entry for 6 July 1947, "Tagebuch Nr. 10."

49. Entry for 21 Sept. 1947, "Tagebuch Nr. 10."

50. LAB E Rep. 200-43, Acc. 3221, Nr. 88.

51. Entry for 4 Nov. 1947, "Tagebuch Nr. 10." On "Eve's daughter," "An Eva," dated 6 June 1932, "Gedichtsammlung, 5 Buch: 1. I. 1920–April 1947," LAB E Rep. 200-43, Acc. 3221, Nr. 29.

52. Entry for 4 Nov. 1947, "Tagebuch Nr. 10."

53. Entry for 23 Sept. 1958, "Tagebuch Nr. 18."

54. Entries for 20 Aug. 1965 and 15 Apr. 1966, "Tagebuch Nr. 19."

55. Atina Grossmann, *Jews, Germans, and Allies: Close Encounters in Occupied Germany* (Princeton, 2009), p. 49. On the confirmation, see the 1963 photograph in LAB E Rep. 200-43, Acc. 3221, Nr. 93.

56. Entries for 18 Mar. 1961, "Tagebuch Nr. 18"; 1 Jan. 1972, "Tagebuch Nr. 21"; and 24 Dec. 1975 and 22 Mar. 1977, "Tagebuch Nr. 22."

57. Entry for 13 Aug. 1945, "Tagebuch Nr. 9."

58. Entry for 20 June 1948, "Tagebuch Nr. 11." See also entries for 16 Oct. 1949, "Tagebuch Nr. 13"; 3 July 1952 and 25 Mar. 1953, "Tagebuch Nr. 14"; and 23 Sept. 1958, "Tagebuch Nr. 18."

59. See entries for 31 Oct. 1981, "Tagebuch Nr. 23"; and 3 July 1965, "Tagebuch Nr. 19."

60. Entry for 23 Jan. 1929, "3. Buch"; Louis Begley, *The Tremendous World I Have Inside My Head: Franz Kafka; A Biographical Essay* (New York, 2008), p. 30; entry for 15 Aug. 1911 in Franz Kafka, *The Diaries of Franz Kafka, 1910–1913,* ed. Max Brod (New York, 1948), pp. 60–61.

61. Entries for 6 Oct. 1933, "4. Buch"; and 30 Nov. 1947, "Tagebuch Nr. 10."

62. Michael J. Cowan, *Cult of the Will: Nervousness and German Modernity* (University Park, PA, 2008), pp. 111–112, 158–159.

63. Entry for 3 Oct. 1942, "7. Buch."

64. Entries for 14–19 Jan. 1954, "Tagebuch Nr. 14."

65. Entry for 26 Jan. 1954, "Tagebuch Nr. 15."

66. Entry for 26 Jan. 1954, "Tagebuch Nr. 15."

67. See entries for 12 Oct. 1975, "Tagebuch Nr. 22"; and 20 May 1974, "Tagebuch Nr. 21."

68. See entries for 31 Dec. 1978 and 1 June 1979, "Tagebuch Nr. 23."

4. The Amateur Scientist

1. Entries for 30 Dec. 1916 and 2 Jan. 1917, "2. Buch."

2. Entry for 21 June 1939, "5. Buch."

3. David Elliston Allen, *The Naturalist in Britain: A Social History* (London, 1976), pp. 4, 12.

4. Andreas Daum, *Wissenschaftspopularsierung im 19. Jahrhundert: Bürgerliche Kultur, naturwissenschaftliche Bildung und die deutsche Öffentlichkeit, 1848–1914* (Munich, 1998), pp. 332–333.

5. Albert J. Klee, *The Toy Fish: A History of the Aquarium Hobby in America—The First One-Hundred Years* (Pascoag, RI, 2003), p. iii.

6. Paul Nitsche, *Das Import von lebenden Fischen* (Berlin, 1901), p. 7; Philip F. Rehbock, "The Victorian Aquarium in Ecological and Social Perspective," in *Oceanography: The Past,* ed. Mary Sears and Daniel Merriman (New York, 1980), pp. 533–554; and Bernd Brunner, *The Ocean at Home: An Illustrated History of the Aquarium* (New York, 2005), pp. 74–75.

7. Gerhard Nebel, "Das Aquarium," in *Von den Elementen* (Wuppertal, 1947), p. 46; Christopher Hamlin, "Robert Warington and the Moral Economy of the Aquarium," *Journal of the History of Biology* 19:1 (Spring 1986), p. 132; and Richard Dawkins, *The Greatest Show on Earth: The Evidence for Evolution* (New York, 2009).

8. See entries for 26 Aug. 1905, 13 Jan. 1906, 27 Dec. 1912, and 22 May and 16 Oct. 1906 in W. N. P. Barbellion, *The Journal of a Disappointed Man* (New York, 1919), pp. 7, 8, 11, 13, 73. See also Richard M. Swiderski, *Multiple Sclerosis through History and Human Life* (Jefferson, NC, 1998), pp. 104–114.

9. Entries for 29 Dec. 1943, "Tagebuch Nr. 8"; and 2 Feb. 1943, "7. Buch."

10. See Christian Brüning, *Leben und Weben in Wald und Feld* (Stuttgart, 1909); Karl Kräpelin, *Naturstudien in Wald und Feld* (Leipzig, 1902); and Brüning, *Wanderungen durch die Natur* (Stuttgart, 1907), excerpted in the entries for 3, 8, 11, 12, 13, 14, 17, and 20 Feb. 1918 in "Wissenschaftliches Notizen-Tagebuch, 24. XII. 1917–20. II. 1918, 2. Buch," LAB E Rep. 200-43, Acc. 3221, Nr. 41.

11. Entry for 16 Feb. 1916, "1. Buch."

12. Entry for 16 Feb. 1916, "1. Buch."

13. See "Lektüre Tagebuch 1913–1922; 1. Buch," LAB E Rep. 200-43, Acc. 3221, Nr. 31.

14. Entry for 13 Aug. 1945, "Tagebuch Nr. 9."

15. Entries for 21 June 1939, "5. Buch"; and 14 May 1916, "1. Buch"; as well as "Lektüre Tagebuch 1913–1922; 1. Buch," LAB E Rep. 200-43, Acc. 3221, Nr. 31.

16. Entry for 30 May 1956, "Tagebuch Nr. 15."

17. Untitled poem dated 5 Jan. 1917, copied out in entry for 26 Apr. 1941, "6. Buch."

18. See entries for 21 Feb. 1950, "Tagebuch Nr. 14"; 30 Apr. and 30 Sept. 1957, "Tagebuch Nr. 16"; 5 and 6 Nov. 1957, "Tagebuch Nr. 17"; 5 Sept. 1958, "Tagebuch Nr. 18"; and 5 Feb. 1971, "Tagebuch Nr. 21." On Halley's Comet, see *BZ am Mittag*, no. 114, 19 May 1910.

19. Entry for 28 Jan. 1949, "Tagebuch Nr. 12."

20. Entry for 22 Mar. 1931, "3. Buch."

21. Entries for 19 Nov. 1939, "5. Buch"; and 2 and 19 Mar. 1934, "4. Buch."

22. Entry for 12 Mar. 1973, "Tagebuch Nr. 21."

23. Entry for 23 Sept. 1938, "5. Buch."

24. Entry for 23 Sept. 1938, "5. Buch."

25. Entry for 16 Jan. 1929, "3. Buch."

26. Entry for 22 Mar. 1931, "3. Buch."

27. Daum, *Wissenschaftspopularisierung im 19. Jahrhundert*, pp. 258, 259n81. See also Alfred Döblin, *Alexanderplatz, Berlin*, trans. Eugene Jolas (New York, 1931), p. 172.

28. Entries for 2 Nov. 1933 and 5 May 1934, "4. Buch."

29. Entry for 5 May 1934, "4. Buch."

30. Entry for 25 Nov. 1961, "Tagebuch Nr. 19."

31. Anne Harrington, *Reenchanted Science: Holism in German Culture from Wilhelm II to Hitler* (Princeton, 1996), p. xx.

32. Entry for 13 Sept. 1940, "6. Buch."

33. Entry for 10 Oct. 1916, "2. Buch."

34. Entry for 19 Aug. 1924, "3. Buch." The phrase is repeated three times in Friedrich Nietzsche, *Thus Spoke Zarathustra*, trans. Walter Kaufmann (New York, 1966), pp. 37, 57, 198: in the speeches "On Enjoying and Suffering the Passions," "On the Friend," and "On Old and New Tablets." According to the reading diaries, Göll read Otto te Kloot's hagiographic biography *Friedrich Nietzsche* (Berlin, 1914) in 1920 and Hans Vaihinger's *Nietzsche als Philosoph* (Berlin, 1902) in 1923, the year before he read *Zarathustra*. See "Lektüre Tagebuch 1913–1922; 1. Buch," LAB E Rep. 200-43, Acc. 3221, Nr. 31; and "Literatur—Tagebuch" [1923–1943], ibid., Nr. 32.

35. Entry for 19 Aug. 1924, "3. Buch."

36. Entry for 3 Feb. 1918, "2. Buch."

37. Friedrich Nietzsche, "On Truth and Lie in an Extra-moral Sense," in *Nietzsche and the Death of God,* trans. and ed. Peter Fritzsche (New York, 2007).

38. Entries for 14 and 21 Dec. 1950, "Tagebuch Nr. 14."

39. Entry for 26 Dec. 1958, "Tagebuch Nr. 18."

40. Entries for 16 and 18 Dec. 1934, "4. Buch."

41. Friedrich Nietzsche, *Beyond Good and Evil,* trans. Walter Kaufmann (New York, 1966); and "On Truth and Lie in an Extra-moral Sense," in *The Portable Nietzsche,* ed. Walter Kaufmann (New York, 1954).

42. Entry for 28 Aug. 1955, "Tagebuch Nr. 15."

43. Entry for 28 Aug. 1955, "Tagebuch Nr. 15."

44. Entry for 18 Dec. 1934, "4. Buch."

45. Friedrich Nietzsche, "The Lie," in *Human, All Too Human,* trans. R. J. Hollingdale (Cambridge, 1986), p. 40 (section 54 in "On the History of the Moral Sensations").

46. Entry for 28 Aug. 1955, "Tagebuch Nr. 15."

47. Entry for 20 Jan. 1955, "Tagebuch Nr. 15."

48. Entry for 4 Dec. 1970, "Tagebuch Nr. 20."

49. Entry for 20 Jan. 1955, "Tagebuch Nr. 15."

50. Entry for 1 Dec. 1949, "Tagebuch Nr. 13."

51. Quoted in Hayden White, *Metahistory: The Historical Imagination in Nineteenth-Century Europe* (Baltimore, 1973), p. 199.

52. Entry for 19 Dec. 1934, "4. Buch."

53. Entry for 16 Jan. 1974, "Tagebuch Nr. 21."

54. Entry for 6 Nov. 1950, "Tagebuch Nr. 14." See also Thomas Kuhn, *The Structure of Scientific Revolutions* (Chicago, 1962).

55. Entry for 21 Oct. 1950, "Tagebuch Nr. 14."

56. Entry for 23 Jan. 1934, "4. Buch."

5. Franz Göll Writes German History

1. Entry for 18 Mar. 1944, "Tagebuch Nr. 8."

2. Eberhard Jäckel, *Das deutsche Jahrhundert: Eine historische Bilanz* (Stuttgart, 1996).

3. Entry for 9 Nov. 1936, "Allgemeines Notizentagebuch, 22. VII. 1934–4. X. 1939, 8. Buch," LAB E Rep. 200-43, Acc. 3221, Nr. 50.

4. Entry for 14 Jan. 1919, "3. Buch."

5. Entry for 11 July 1919, "3. Buch."

6. Entry for 11 Sept. 1921, "3. Buch."

7. Entries for 1 Jan. and 11 July 1919, "3. Buch."

8. Entry for 11 Sept. 1921, "3. Buch."

9. Thomas Mann, "Okkulte Erlebnisse," in *Essays II: 1914–1926,* ed. Hermann Kurzke (Frankfurt, 2002), p. 612. See also Monica Black, *Death in Berlin: From Weimar to Divided Germany* (New York, 2010), p. 64; Mann, "Drei Berichte über okkultistische Sitzungen," in *Essays II,* pp. 587–602; and Elizabeth Boa, "The Trial of Curiosity in *Der Zauberberg,*" *Oxford German Studies* 38 (2009), p. 183.

10. Entry for 6 Oct. 1921, "3. Buch."

11. Peryt Schou, "Die Schrecken und das Heil des kommenden 'uranischen' Zeitalters," and Arthur Grobe-Wutischky, "Deutschlands Zukunft im Lichte alter und neuer Prophezieungen," *Psyche* 5 (1920–21); Hans Hauptmann, "Die Karma des Deutschen Volkes," and Maria B., "Ein Schmetterling als Gruss aus dem Jenseits," *Psyche* 6 (1922).

12. Entry for 11 Sept. 1921, "3. Buch."

13. Entry for 3 Sept. 1944, "Tagebuch Nr. 8."

14. Entries for 22 July 1920, "3. Buch"; and 18 Mar. 1944, "Tagebuch Nr. 8."

15. "Ein Weg zur Rettung," entry for 5 Mar. 1922, LAB E Rep. 200-43, Acc. 3221, Nr. 48. The manifesto was written a year earlier: see entry for 20 Feb. 1921, "3. Buch."

16. Entries for 10 Sept. 1935, "4. Buch"; and 4 Nov. 1947, "Tagebuch Nr. 10."

17. Paul Nolte, *Die Ordnung der deutschen Gesellschaft: Selbstentwurf und Selbstbeschreibung im 20. Jahrhundert* (Munich, 2000), pp. 395–396.

18. Entry for 6 Nov. 1921, "3. Buch."

19. Entry for 22 Dec. 1922, "3. Buch."

20. Entry for 10 Jan. 1922, "3. Buch."

21. Entry for 6 Nov. 1921, "3. Buch."

22. Entries for 16 Jan. 1929 and 18 July 1932, "3. Buch."

23. Entry for 2 Feb. 1922, "3. Buch."

24. Entry for 10 Feb. 1930, "3. Buch."

25. Entry for 22 Mar. 1931, "3. Buch."

26. Entries for 29 and 16 Sept. 1919 in Victor Klemperer, *Leben sammeln, nicht fragen wozu und warum: Tagebücher, 1918–1924* (Berlin, 1996), pp. 188, 179.

27. Entry for 20 Nov. 1929, "3. Buch."

28. Entry for 10 Oct. 1932, "3. Buch."

29. Saul Friedlander, *Nazi Germany and the Jews: The Years of Persecution, 1933–1939* (New York, 1997), p. 3.

30. See Peter Fritzsche, *Germans into Nazis* (Cambridge, 1998).

31. Entries for 14 Nov. 1947, "Tagebuch Nr. 10"; and 25 Oct. 1944, "Tagebuch Nr. 8,"

32. Transcript of Göll's letter to Hindenburg, dated 1 Oct. 1932, "Allgemeines Notizentagebuch, 10. II. 1923–2. X. 1933, 7. Buch," LAB E Rep. 200-43, Acc. 3221, Nr. 49.

33. Entry for 20 Sept. 1932, "3. Buch."

34. Entries for 20 Sept. and 7 Dec. 1932, "3. Buch."

35. Entry for 8 Nov. 1947, "Tagebuch Nr. 10." See the entry for 2 Nov. 1944, "Tagebuch Nr. 8," for confirmation of his presence.

36. Entry for 23 July 1933, "4. Buch"; and the transcript of Göll's letter to Hindenburg, dated 1 Oct. 1933, "Allgemeines Notizentagebuch, 10. II. 1923–2. X. 1933, 7. Buch," LAB E Rep. 200-43, Acc. 3221, Nr. 49.

37. Entry for 10 Sept. 1935, "4. Buch."

38. "Literatur—Tagebuch" [1923–1943], LAB E Rep. 200-43, Acc. 3221, Nr. 32.

39. Entry for 28 Dec. 1935, "4. Buch"; entry for 9 Nov. 1936, "Allgemeines Notizentagebuch, 22. VII. 1934–4. X. 1939, 8. Buch," LAB E Rep. 200-43, Acc. 3221, Nr. 50.

40. Entry for 8 Feb. 1946, "Tagebuch Nr. 9."

41. Entry for 11 Dez. 1947, "Tagebuch Nr. 10." See also entry for 1 Feb. 1958, "Tagebuch Nr. 17."

42. Entry for 8 Feb. 1946, "Tagebuch Nr. 9."

43. Entry for 8 Nov. 1947, "Tagebuch Nr. 10."

44. Entries for 8 and 10 Nov. 1947, "Tagebuch Nr. 10."

45. Entry for 25 Oct. 1944, "Tagebuch Nr. 8."

46. Entry for 23 Aug. 1933, "4. Buch."

47. Entry for 28 Dec. 1935, "4. Buch."

48. Entry for 2 Mar. 1939, "5. Buch."

49. Entries for 7 Dec. 1947, "Tagebuch Nr. 10"; and 5 May 1934, "4. Buch."

50. Entries for 6 Apr. 1940, "6. Buch"; 24 Nov. 1947, "Tagebuch Nr. 10"; and 25 Oct. 1944, "Tagebuch Nr. 8."

51. Entry for 30 Mar. 1938, "5. Buch."

52. Ernst Jünger, *Das abenteuerliche Herz: Figuren und Capriccios,* in *Sämtliche Werke,* vol. 9 (Stuttgart, 1979), p. 184.

53. Entry for 4 Nov. 1941, "6. Buch."

54. See, for example, entries for 24 and 25 June and 21 Oct. 1941 in Lisa de Boor, *Tagebuchblätter: Aus den Jahren 1938–1945* (Munich, 1963), pp. 79, 88.

55. *Das Schwarze Korps,* 22 Feb. 1945.

56. Entry for 14 Nov. 1937, "4. Buch."

57. Entry for 27 Feb. 1939, "6. Buch."

58. Entry for 10 Nov. 1947, "Tagebuch Nr. 10."

59. Entry for 25 Nov. 1938, "5. Buch."

60. Entry for 14 Nov. 1937, "4. Buch."

61. Entry for 10 Mar. 1938 in Erich Ebermayer, . . . *Und morgen die ganze Welt: Erinnerungen an Deutschlands dunkle Zeit* (Bayreuth, 1966), p. 244.

62. Entry for 13 Apr. 1938, "5. Buch."

63. Entry for 12 Oct. 1938, "5. Buch."

64. Entries for 14 Dec. 1938, "5. Buch"; and 30 May 1941, "6. Buch." On Jewish *Raffinesse,* see the entry for 18 Feb. 1944, "Tagebuch Nr. 8."

65. Entry for 5 Mar. 1943, "7. Buch." Göll misdated the pogrom of 9–10 November 1938.

66. Entry for 26 July 1940, "6. Buch." The original reads: "Früher ging es uns gut, heute geht es uns besser; es wäre aber besser, es ginge uns wieder gut."

67. Entry for 3 July 1941, "6. Buch." See also Paul Celan, "Deathfugue," in *Selected Poems and Prose of Paul Celan,* John Felstiner, ed. (New York, 2001), pp. 30–33.

68. Entry for 4 June 1944, "Tagebuch Nr. 8."

69. Entry for 17 Jan. 1977, "Tagebuch Nr. 22"; and "Ein Weg zur Rettung," dated Feb. 1921 and transcribed in the entry for 5 Mar. 1922, "Allgemeines Notizentagebuch, 1. I. 1921–9. II. 1923, 6. Buch," LAB E Rep. 200-43, Acc. 3221, Nr. 48.

70. Entry for 27 Feb. 1939, "6. Buch."

71. See entries for 27 Feb. 1939, "5. Buch"; and 26 July 1940, "6. Buch."

72. Entry for 26 July 1940, "6. Buch."

73. Entry for 18 Apr. 1948, "Tagebuch Nr. 11."

74. Entry for 11 July 1948, "Tagebuch Nr. 12."

75. Photograph inserted near entry for 18 Apr. 1948, "Tagebuch Nr. 11."

76. Entries for 15 Dec. 1947, "Tagebuch Nr. 10"; and 2 Jan. 1940, "5. Buch."

77. Entry for 12 June 1933, "4. Buch." See also Ernst Kretschmer, *Geniale Menschen* (Berlin, 1929), p. 90, cited in entry for 1 Feb. 1935, "Allgemeines Notizentagebuch, 22. VII. 1934–4. X. 1939, 8. Buch," LAB E Rep. 200-43, Acc. 3221, Nr. 50.

78. Entries for 15 July 1941, "7. Buch"; and 7 June 1949, "Tagebuch Nr. 13."

79. Entry for 1 June 1933 in Karl Dürkefälden, *"Schreiben wie es wirklich war . . .": Aufzeichungen Karl Dürkefäldens aus den Jahren 1933–1945,* ed. Herbert and Sibylle Obenaus (Hannover, 1985), p. 54.

80. Margarete Hannsmann, *Der helle Tag bricht an: Ein Kind wird Nazi* (Hamburg, 1982); Eva Sternheim-Peters, *Die Zeit der grossen Täuschungen: Mädchenleben im Faschismus* (Bielefeld, 1987), p. 16.

81. Georg Hensel, "Der Sack überm Kopf," in *Meine Schulzeit im Dritten Reich: Erinnerungen deutscher Schriftsteller,* ed. Marcel Reich-Ranicki (Munich, 1984), p. 129.

82. Hannsmann, *Der helle Tag bricht an;* Sternheim-Peters, *Zeit der grossen Täuschungen,* pp. 15–16.

83. Entry for 12 Mar. 1938, "4. Buch."

84. Ludwig Eberlein, "'Entartete Kunst: Die aufsehenerregende Ausstellung jetzt auch in Berlin," *Berliner Morgenpost,* 25 Feb. 1938, quoted in Katrin Engelbardt, "Die Ausstellung 'Entartete Kunst' in Berlin 1938: Rekonstruktion und Analyse," in *Angriff auf die Avantgarde: Kunst und Kunstpolitik im Nationalsozialismus,* ed. Uwe Fleckner (Berlin, 2007), p. 105.

85. Entry for 12 Aug. 1923, "3. Buch."

86. Entry for 12 Mar. 1938, "4. Buch."

87. Entry for 23 July 1923, "3. Buch."

88. Entries for 12 Mar. 1938, "4. Buch"; and 25 June 1941, "6. Buch."

89. Entry for 12 Mar. 1938, "4. Buch."

90. Entry for 5 Oct. 1939, "5. Buch."

91. Entry for 2 Nov. 1944, "8. Buch."

92. Entry for 5 Oct. 1939, "5. Buch."

93. Entry for 17 June 1940 in Lore Walb, *Ich die Alte, ich, die junge: Konfrontation mit meinen Tagebüchern, 1933–1945* (Berlin, 1997), p. 184.

94. Entry for 26 July 1940, "6. Buch."

95. Entry for 25 June 1941, "6. Buch." Emphasis Göll's.

96. Entry for 24 June 1941 in *Die Tagebücher von Joseph Goebbels,* ed. Elke Fröhlich, pt. 1, vol. 9 (Munich, 1998–2006), pp. 399–400.

97. Entry for 1 May 1948, "Tagebuch Nr. 11." See also entry for 25 June 1941, "6. Buch."

98. Entries for 25 June 1941, "6. Buch"; and 20 Sept. 1932, "3. Buch."

99. Entry for 10 July 1943, "7. Buch."

100. Entry for 18 Feb. 1944, "Tagebuch Nr. 8."

101. Entry for 4 Feb. 1942, "6. Buch."

102. Entry for 10 July 1943, "7. Buch."

103. Entry for 13 Nov. 1947, "Tagebuch Nr. 10"; and "Luftschutz tut not!" dated 2 Oct. 1933, "Allgemeines Notizentagebuch, 10. II. 1923–2. X. 1933, 7. Buch," LAB E Rep. 200-43, Acc. 3221, Nr. 49.

104. Michael Geyer, "Endkampf 1918 and 1945: German Nationalism, Annihilation, and Self-Destruction," in *No Man's Land of Violence: Extreme Wars in the 20th Century,* ed. Alf Lüdtke and Bernd Weisbrod (Göttingen, 2006), p. 60.

105. Entry for 6 July 1948, "Tagebuch Nr. 11."

106. On this theme, see Christopher Browning, *Ordinary Men: Reserve Police Battalion 101 and the Final Solution in Poland* (New York, 1993).

107. Entries for 1 and 15 June 1948, "Tagebuch Nr. 11." See also the unsigned statement from Springer to Schutzpolizei Gruppenkommando Süd, Erfassungsstelle, 8 Jan. 1940, Franz von Göll's personnel file, Julius Springer Verlag, Berlin.

108. See Göll's salary history in his personnel file, Julius Springer Verlag, Berlin.

109. "Luftschutz tut not!" dated 2 Oct. 1933, "Allgemeines Notizentagebuch, 10. II. 1923–2. X. 1933, 7. Buch," LAB E Rep. 200-43, Acc. 3221, Nr. 49.

110. See entries for 10 July 1948, "Tagebuch Nr. 11"; and 11 July 1948, "Tagebuch Nr. 12." See also Marie-Odile Berne, "A Berlin sous le National-Socialisme: Vie et réflexions de Franz von Göll à travers ses journaux intimes et autre notes," Master's thesis (Université des Paris X Nanterre, 1995), Landesarchiv Berlin 97/356.

111. Adam Tooze, *The Wages of Destruction: The Making and Breaking of the Nazi Economy* (New York, 2007).

112. Günter Moltmann, "Goebbels' Rede zum Totalen Krieg am 18. Februar 1943," *Vierteljahrsheft für Zeitgeschichte* 12:1 (1964), p. 22.

113. Entry for 5 Mar. 1943, "7. Buch."

114. Entry for 5 Mar. 1943, "7. Buch."

115. Entry for 23 May 1945, "Tagebuch Nr. 9."

116. Entry for 26 Nov. 1943, "Tagebuch Nr. 8."

117. Entry for 30 Nov. 1944, "Tagebuch Nr. 8." See also entry for 11 Sept. 1943, "7. Buch."

118. Entry for 5 Mar. 1943, "7. Buch."

119. Entries for 6 Jan., 21 Mar., and 27 Jan. 1945, "Tagebuch Nr. 8."

120. Entry for 19 Feb. 1944, "Tagebuch Nr. 8."

121. Entry for 19 Feb. 1944, "Tagebuch Nr. 8."

122. Entry for 19 Feb. 1944, "Tagebuch Nr. 8."

123. Entry for 2 Nov. 1944, "Tagebuch Nr. 8."

124. Entry for 2 Nov. 1944, "Tagebuch Nr. 8."

125. Entry for 2 Nov. 1944, "Tagebuch Nr. 8."

126. Entry for 13 Jan. 1945, "Tagebuch Nr. 8."

127. Entry for 27 Jan. 1945, "Tagebuch Nr. 8."

128. Entries for 28 July 1944 and 13 Jan. 1945, "Tagebuch Nr. 8." In post-1945 criticism Schiller's poem is sometimes associated with Paul Celan's "Death Fugue."

129. Entry for 14 May 1945, "Tagebuch Nr. 9."

130. Entry for 3 May 1945, "Tagebuch Nr. 9."

131. Atina Grossmann, *Jews, Germans, and Allies: Close Encounters in Occupied Germany* (Princeton, 2007), p. 49.

132. Entry for 3 May 1945, "Tagebuch Nr. 9."

133. Entry for 7 May 1945, "Tagebuch Nr. 9."

134. Entry for 14 May 1945, "Tagebuch Nr. 9."

135. The term he uses is "arme Schlucker." See entry for 21 Mar. 1945, "Tagebuch Nr. 8."

136. Entry for 14 May 1945, "Tagebuch Nr. 9."

137. Primo Levi, *Survival in Auschwitz* (New York, 1996), pp. 105–106.

138. Entry for 18 Feb. 1944, "Tagebuch Nr. 8."

139. Entry for 28 July 1944, "Tagebuch Nr. 8."

140. Entry for 6 Jan. 1945, "Tagebuch Nr. 8."

141. Entry for 30 July 1945, "Tagebuch Nr. 9." See also the entry for 12 July 1945, "Tagebuch Nr. 9."

142. Entry for 5 Oct. 1939, "5. Buch."

143. Entry for 14 Nov. 1947, "Tagebuch Nr. 10."

144. Entry for 24 Nov. 1947, "Tagebuch Nr. 10."

145. Cited in Victor Farias, *Heidegger and Nazism* (Philadelphia, 1989), p. 287.

146. Daniel Morat, *Von der Tat zur Gelassenheit: Konservatives Denken bei Martin Heidegger, Ernst Jünger und Friedrich Georg Jünger, 1920–1960* (Göttingen, 2007), p. 256.

6. Resolution without Redemption

1. Entry for 31 Dec. 1983, "Tagebuch Nr. 23."

2. Entries for 14 and 7 May 1945, "Tagebuch Nr. 9."

3. Entries for 3 and 31 Jan. 1945, "Tagebuch Nr. 8."

4. Entries for 27 Sept. and 19 July 1945, "Tagebuch Nr. 9."

5. Entries for 28 Aug. and 19 July 1945, "Tagebuch Nr. 9."

6. Entry for 19 July 1945, "Tagebuch Nr. 9."

7. Entries for 15 July 1948, "Tagebuch Nr. 12"; and 27 Sept. 1945, "Tagebuch Nr. 9."

8. Entry for 23 Mar. 1947, but part of the memoirs, "Tagebuch Nr. 10." On the Russians, see the note dated 9 June 1945 in Göll's personnel file at Julius Springer Verlag.

9. Varlam Shalamov, "Shock Therapy," in *Kolyma Tales,* trans. John Glad (New York, 1994), pp. 114–115.

10. Entry for 8 May 1946, "Tagebuch Nr. 9."

11. "Wirtschaftsbericht April 1947," in "Franz v. Göll, Berlin-Schöneberg, Roßbachstraße 1, Wirtschaftsbuch 1944–1947," LAB E Rep. 200–43, Acc. 3221, nr. 84.

12. Jürgen Schmidt, ed., *Rote Rüben auf dem Olivaer Platz: Quellen zur Ernährungskrise in der Nachkriegszeit Berlins, 1945–1949* (Berlin, 2008), p. 33.

13. Entries for 7 Mar., 22 June, and 7 Aug. 1947, "Tagebuch Nr. 10."

14. Entry for 7 June 1946, "Tagebuch Nr. 10."

15. Entry for 1 Jan. 1948, "Tagebuch Nr. 11."

16. Entry for 13 Mar. 1948, "Tagebuch Nr. 11." See also George Orwell, "You and the Atomic Bomb," *Tribune* (London), 19 Oct. 1945; see http://www.orwell.ru/library/articles/ABomb/english/e_abomb, accessed 13 Mar. 2010; Walter Lippmann, *The Cold War: A Study in U.S. Foreign Policy* (New York, 1947).

17. Entry for 13 Mar. 1948, "Tagebuch Nr. 11."

18. Entries for 28 Mar. 1949, "Tagebuch Nr. 13"; and 13 Sept. 1948, "Tagebuch Nr. 12." See also Oswald Spengler, *The Decline of the West,* 2 vols. (New York, 1926 [1918, 1922]).

19. Entry for 13 Mar. 1948, "Tagebuch Nr. 11."

20. Michael Bodemann, "Mentalitäten des Verweilens: Der Neubeginn jüdischen Lebens in Deutschland," in *Leben im Land der Täter: Juden im Nachkriegsdeutschland (1945–1952),* ed. Julius H. Schoeps (Berlin, 2001), p. 15.

21. Entry for 18 Feb. 1944, "Tagebuch Nr. 8."

22. Entry for 11 Mar. 1945, "Tagebuch Nr. 8"; and untitled commentary dated "January 1947," in "Allgemeines Notizentagebuch, 14. Juni. 1944–28. Januar. 1947, 12. Buch," LAB E Rep. 200-43, Acc. 3221, Nr. 51.

23. Entry for 2 Sept. 1950, "Tagebuch Nr. 14."

24. On Asia, see, for example, his comments on U.S. military bases in Southeast Asia, entry for 21 June 1976, "Tagebuch Nr. 22."

25. Entry for 5 Nov. 1957, "Tagebuch Nr. 17."

26. Entry for 7 Feb. 1971, "Tagebuch Nr. 21."

27. Entry for 24 Nov. 1976, "Tagebuch Nr. 22."

28. Entry for 23 Sept. 1959, "Tagebuch Nr. 18."

29. Entry for 1 June 1979, "Tagebuch Nr. 23."

30. Entries for 10 Jan. 1962, "Tagebuch Nr. 19"; 21 Nov. 1971, "Tagebuch Nr. 21"; 5 Jan. 1978, "Tagebuch Nr. 23"; 16 Feb. 1971, "Tagebuch Nr. 21"; and 9 Dec. 1979, "Tagebuch Nr. 23."

31. Entries for 23 Dec. 1971, "Tagebuch Nr. 21"; and 31 Oct. 1981, "Tagebuch Nr. 23."

32. Entry for 3 July 1965, "Tagebuch Nr. 19"; Fernando Pessoa, *The Book of Disquiet: A Selection,* trans. Iain Watson (London, 1991), p. 76.

33. Entries for 23 June 1978, "Tagebuch Nr. 23"; and 8 Jan. 1976, "Tagebuch Nr. 22."

34. Entries for 12 June and 5 Aug. 1970, "Tagebuch Nr. 20."

35. Entry for 17 Jan. 1977, "Tagebuch Nr. 22."

36. See, for example, his discussion of Bernard Goldstein's book on the destruction of Polish Jewry, *Die Sterne sind Zeugen* (Munich, 1965), in entry for 29 Apr. 1958, "Tagebuch Nr. 17."

37. Entry for 28 Feb. 1946, "Tagebuch Nr. 9."

38. Entries for 20 Sept. 1956, "Tagebuch Nr. 15"; and 12 Mar. 1958, "Tagebuch Nr. 17."

39. Entries for 7 Sept. 1970, "Tagebuch Nr. 20"; and 27 and 30 Nov. 1976, "Tagebuch Nr. 22."

40. Entries for 28 Feb. and 6 Mar. 1975, "Tagebuch Nr. 22."

41. Entry for 21 Oct. 1977, "Tagebuch Nr. 22."

42. Entry for 12 June 1981, "Tagebuch Nr. 23."

43. Frank Biess, " 'Everybody Has a Chance': Nuclear Angst, Civil Defence, and the History of Emotions in Postwar West Germany," *German History* (2009), pp. 215–243.

44. Quoted in Dubravka Ugresic, *The Ministry of Pain* (New York, 2005), p. 76.

45. Entries for 23 Jan. 1955, "Tagebuch Nr. 15"; and 25 Mar. 1958, "Tagebuch Nr. 17."

46. Entry for 15 Jan. 1958, "Tagebuch Nr. 17."

47. Entries for 15 Jan. and 25 Mar. 1958, "Tagebuch Nr. 17." Emphases are Göll's.

48. Entries for 25 and 29 Mar. and 15 Apr. 1958, "Tagebuch Nr. 17"; and 2 June 1958, "Tagebuch Nr. 18."

49. James Sheehan, *Where Have All the Soldiers Gone? The Transformation of Modern Europe* (Boston, 2008).

50. Entries for 18 Nov. 1957, "Tagebuch Nr. 17"; and 18 Nov. 1959, "Tagebuch Nr. 18."

51. Entry for 16 Mar. 1970, "Tagebuch Nr. 22."

52. Entry for 12 Oct. 1949, "Tagebuch Nr. 13."

53. Entry for 18 Sept. 1957, "Tagebuch Nr. 16." See also "Sozialistische 'Verkaufskultur,'" *Die Zeit*, no. 47, 23 Nov. 1962.

54. Entries for 12 June 1965, "Tagebuch Nr. 19"; and 5 Apr. 1972, "Tagebuch Nr. 21."

55. See Günter Gaus, *Wo Deutschland liegt* (Hamburg, 1983).

56. Stephen Brockmann, *Literature and German Reunification* (Cambridge, UK, 1999), p. 43.

57. Entries for 1 Feb. and 7 Dec. 1967, "Tagebuch Nr. 19"; and 21 Mar. 1970, "Tagebuch Nr. 20."

58. See entries for 13 Sept. 1948, "Tagebuch Nr. 12"; and 18 Sept. 1960, "Tagebuch Nr. 18."

59. Entry for 8 Dec. 1970, "Tagebuch Nr. 20."

60. Entries for 14 Dec. 1977, "Tagebuch Nr. 23"; and 18 Jan. 1971, "Tagebuch Nr. 21."

61. Entry for 20 Dec. 1970, "Tagebuch Nr. 20."

62. Entry for 18 Nov. 1957, "Tagebuch Nr. 17."

63. Entry for 16 Apr. 1977, "Tagebuch Nr. 22." See also entries for 13 Jan. 1949, "Tagebuch Nr. 12"; and 14 Sept. 1978, "Tagebuch Nr. 23."

64. Entries for 2 May 1956, "Tagebuch Nr. 15"; 6 Sept. 1977, "Tagebuch Nr. 22"; and 3 Feb. 1970, "Tagebuch Nr. 20."

65. See entries for 5 Sept. and 23 Nov. 1948, "Tagebuch Nr. 12"; and 7 Feb. 1971, "Tagebuch Nr. 21."

66. Entry for 28 Sept. 1971, "Tagebuch Nr. 21." See also entries for 21, 24, and 28 Jan. 1938, "4. Buch"; and 21 Oct. 1950, "Tagebuch Nr. 14."

67. Entry for 5 Feb. 1953, "Tagebuch Nr. 14."

68. Entries for 21 Oct. 1950, "Tagebuch Nr. 14"; and 16 Jan. 1949, "Tagebuch Nr. 12."

69. Entries for 15 Jan. 1976, "Tagebuch Nr. 22"; and 21 Nov. 1978, "Tagebuch Nr. 23."

70. Entries for 16 Feb. 1939, "5. Buch"; and 25 Feb. 1957, "Tagebuch Nr. 16."

71. Entries for 16 Jan. 1949, "Tagebuch 12"; and 25 Mar. 1969, "Tagebuch Nr. 20."

72. Entry for 4 Dec. 1971, "Tagebuch Nr. 21."

73. Entries for 14 Dec. and 10 Apr. 1966, "Tagebuch Nr. 19."

74. Entries for 1 Nov. 1979, "Tagebuch Nr. 23"; and 26 Dec. 1972, "Tagebuch Nr. 21."

75. E. P. Sanders, *Jesus and Judaism* (Philadelphia, 1985), p. 319.

76. Charlotte Allen, *The Human Christ: The Search for the Historical Jesus* (New York, 1998).

77. Entry for 19 Nov. 1956, "Tagebuch Nr. 16."

78. See Robert Wright, *The Evolution of God* (New York, 2009).

79. Entry for 24 May 1965, "Tagebuch Nr. 19."

80. See Susan Gubar, *Judas: A Biography* (New York, 2009).

81. José Saramago, *The Gospel according to Jesus Christ* (New York, 1994), pp. 320–321. Göll developed the basic themes of his search for the historical Jesus in the 1950s and embellished them in the decades that followed. See entries for 19 Nov. and 18 Dec. 1956, "Tagebuch Nr. 16"; 16 Feb. 1968, "Tagebuch Nr. 19"; 26 Dec. 1972 and 19 Mar. 1974, "Tagebuch Nr. 21"; 14 Oct. 1977, "Tagebuch Nr. 22"; and 6 Nov. 1977 and 1, 3, 6, 8, and 16 Nov. 1979, "Tagebuch Nr. 23."

82. Entries for 11 Sept. 1966, "Tagebuch Nr. 19"; and 10 Jan. 1957, "Tagebuch Nr. 16."

83. Entry for 16 Feb. 1968, "Tagebuch Nr. 19."

84. Entries for 16 Apr. and 9 May 1977, "Tagebuch Nr. 22."

85. Entry for 6 Jan. 1981, "Tagebuch Nr. 23." On the afterlife, see Elisabeth Noelle and Erich Peter Neumann, eds., *Jahrbuch der öffentlichen Meinung, 1957* (Allensbach, 1957), p. 130.

86. Entries for 6 Feb. and 24 Apr. 1916, "1. Buch"; and 15 Oct. 1945, "Tagebuch Nr. 9."

87. Entry for 28 Feb. 1946, "Tagebuch Nr. 9." See also Monica Black, *Death in Berlin: From Weimar to Divided Germany* (New York, 2010), pp. 34, 243.

88. Entry for 27 Sept. 1945, "Tagebuch Nr. 9."

89. On "Tante Paula," see http://www.fotocommunity.de/pc/pc/display/8969946, accessed 29 Dec. 2009.

90. Marie-Odile Berne, "A Berlin sous le National-Socialisme: Vie et réflexions de Franz von Göll à travers ses journaux intimes et autre notes," MA Thesis (Université des Paris X Nanterre, 1995), Landesarchiv Berlin 97/356.

91. Entry for 5 June 1935, "4. Buch."

92. Peter Fritzsche, "Talk of the Town: The Murder of Lucie Berlin and the Production of Local Knowledge," in *Criminals and Their Scientists: The History of Criminology in International Perspective*, ed. Peter Becker and Richard Wetzell (Cambridge, UK, 2005), pp. 377–398.

93. Entry for 5 June 1935, "4. Buch."

94. See George E. Vaillant, *Adaptation to Life* (New York, 1977); and Joshua Wolf Shenker, "What Makes Us Happy," *Atlantic*, June 2009.

Index

Adenauer, Konrad, 205
Adorno, Theodor, 16
Air raids, 132, 156, 169–178, 207–208
Amboss, Carl, 199
Amboss, Margarete (cousin), 95–96
Ambosses (relatives), 14, 34, 44–46, 111,
   199, 200, 220
Amiel, Henri-Frédérick, 24
Anschluss (Austria), 147, 154–155, 164,
   168
Ant colonies, 21, 112, 168
Anti-Semitism, 139, 142–144, 146, 148,
   156–158, 166
Apartment, 51, 68, 175, 180–181
Aquarium, 55, 102, 108–110, 111–112, 115
Art, 52, 162–163

"Aryans," 43, 99, 137, 160
Astronomy, 20, 123, 130
Autobiography, 59–60, 74–77, 218–219,
   222–223

Barbellion, W. N. P., 24, 110
Baumeister, Roy, 26
Berlin, 1–2, 51, 53, 54–55, 67–69, 81–82,
   175–176, 188–190, 197–198, 203,
   209–210
Berlin, Lucie, 221
Berlin Wall, 198, 210
Berne, Marie-Odile, 220–221
Biberkopf, Franz, 3, 23, 98
Bicycling, 103–104
Birnbaum, Karl, 28

Black market, 191–192
Bodemann, Michael, 195
Bölsche, Wilhelm, 9, 17, 20–21, 109, 115, 117, 121
Bolshevism. *See* Soviet Union
Brandt, Willy, 204, 211
Brehm, Alfred, 18, 109, 119
Bumke, Oswald
Büsscher, Alice, 92–94, 100

Carnegie, Dale, 37
Celan, Paul, 157
Cemeteries, 220
Charcot, Jean-Marie, 81
Childhood, 129–130; Franz Göll's, 35–36, 40, 63–64, 65–66, 88, 225
Christel, 100–101
Christianity, 197, 214–218
Cohn, Norman, 215
Cold War, 6, 113, 194, 198, 203–209
Colonialism, 10, 166, 183, 193
Communists, 137, 144–145. *See also* Soviet Union
Concentration camps, 159
Confirmation, 9, 101
Copernicus, Nicolaus, 20, 23, 114, 123, 130, 214

Darwinism, 5, 17, 110, 115, 117, 118–119
Democracy, 135–136, 200–201, 211–212
Détente, 8, 204, 211
Diaries, 10–13, 24
Dietrich, Marlene, 2
Dix, Otto, 163–164
Döblin, Alfred, 3, 98, 119
Dreams, 49–50
Durant, Will, 9
Dürkefäldens, 161

Eakin, Paul John, 10
Ebermayer, Erich, 154
Education, of Franz Göll, 13
Eichendorff, Joseph von, 14, 16
Employment, Franz Göll's, 36–39, 57–58, 66, 187, 190–191, 192, 199
Entropy, 121–122
Euthanasia, 152–153
Exhibit of Degenerate Art, 134, 162–164
Extraterrestrial life, 197

Fallada, Hans, 70
Feminism, 91–92
Flex, Walter, 136
Foreign workers, 198, 201–202
Fortune tellers, 14–15, 37, 66
Frederick II, 52, 125
Freud, Sigmund, 26, 81, 117

Gaulle, Charles de, 4
Genius, 123–126
German Democratic Republic, 198, 208–210
German Revolution, 132, 135–137
German Women's Fund for Children, 15, 34, 39, 64, 108
Gibson, Mel, 216
Ginzburg, Carlo, 23–24
God, 128, 131, 213–214. *See also* Religion
Goebbels, Joseph, 173, 178, 179
Goering, Hermann, 160, 178
Goethe, Johann Wolfgang von, 17, 22, 24, 201
Göll, Anna von (mother), 14, 46, 60, 62, 78–84, 192
Göll, Franz von (father), 4, 13–14, 46, 61–62, 220
Göll, Gerhardt von, 4

Göll, Gertrude von (grandmother), 4,
  61–62
Gosse, Philip Henry, 109
Grant Study, 225
Great Depression, 5, 144–145

Haeckel, Ernst, 17, 115, 117, 121
Harrington, Anne, 121
Hebbel, Friedrich, 22, 24
Heidegger, Martin, 8, 185, 230n6
Heredity, 42–48, 122, 160–161
Heyse, Paul, 20, 22
Hindenburg, Paul von, 145, 147
History, 116–117, 133, 141, 146–147, 191,
  211–212
Hitler, Adolf, 117, 147–149, 160, 161–162,
  178, 179, 182, 188, 212
Hocke, Gustav, 10
Holocaust, 133, 157, 185, 201
Homosexuality, 98–99, 159
Hospitalization, 104–107
Household accounts, 50–59, 60–61, 74–76
Humor, 177–179

Imperialism. See Colonialism
Inflation, 52, 53, 57–58, 69, 142
Inman, Arthur, 24, 90

Jehovah's Witnesses, 159, 213
Jesus Christ, 216–219
"Jewish star," 157
Jews, 99, 120–121, 134, 139, 142–144,
  145–146, 151, 156–158, 201
Johanni-Bund, 20, 55, 136
Judas, 217–218
Julius Springer Publishers. See Springer
  Publishers
Jünger, Ernst, 49, 152

Kafka, Franz, 24, 49, 103
Käthe (nurse), 105–106
Kazantsakis, Nikos, 218
Keller, Gottfried, 11
Klemperer, Victor, 10, 54, 61, 142–143
Knowledge, idea of, 19–20, 115, 126–131,
  213–214, 219–220
Kretschmer, Ernst, 26–28, 36, 45, 125,
  161
Kriegskinderspende deutscher Frauen. See
  German Women's Fund for Children
Kristallnacht, 156, 174
Kronfeld, Arthur, 26
Kuhn, Thomas, 131

Lagerlöf, Selma, 22
Landwehr, Else, 95
Landwehr, Margarete, 95
Last testament, 220–221
Lauffer, Herbert, 2
Leber, Julius, 2
Lejeune, Philippe, 61
Lesbianism, 98
Levi, Primo, 182
Lhotzky, Heinrich, 25
Libraries, 16–17, 23, 199
Lippmann, Walter, 194
Liskow, Hermann (grandfather), 48,
  62–63, 220
Liskows (relatives), 44, 46, 48, 96
Lorenz, Konrad, 111
Löwith, Karl, 213

Mann, Thomas, 20, 42–43, 136–137
Marti, Fritz, 22
McGurl, Mark, 11
Meissner, Hildegard, 96–100
Melville, Herman, 225

Meteorology, 19, 55, 114–115
Meyer, M. Wilhelm, 20
Mieze, 98
Military service, 7, 171, 220
Monism, 121–122, 213
Movies, 19, 53–54, 200
Mührke, 97
Müller, Rudolf, 200, 221–222
Mussolini, Benito, 161, 179

Napoleon, 160
Natural history. See Science
Nazis, 5, 7, 41, 121, 133–134, 149–151,
    167–168, 182, 184–185, 215; May Day,
    132; opposition to, 148, 158–159, 167;
    postwar apologia, 194–195; racial
    legislation, 43–44, 152–153, 155–156;
    rise to power, 137, 144–146, 147–148;
    worldview, 120, 139, 150–154, 158,
    167–168
Nebel, Gerhard, 109–110
Nietzsche, Friedrich, 17, 124, 125,
    127–128, 219
Nolte, Paul, 139
Nooteboom, Cees, 205
North Altantic Treaty Organization,
    205–206
Nuclear arms, 6, 204–209, 212–213, 222

Occultism, 20, 37, 42–43, 55, 136–137. See
    also Fortune tellers
Orwell, George, 194
Ostpolitik. See Détente
Otterstein, Brigitte, 102, 112, 161

"Path to Salvation, A," 15, 138–140, 143,
    146, 155
Penzig, Rudolf, 25

Pessoa, Fernando, 11–12, 24, 200
Philipp, S., 21, 23, 107, 117, 184
Photography, 30, 97–98, 100
Poetry, 14, 15, 34, 37, 84–86, 92–94, 97,
    107, 113–114, 176–177, 179
Popkin, Jeremy, 9
Postcards, 18, 30, 67
Propaganda, 154–155, 166–167, 176
Psyche, 137
Psychology, 26–28, 41, 48–50, 89
Pynchon, Thomas, 4

Racism, 195–197, 201–202
Radek, Karl, 137
Reading, 9, 13, 16–18, 20–24, 25, 28,
    56–57, 111, 124, 137–138, 148, 216
Reagan, Ronald, 204, 222
Red Army Faction, 203
"Red Island." See "Rote Insel"
Reich Coal Distribution Office, 34, 37,
    39, 51, 52, 65, 94–95, 135
Reichsstrasse 1, 1–2
Religion, 127–128, 213–216
Remarque, Erich Maria, 161–162, 163
Renan, Ernst, 216
Resistance-accommodation theory, 116,
    118
Rossmässler, Emil Adolf, 109
"Rote Insel," 2, 113
Roth, Joseph, 15
Russia. See Soviet Union

Sajo, Karl, 21, 112
Sass, Lewis, 11
Schauwecker, Franz, 162
Schiller, Friedrich, 17, 179, 193, 195
Schmiedel, Otto, 216
Schmöckwitz, 81–82

Schöneberg, 2, 16, 34, 51, 67, 197–198
Schopenhauer, Arthur, 125
Schreber, Daniel Paul, 24
Schuster, Margarete, 94–95
Schweitzer, Albert, 216
Science, 8, 18–19, 55, 110–112, 224; Göll's
    scientific worldview, 112–113, 115–122,
    155, 183, 185–186
Scorsese, Martin, 216, 218
Seigel, Jerrold, 11
Sexuality, 78–79, 86–92, 97, 99–100, 135
Shalamov, Varlam, 191
Social Democrats, 135, 138. *See also*
    Brandt, Willy
Society for Research into Psychology
    and the Occult, 20, 37, 55, 136–137
Socrates, 129
Soviet Union, 7, 151, 153–154, 166, 168,
    180–181, 182–183, 194, 193–194
Spengler, Oswald, 194
Springer Publishers, 38–39, 48,
    50, 51, 60, 64–65, 113, 171, 175,
    190, 199–200, 221
Stab-in-the-Back Legend, 137
Stalin, 160
Stalingrad, 172, 179
Stamulla, Inge, 101–102
Staudacher, Walther, 22–23
Strength through Joy, 55–56, 71–73, 75,
    132, 159–160, 172
"Struggle for existence," 5, 8, 25, 47,
    118–120, 133, 135–136, 140–141, 152–153,
    183–184, 189. *See also* Darwinism
Sudetenland, 155

Theater, 54
Tinbergen, Niko, 111
Tocqueville, Alexis de, 130
Treaty of Versailles, 7

Unification, 205, 208–209, 212
United States, 183, 184, 193–194,
    205–206, 210

Vacations, 9, 55–57, 70–74. *See also*
    Strength through Joy
Volkssturm, 172

Wasko, Klara, 2, 14–15, 34, 78, 84–88, 92
Weber, Carl Maria von, 72
Weimar Republic, 134–146
Weininger, Otto, 17, 25, 79, 86–87,
    90, 96
Wells, H. G., 9
Winter Aid, 159
World War I, 5, 13, 117, 134–135, 161–162
World War II, 5, 113; and the battle for
    Berlin, 132–133, 179–181; invasion of
    France, 165–166; invasion of Poland,
    164–165; invasion of the Soviet Union,
    157, 163, 166–167; and the memoirs, 59,
    61, 68, 70
Wulkow, Eva, 96–100

Youth, 202–203, 210

Zahn, Ernst, 20, 22
Zeugens, von (cousins), 160
Zöberlein, Hans, 163